my foreign cities

LIVERIGHT PUBLISHING
CORPORATION

a division of

W. W. NORTON & COMPANY

NEW YORK • LONDON

my foreign cities

a memoir

e l i z a b e t h   s c a r b o r o

In writing this book, I have tried to respect the privacy of the people described in its pages. I have used real names when I could, in recognition of those who lived this life out with me. I have kept the names of those who've died, after asking their families. Several people important to this story share the same names, and I have changed their names to avoid confusion.

"I Wonder Love" by Pedro Salinas, original text © Herederos de Pedro Salinas, English translation © 1986 by Perry Higman. Reprinted by permission of City Lights Books.

For information about permission to reproduce selections from this book, write to Permissions, Liveright Publishing Corporation, a division of W. W. Norton & Company, Inc., 500 Fifth Avenue, New York, NY 10110

For information about special discounts for bulk purchases, please contact W. W. Norton Special Sales at specialsales@wwnorton.com or 800-233-4830

Manufacturing by RR Donnelley, Harrisonburg, VA
Book design by Barbara M. Bachman
Production manager: Anna Oler

LIBRARY OF CONGRESS CATALOGING-IN-PUBLICATION DATA
Scarboro, Elizabeth.
My foreign cities : a memoir / Elizabeth Scarboro. — First edition.
pages cm
ISBN 978-0-87140-338-4 (hardcover)
1. Scarboro, Elizabeth. 2. Scarboro, Elizabeth—Marriage.
3. Authors, American—20th century—Biography. I. Title.
PS3569.C315Z46 2013
818'.603—dc23
[B]
            2012042010

Liveright Publishing Corporation
500 Fifth Avenue, New York, N.Y. 10110
www.wwnorton.com

W. W. Norton & Company Ltd.
Castle House, 75/76 Wells Street, London W1T 3QT

1 2 3 4 5 6 7 8 9 0

for theo and tess

my foreign cities

STEPHEN AND I DROVE UP BOULDER CANYON IN HIS OLD Jeep, its doors taken off for summer. I rested my bare foot where the passenger door should have been. We were looking for a waterfall where the river crossed under the road and created a small pool on the opposite side. There were three cars parked in the dirt pullout already, other kids and tourists. We stripped to our bathing suits and stepped carefully across the jagged rocks to the river. On the other bank, about thirty feet high, was a small rock ledge, the perfect place to jump from. You didn't want to jump out too far, you had to almost step off, so you landed in the deepest part of the river.

We waded into the water, swam against the current, to the rocks on the other side. We sat for a minute in the sun, waiting for our feet to dry before we started the climb. I had thought about wearing shoes, but as we began I was relieved to be barefoot, I pressed my feet into the rough surface, gaining traction. Stephen climbed slowly above me. He stopped for a second and I glanced down. I remembered hearing that jumping was the easy way down, and now I knew why. Climbing down, with the rocks slightly wet, and the river below, would be treacherous.

At the ledge, I told Stephen to go first. I moved back and watched as he stood in front of me. Beyond him, I could see the other side of the canyon, dusty red rocks stretching into the sky. His shoulders relaxed, and he stepped off. A splash below.

I stood perched on the edge of the rock, my feet clinging. It was a delicate matter, to land in the spot where the river ran deep. Too far and I would hit the bank, not far enough and I would tumble down the rocks. I counted to three, over and over in my head. The river began shrinking. I could hear people calling up to me, the kids yelling jump and the tourists yelling get down. I could see Stephen, his shoulders just above the water, wet from making the leap seconds before. One step out and I fell through the air, wind rushing against my arms.

chapter one

ELITCH'S AMUSEMENT PARK, THE HOT PAVEMENT LITTERED with popcorn flakes and beer can tabs. Early August it teemed with kids—Denver kids of course, and kids from the suburbs, but also kids from the large and small towns that ran along I-70 and I-25, kids with driver's licenses and summer jobs, looking for places to congregate on their days off, hitting the water park one week and the amusement park the next, and making the late-night trek to Slashers on Sundays for all-ages headbanging, drinking in the car since you couldn't once you were inside.

We'd driven the freeway to get there, the thirty-minute stretch of plains between Boulder and Denver, the mountains behind us still dark blue in the late morning. The five of us had squeezed into my old green and white Dodge Colt, which was filled with our sunglasses, notebooks, hairbands and sneakers. I'd spent all summer hostessing at Fred's Restaurant to earn the money to buy the car, only to have my friends own it, too. This was the way things were between us, too communal, clothes and ambitions and boyfriends shifted around or stolen, depending on your point of view.

The ground was thick with dust, ticket stubs stuck here and there in rivulets of slushie. We wandered through the stands, a little depleted. Last night had been a full moon and still warm at midnight, and we'd snuck out late, wandered through the Hill to the university campus. We'd circled the stadium and found a place where the fence dipped, helped each other pass between the chain-link and the barbed wire. The field had been bathed in moonlight, the giant letters COLORADO glowing at one end. We'd done roundoffs on the AstroTurf and then lay on the curved alphabet, each taking a letter for ourselves, until the stadium lights had flashed on and we'd had to run. I'd lost track of time and gotten home late, slipping through the sliding glass door to my basement bedroom just as my mom had come down the stairs to do early morning laundry. I'd been under my covers, eyes closed, still in my jeans as she'd padded into my room, paused for a long minute and then checked the lock on the sliding door.

Now, in the amusement park, I walked with my friend Caitlin, telling her about my close call. We'd slowed down by the Tea Cups, which we'd loved when we were little, until the time when we'd thrown up in unison. She frowned, pushing her long red hair back from her temples. "Your mom stood right over you and you kept your eyes closed?"

I couldn't help it—I lied to my parents too easily; I liked being two people, leading two lives. Caitlin was a habitual truth-seeker. We'd been friends since we were three, and at some point, before we knew about sex, we'd each made the mistake of walking in on our parents. I'd faked sleepwalking and denied that it had ever happened, while Caitlin had turned the lights on and demanded that her parents tell her what was going on.

By midafternoon, the peak of the heat, the bottoms of my feet were sliding in my sandals. A Western-themed shooting game, bales of hay stacked and tied, with a bull's-eye hanging in front. We were on the old end for rides and games, when half of being here was the suspense of seeing what would happen if all of us were together. Though my stomach had dropped in the car when I'd found out who "all of us" entailed. My ex-boyfriend Amani was coming, since his friend was dating mine.

I'd met him at school but the first time we'd talked was at a Red Rocks concert in the pouring rain, both of us wearing garbage bags with holes ripped out for our heads. He'd been comfortable, and his quiet self-assurance had stood out in a sea of trying-hard sixteen-year-olds. His biological father was from Tanzania, and maybe it was growing up biracial in a mostly white town, or maybe it was being raised Buddhist, but he saw everything and everyone with a little distance. He was smart but didn't make a point of it, and artistic in a careful rather than free-form way. We'd been inseparable for ten months, which was probably too long for any high school couple, but he'd seen the end coming first, which I still hated to think about.

I glanced over at Eve, wondering if she was grumbling too. She was deep in concentration at the ring toss, her dark brown ponytail hanging still between her shoulder blades. I watched as she floated the rings through the air, nailing four out of the five. Then she relaxed, talking with the guy who ran the booth. Eve had two older brothers, and she could joke, flirt, or wrestle her way through almost anything. I couldn't hear what she was saying, but I could see the guy laughing, and I was pretty sure that minutes from now he'd be giving us all a free round. Still, underneath she was probably having her own trepidation. She'd broken up with Stephen in May, and spent the summer volunteering for the Student Conservation Corps in Idaho, repairing fences. Stephen supposedly knew it was over, but while she'd been gone, he'd written her lots of letters.

I turned to see the group of boys in the distance, near the roller coaster. They hadn't seen us yet, and they were caught up in something between them, laughing. Even from here I could see Amani, low-key and self-possessed, his graceful, easy stride. And then I saw Stephen next to him, cackling, gesturing wildly, his blond hair shaggy, his leaned-back, duck-footed walk.

To my relief, summer relaxed all divisions. Eve teased Stephen and he laughed rather than flinching. I walked comfortably next to Amani. We took turns putting quarters in the fortune-teller vending machine, reading the tiny white strips. Caitlin would travel around the world. Amani would have great wealth.

Stephen hesitated when it came to his turn. When he was seven, a carnival fortune-teller had studied his palm, squinted up at him, and pushed his hand away. Like any kid, he'd been secretly sure she would look at his palm and see great things. He'd been interested in space travel; he'd organized football scrimmages and trips to caves. Maybe his future would be full of the adult versions of these things, scientific discoveries, or even a stint as the Colorado Buffs quarterback. The fortune-teller had shaken her head. "The lifeline's cut," she'd said. He'd been scared right afterwards, and then he'd hated her. In spite of himself, he wondered if she'd known somehow. He imagined her staring through his skin, deep into his cells, *cystic fibrosis* flashing out at her from the rest of his DNA.

But he was strangely healthy. He took enzymes with his

meals, and though his cough was deep, every time he went to the clinic in Denver the doctor told him his lungs were as good as any kid's on the street. He'd given up on football, but other dreams were there, even closer, almost plans now. He'd decided that fortune-telling was a scam, just as he'd decided there was no such thing as fate. Having CF was random bad luck. I'd asked him about it, and he'd said that it had to happen to some-body—he guessed that he was the somebody. I'd been surprised not to hear, *Why me?* But then maybe *Why me?* was for people who weren't born with bad luck but were struck by it later, whose lives had gone well up to a point, who'd assumed they understood the order of things. For Stephen, from the begin-ning, there was no understanding the order of things. Years later, in a bookstore, we'd come across a book titled *When Bad Things Happen to Good People*. Stephen would laugh in dis-belief, and then get sort of pissed off. People were surprised by this? Who were these people? In fairness, it was more compli-cated than that, it was an emotion, not an idea: *why me?* It was an emotion we all expected Stephen to have, which says a lot about how far removed he was from the rest of us.

Still, he slipped a quarter in the machine. He couldn't stop himself from opening fortune cookies either. In his wallet, hid-den in the back pocket, he collected good omens. "You will live a long and happy life." "Your wealth is your health." He stopped for pennies, too. Maybe he didn't believe in good luck, but he wasn't going to ignore it if it crossed his path.

"You are young at heart," he read aloud. I shrugged. He was young, period. Caitlin thought it meant that Stephen would stay young at heart as he grew older. There was no future tense in the fortune, but she liked the idea, she could see him running around mischievously, while the rest of us became serious.

I put my quarter in the machine and silently willed it to dispense something good, something exciting, something full of adventure. I couldn't tell exactly what my future was going to hold, because that was the point of a future, you didn't know. In English class, when we'd been asked to write on the subject, I'd scrawled, "I plan to avoid marriage and children at all costs." I pictured myself as an international journalist, moving from country to country and boyfriend to boyfriend.

Though for now, my affairs and adventures were local. I'd slip out at night to meet my friends, and we'd climb fire escapes, sit on rooftops and feel the streets and minutes spread out eerie and vacant around us, the time of night when our town was truly ours. The safety of our town allowed us a kind of freedom that most teenage girls never got to have, I'd realize later. There were near misses—the slightly volatile guy who dealt us Ecstasy, the older man who followed us home and lingered in the bushes, the frat boys who cornered me when I delivered pizza. But for the most part, as long as we did our sneaking around in a pack, we were fine.

Maybe it was these small, early adventures that made me desire their adult counterpart. Men seemed to have all the privileges in the department of adventure—if and when they settled, they did so reluctantly. Why did they get to be the reluctant ones? And why did they get to be seen as "tied down"? From what I could see, women were so tied down you wouldn't even think of it as tied down, because where were they going to go? Nowhere without us, their children, that was for sure. I had a chip on my shoulder about all this. It wasn't that I wanted to be a boy, it was that I wanted to be a girl with the internal sensibility that came with being a boy, that distance, that gravitation toward self-fulfillment.

I read my fortune: I would have five children. "It's not that bad," Caitlin said, "it'd be your family but one more." Eve was impatient with the idea of fortunes in general, and she urged us toward the rides.

I sat next to Stephen on the Sky Ride, just the two of us in an open metal seat, inching along high above the amusement park. None of our friends had been interested in a ride this slow, and I imagined them down there, smirking. I dangled my feet, remembering the bridge over the crocodile pit at the zoo, my two-year-old sister's sandal flying off, my mom peering down into the water, as if considering snatching the shoe back with her hand. I stretched my toes out to keep my sandals on, clacked them against my heels a few times, and finally leaned over and took them off, stuck them between my hip and the seat. Stephen and I were already squished, leaning away from each other, our outside arms hanging out of the chair. No one was up here with us, but we still made a point of our physical separation.

It wasn't what everyone thought, but then, what was it? We'd met in history class, sitting across the aisle from each other, Stephen in his jeans and flannel shirt, leaning back in his seat, his dark brown eyes alert, shifting between mischief and judgment. I'd thought he was sort of funny but sort of an asshole; he had the kind of confidence that made me jump into class discussion against my will to shut him down. But then he'd started going out with my friend Carla, so we'd been forced to reach a truce, still arguing in class but amiable on the weekends.

This summer, with everyone else out of town, we'd started talking on the phone. We were both sheepish about having a friend of the opposite sex. I was doubly sheepish since Amani and I had just broken up, since Stephen had gone out with both Eve and Carla by now. We wandered around town, climbing buildings, going to the occasional movie. Our friendship was perfect; I could spend the night at his house without anything happening. We'd lie far apart in our T-shirts and sweats, talking about everything. When I'd have a fight with my parents, I'd call him, and he'd pick me up in the Land Cruiser. We'd wander through the graveyard on Ninth Street, teasing each other, arguing, reading the headstones.

But the perfect balance of our friendship was getting harder to maintain. I was having trouble concentrating at the moment, with his leg next to mine, especially where our skin was touching. I could move my leg away—the momentary smack of separation and then the freedom to think about other things—but I didn't want to do that. This was as much as I was comfortable admitting—I didn't want to move my leg. He wasn't moving his leg either. He didn't seem to be thinking about it, but then, who knew.

The city of Elitch's and beyond, the black roofs of the one-story brick houses that took up where the amusement park left off, their chimneys and square grass yards, jungle gyms in the back, too hot to climb. Somewhere around here, the hospital where I was born—St. Anthony's, famous in our family for allowing my dad to be in the delivery room back when no one else would let him.

"Saving that fortune?" Stephen asked me.

"You want it?"

He smiled. "You should keep it. You never know."

"You're saying I'll accidentally get pregnant, five times?"

"You'll be married with kids, no question."

"How much do you want to bet?"

"A hundred dollars."

"But how am I going to find you to collect?"

"You don't think we'll stay in touch? How insulting."

I laughed. "You think your wife will be okay with that?"

"She won't mind, you'll be married, too."

"Fine. A hundred dollars."

I made a mental note to write it down in my journal, so I could be sure to keep track, and get him to pay up. Below us, the octopus threw its arms around, waving eight little cradles of humans in the air. Soon, the sky would darken in one swift move, clouds heavy as cars, and then the downpour, cracks of thunder echoing. For an hour the rides would clear, the crowds would huddle in the hot dog stands, drenched, waiting for the lightning to pass. And after the rain, damp air would rise from the asphalt, hover about a foot high, carrying the smell of wet hay.

Stephen hooked his foot over mine. This was within the realm of our friendship, though admittedly near its outer edges. I offered him a sip of my root beer.

chapter two

THERE IS THE TENSION BETWEEN WHAT I SAW THEN AND what I see now. If I'd been sixteen, or seventeen, or eighteen and writing this, I wouldn't have included much about cystic fibrosis at all. I realized this when I mentioned to a friend that I wanted to introduce Stephen as he was when I met him—healthy. "He was never healthy," my friend said. But we thought of him as healthy; we thought of him the way he thought of himself. The illness was like bad eyesight—as long as he made small accommodations for it, he was fine. And because of this, things slipped by me.

The time we were all over at our friend Joaquin's house, for example. Stephen sat in the kitchen talking with Joaquin's mom. She was saying something about feeling middle-aged, and Stephen replied that at seventeen, he was middle-aged too. They decided to get their midlife crises over with together, and sat at the kitchen table, yelling a good long yell. Stephen was already at home in the short-life part of his illness. And he probably understood his middle age in the same way Joaquin's mom understood hers: her knees might have been creaking but she didn't expect to die tomorrow, or in the next few years. Maybe this is the best way to convey how Stephen felt about death at seventeen—it's the way the rest of us feel at forty.

Then there was the weight of Stephen's moving away from home. He came into English class once grumbling because his dad wanted him to stay in town for college. He'd worked hard to get good grades, he'd gotten into UC Berkeley. His dad said his objections were financial. Stephen came up with a whole plan, how he'd take out loans, go to California, and get in-state tuition as soon as he could. His dad acquiesced. Years later, a family friend would come up to Stephen at his dad's memorial. *Your dad was worried sick when you went off to college,* he'd say. It's only now that I link these two memories. Stephen was doing well, but his dad was a doctor, after all.

In high school, I didn't give much thought to Stephen's parents. They were the Parents, the backdrop, like mine. When I look back, I think of them more than I think of anyone else.

Gus and Fran were both heartbreakers, and maybe this was how they met, seeing as they were from such different worlds. Gus had grown up in Albuquerque, part of a modest, close-knit family. The only picture I ever saw from his childhood was the one found tucked into his father's wallet after his father had died. Gus is two in the picture, laughing, taking a bath in a metal pail on the family's wooden porch. Fran had grown up in Santa Fe, but her father was from a long-established family in Tennessee. He'd died in battle near the end of World War II, and twelve-year-old Fran had accepted his medal of honor.

Fran's mother was, to put it mildly, mean. Fran had escaped home, bouncing from boarding school to her grandparents in Tennessee.

They were settled by the time they had Stephen. He was the baby of the family—eight years younger than his sister Tinka, six years younger than his brother Clay—and doted on. He adored his sister and idolized his brother. He adopted Clay's music, his clothes, his walk. Clay, like Stephen, gestured with abandon and said exactly what was on his mind. Tinka was more understated and generous to a fault, but she had a mis-chievous, infectious laugh, which her brothers loved to draw out of her. They'd reenact moments from childhood, getting fully into character, or caricature. They'd be Tinka hissing as a surly teenager, or their grandma holding her arms in the air, explaining why she had to give up her beehive hairdo ("I can't reach my hair no more"), or Clay in his cowboy phase ("Don't touch mah hat"). They exaggerated for effect, which took me a while to grasp. Clay liked to tell the story of hiking in Santa Cruz and seeing our friend Josh fly by on his mountain bike, naked, and career into a ditch. Only recently did I realize that the "naked" part had been added in.

Fran would feign dismay at their more inappropriate jokes, her dark brown eyes widening in disapproval, carrying a glint of appreciation underneath. She had a way of effortlessly acing social conventions while simultaneously treating them with a certain disregard. While her kids liked to talk everything to death, Fran was more private. She took care of people discreetly. Instead of asking you how you were doing, she'd find the one small thing you needed, and get it for you. When she was agi-tated, she went off by herself and then reappeared, her lipstick refreshed.

I imagine her sitting in the doctor's office with Gus, Stephen on her lap, all those years ago, just after Stephen had turned one. In Stephen's version of his diagnosis, he ate and ate, and his babysitter was so proud that she kept feeding him until suddenly it all streamed out the other end. He liked to tell this as a story, imitating the spooning of the food, the baby-voice encouragement of the sitter, the disgusted shock on her face moments later. His doctor, looking for the root of the problem, ran several tests, and discovered he had cystic fibrosis. At that time, in 1970, the doctors probably didn't expect him to live to ten. Did they tell his parents that? Now, they probably would, I'd guess they'd lay the odds out, the tiniest of percentages.

I imagine Fran, carrying this around while carrying him around, watching him toddle and then race around the house, getting into trouble, because he was always getting into trouble. Trying to make every meal as caloric as possible. Wondering if and when to tell him and his brother and sister, in the odd moment she had time to stop and think.

Stephen knew, as a kid, that he had cystic fibrosis, but it wasn't talked about much. His parents let him do everything healthy kids did. His mom always says it wasn't a choice; he was stubbornly independent. When he was eleven he'd call his friends himself and get them to come to the park for soccer or football. By high school he was rock climbing, caving, scuba diving. I imagine his parents watching him fly down the ski slope at six, wondering what was in store. Or pointedly not wondering? His mom told me later, it wouldn't have helped to think about it all the time; she put it out of her mind. This seems impossible to me as a parent, but familiar to me as a person who loved Stephen too.

And then there are my parents. They must have been looking ahead, and they must have known that I wasn't. But they were as restrained with me as Stephen's parents were with him. I never wondered about this, though other people have brought it up over the years. Looking back, it doesn't seem out of character. They had confidence in their children's abilities to handle what came our way, and they're not big worriers. My mom in particular is deeply optimistic, not just in terms of where life might be headed, but in how she interprets what actually happens. A few years ago, when she fell down the stairs and got a concussion, she saw it as a chance to learn to slow down. She is a chronic jerry-rigger because she's pretty sure she can fix anything. I remember watching her crawl under my grandparents' A-frame cabin with a flashlight to disconnect the sink pipes so she could search for her missing contact lens.

My dad's faith in life is a little darker. When he was eleven, he was hit by a car and landed in a coma for two weeks. After he woke up, he had to learn to talk and walk and read again. He was depressed and lonely, and he spent a long time wondering whether life was worth living. He told us this story many times when we were kids, probably imagining the day when we might come up against our own difficulties.

He comes alive in the face of a challenge, which made him useless to complain to, growing up. In college, when I told him I wanted to transfer to Santa Cruz from the University of Chicago because I thought I'd be happier, he shook his head. "I've ruined my kids," he said. "Whoever told you that life's about being happy?"

It should also be mentioned that my parents are romantics. They are seventy years old, and if you bring up the name of the woman who danced with my dad at a party forty years ago my mom still gets a steely glint in her eye. They met when they were sixteen and got married when they were twenty-one, their senior year at Colorado College. Growing up, I figured they were a product of their generation, but now I can see that they were also both unusually serious at a young age. In their wedding pictures, my mother looks serene and confident, my dad like a terrified teenager. His parents had gotten divorced when he was eleven, after a very unhappy marriage. And still he gives the same toast every year on their anniversary. This year will be their fiftieth, and he will raise his glass, and say, "We made it through another year."

I asked my dad once what he thought about me and Stephen, back in the beginning. He said he admired me for what I was doing, which is a little strange, since we both know I didn't know what I was doing. He said there was that One Time he talked to me about it, which I only vaguely remember. He said something like, "You're going to have to figure out what you want to do about Stephen." I remember feeling insulted. I thought he was talking about getting into a relationship so young, and how this might limit what I decided to do after college. (This was what I worried about—how a relationship might compromise my independence.) My dad said, most of all, I always did what I wanted to do anyway.

Which is true, and brings up the question of me. The question everyone asks, when they find out that CF is a condition you're born with. You *knew*, all along? And maybe they're thinking the same thing I thought about Stephen when I first met him: Who are you then, if this is true?

Strangely, back then, CF hardly played into the equation at all. It might have been that I was deep in my vow never to commit to one person for too long, much less get married. Like most teenagers, I wanted to do the opposite of what my parents had done. My first childhood ambition had been to be a spy—I'd told my mom to throw away my baby clothes, which she'd been saving for my future daughter. The spy dream had faded, but the aversion to a settled life had stuck. It might have been that at nineteen, a two-year relationship is long, much less a ten-year relationship, and I assumed we'd break up long before life might do the breaking for us. And maybe it was simpler than all this— I fell in love with him, the way you do, and it stuck.

But I must have been serious about not feeling the need for security in my future, and this is probably for the same reason that a healthy person can afford not to think about health or a rich person about money. I had so much security I didn't even notice it was there. *Your family operates like an organism,* Caitlin said to me in high school. And it was true. We were bound up in each other's happiness, and even though I fought against it sometimes, I couldn't imagine a life that worked any other way.

There were four of us kids, and I was the oldest. My sister Catherine and I were two years apart, inseparable and constantly at each other's throats. My parents had to make a rule that we couldn't touch each other, and still when their backs were turned we drew blood. We held secret worlds between us—spy clubs and endless adventure games. And when our brother and sister came along, we claimed them and indoctrinated them in our ways. John was equal parts lost-in-thought and mischievous, Jean feisty and able to carry her own weight. When she was four, Catherine and I had to pay her to be in a family play, and she held out for a five-dollar bill.

When I think back to the four of us, I see us lying in the small loft space of that A-frame cabin my grandparents built in Breckenridge, with logs they'd skinned and a stove they'd ordered from Sears. The stairs to the loft were narrow and steep, and being the oldest, I slept by them in case one of the younger kids started sleepwalking or needed to pee in the middle of the night. Our beds were squished together, but that was the way we liked it.

My siblings all knew about Stephen's illness, but I'd guess they didn't think about it much. He was the boyfriend of their older sister, not a potential new family member. We were young enough that we couldn't imagine the family *having* new members. He was an enjoyable temporary interloper. As I became close to him they became close to him, and by the time his illness counted, they understood that I was in deep.

HOW DID HIS illness count, and when? I remember the books Eve checked out from the library, when she and Stephen were going out, when he and I were just starting to become friends. The group of us huddled around the library table, trying to get our bearings. From what we could decipher, Stephen was missing a crucial enzyme, and this allowed mucus to build up in his lungs and his digestive system, until it eventually made it impossible for him to breathe. It was strange, though, because he looked nothing like the kids in the book; it seemed like he should have been worse off.

I had decided that if he brought it up I would say I knew, but otherwise I wouldn't. One day we walked to the corner store during our class break, and he took out a handful of pills. My heart began racing, but it seemed too pointed to ignore the horse pills he was downing with his Coke. "Eve told me about those," I admitted.

"I figured," he said. He paid for his beef jerky. I bought my cup of coffee and we headed back across the street toward school. He coughed his signature guttural cough, which I'd somehow assumed was from chewing tobacco.

"So it's true for everyone," I ventured, "the dying young part?"

He nodded. "Me and Jim Morrison, but probably not that young."

I pictured Jim Morrison near the end of his career. Heavyset, bearded, his face no longer chiseled but loose. Old, a full adult, so far from where we were now. I was flooded with relief. Still, I wasn't sure what I was supposed to say. I'm sorry? Once, Stephen and I had been talking about a girl in our science class who annoyed him. I thought she deserved a break; I'd heard she lived in a group home. Stephen gave me a dirty look when I brought this up. "Do you think she wants you to feel sorry for her?" he'd spat. "If she's irritating, she's irritating, like anybody else." Suddenly he was on her side, his dislike a show of solidarity. This was the light he'd want to be seen in, so I tried to see him that way, like his circumstances were just circumstances, nothing to shrink from. I went ahead and asked. "How long will you live, do you think?"

He thought about it for a second. "At least till I'm thirty, I could make it to forty but I'm not sure."

"Do you think about it a lot?"

"It's a long way off. And you never know what will happen. I could spend all this time worrying about it and end up getting hit by a bus."

Months after this conversation we sat on his couch, watching *Harold and Maude*, arguing about whether we could go out. He was in favor; I was worried about ruining our friendship, about what my friends would think. "Maybe in a month," I told him, thinking by then I'd have it all figured out. That night we tried to sleep like we had been all summer, far apart, the alarm set for five so I could get home before I was missed. We lay with our eyes closed, my hand resting loosely on his shoulder, the threads of his T-shirt like pinpricks. And then I couldn't help it; I touched his face. He kissed my fingers, which had found their way to his mouth, and pulled me close to him. *Short month*, he said, a little garbled. I laughed, and moved my hand to kiss him. We were not tentative or even gentle. Within seconds we had taken all our clothes off, tangled ourselves fiercely and were not letting go. We found ourselves halfway off the bed, my hair hanging down to the carpet; we suddenly realized where we were and felt silly, we laughed and then became shy, just looking at each other as he pulled me up. The alarm went off, and we were shocked that five hours had gone by. It seemed a good sign. I drove home and snuck in the basement door, went to bed and couldn't sleep.

I remember thinking that if we stayed together as long as possible we'd last a year, until we went off to college. The best way to go to college, the only way, was to go unattached. I imagined us as adults. Stephen would be settled, and I'd pass through the town where he and his wife lived, stopping by to say hello. She'd be annoyed, and Stephen and I would be nostalgic; he for being young and free and running around with me, and me, for being with him.

But it turned out we barely lasted three months. In December, one snow day, Stephen told me that he thought we'd been better as friends. I stared at him indignantly.

"I told you this would happen," I said, "we ruined a great friendship for nothing."

"You were right."

"That's it, I was right?" I shook my head in disbelief, furious with both of us.

Second semester began, and as luck would have it, we were in the same English class, and assigned neighboring seats. The first week I sat stiffly at my desk, ignoring him. But at some point our shared sensibility got the better of us. He scrawled a sarcastic comment in his notebook, and pushed the notebook toward the edge of his desk. I read it and begrudgingly wrote back. One night, one of us called the other for the homework and we slipped into our old way of talking. Soon we were teased at school for being friends again. We laughed about the fact that we had tried to go out. How could we have been that stupid?

In the fall, we both left for college, and it was harder than we wanted to admit to say goodbye. We wrote each other letters, chronicling our new lives. Stephen wrote about the drive cross-country, following I-80 through the plateaus of Wyoming and the salt flats of Utah to reach California. Arriving in Berkeley to find he had no student housing. He'd ended up in a fraternity, which I looked forward to teasing him about, even though he claimed it was more of a hippie co-op. The house was a large dark wooden bungalow, and he liked the people there, though he hated the Grateful Dead and they were disgusted by his Jif peanut butter and Oreos. He thought they were secretly happy; he kept waking up to find his food box pilfered.

I wrote to Stephen about the University of Chicago, the way it appeared from the taxi window, a tiny square plot dwarfed by the vast city surrounding it. The campus looked like it had been picked up from another century and set down here by mistake, with its formidable stone buildings, gargoyles peering down from their roofs. I wrote to Stephen about being equally, though differently, out of place. People here were studious and intent; they considered pot a drug. After dinner, it was only a question of which library.

I told him about my new friend Kristie, and the morning our friendship came into being, on a run to Lake Michigan after pulling an all-nighter. The darkness had been lifting, the streets were wet with leaves, and our feet had brushed against them, the only sound on the South Side of Chicago. I told him I'd met a guy named Paolo. I didn't tell him, as I would another friend, that we'd met sitting on the basement floor of a Halloween party, drunk, Paolo dressed as a Smurf. I did not say that we kissed sloppily, and when I looked in the mirror my face was smudged everywhere with blue. Stephen liked Carolyn, a girl in his architecture studio, and I wondered about what I wasn't hearing.

Then in May, he came to visit me in Chicago. He got off the airport shuttle in front of Woodward Court. He was wearing his faded black Berkeley sweatshirt and his old Levi's, and carrying a duffel bag. The leaves on the tree behind him were painfully green. We couldn't stop smiling, which made it hard to talk. In my room, lying on my bed, we pulled at each other's clothes and started kissing, but every time our eyes met we started laughing, and we were rendered helpless. Stop making me laugh—I'm not doing anything—maybe if we both look away at the same time—okay, ready—you looked too soon—it's your fault, I heard you trying not to laugh—I couldn't help it—okay really, just come here. I was in love with this person. I'd been here with him before and I could feel the difference. My mattress was on the floor, tucked into the corner below the medicine cabinet on my side of the room. From there I could see the aluminum window frame, the low gray sky.

Later we sat in Morry's Deli staring at the gigantic paintings of the former deans of the university. The room, with its high ceilings and dark red carpet, was porous and breathing. How did we explain that, explain the way life appeared backlit all of a sudden? We gave up and just paid attention, wandering around the city, taking it all in.

The night before he left we lay squeezed in my single bed, trying not to fall asleep. We listened to "Murmur," comparing our different versions of the lyrics song by song. We made fun of the ways we'd each changed since we'd moved to our new cities. I teased Stephen about growing his hair, becoming more liberal by the minute. He teased me for my newfound interest in philosophy, for defending my school's emphasis on the classics. "My job is to help you take life less seriously," he said. I became indignant, then sleepy, and the next thing I knew it was morning, and time to say goodbye.

I'd found myself in the middle of something I'd sworn I'd never do. I was in love, long-distance. Long-distance relationships had always seemed like a joke—how could you be with someone who wasn't there? We vowed to see other people; we promised that we couldn't predict what was going to happen. A person could easily change in a few months, and when they did, you were not required to like the person they'd become. But the problem was, we kept liking each other, every time one of us showed up in the other's city.

Looking back, this is when you'd think the illness would figure in. And it did, but exactly how is harder to puzzle out. One day, I slipped in late to my biomedical ethics class to see the words "genetic engineering" written on the board. Every week the professor, who held both a medical and a law degree, lured us into fiery debates on current issues. Today, he announced, we'd be talking about the research done on cystic fibrosis. I thought about last week's abortion discussion, the few quiet people in the room. I sank low in my seat as my classmates argued about whether babies with cystic fibrosis should be born, whether it was a good thing people with the illness couldn't reproduce. Now that people with it were living longer, was it worth pouring money into research on the final stages, on trying to keep them alive? They were expensive. I was sweating. I thought about Stephen, how he joked that if amniocentesis had been invented ten years earlier, he never would have been born.

I watched my professor as the class went on. I'd liked him so far, he was arrogant but he worked hard, he didn't shy away from the big questions. I went up to him after class. "Do you know where I could find out more about cystic fibrosis?" I asked him. It wasn't what I'd meant to say.

"You know someone who has it?" he asked me.

"My boyfriend. I mean, sort of, he lives in California."

He nodded and glanced at his watch. Then he suggested that we go over to Crerar, the medical library. I knew he juggled teaching with medical residency; usually he flew out of class to catch the train to the hospital. But he pretended to have the time, and now I couldn't convince him that I was fine and could look it up on my own.

In the library, he printed out a list of references with article summaries. He looked at me carefully, the paper in his hand. "As your professor, I could just hand you this list," he said. "But as a doctor, I won't feel right until I ask you to promise me something first."

"What?"

"That you'll think about whether you want to know this information."

Something in me sank.

"Everybody with this illness is affected differently," he said.

"There won't be a chart that can predict how long your boy-friend will live."

I rolled the list into a scroll. For weeks I kept it in my back-pack, and then I went into the shelves of Crerar and found a book or two. The people in the books looked nothing like Ste-phen, and I stopped short of reading the accompanying text. I felt superstitious, struck by the feeling that words mattered, that learning one version of the possible future, articulating it as a reality, made it more likely to happen. When I got home I set the list on the left corner of my desk, in my pile of things to read in my free time. After a while, I just kept it in my middle desk drawer. I imagined showing it to Stephen the next time he vis-ited. I wondered what he would say; whether he'd be surprised that I'd wanted to look all this up, whether he'd be tempted to read the books or to throw the list away.

IN THE SPRING of our junior year, Stephen came to live with me in the apartment I shared with friends on South Hyde Park Bou-levard. He'd set up a semester-long internship at an architecture firm downtown. I worried about splitting my time between him and my friend Kristie, about whether the two of them would get along. As usual, the things that I worried about were not the things that went wrong.

Stephen and Kristie got along fine. In fact, they became good friends. Sunday mornings, I found myself sandwiched between them on the couch, watching back-to-back episodes of *The Brady Bunch* (the show Kristie loved, and Stephen loved to hate). But Stephen and I couldn't go a day without fighting. We fought over everything that wasn't important. We argued about when to turn out the light, when to go to bed and when to get up, who chose the music first thing in the morning. He got suddenly energetic late at night, just when I plummeted. He teased me too much in front of my friends, then I snapped at him, and he became embarrassed and hurt. My messiness frustrated him, the giant pile of clothes in the corner, the stacks of paper covering the floor. I felt insulted that he couldn't see my efforts: that I'd consolidated the clothes into a single pile, kept my papers by the desk instead of spreading them around the room the way I always had before.

Mornings we woke up hopeful. From our bed, which we had moved into the corner and cloistered off with vertically hung tapestries, the day looked promising. Some days we made it until dark. But we never made it all the way without yelling at each other, quietly yelling, whisper-yelling because we were living with four other people. We fought for twenty-one days. The twenty-second day, we lay in bed, exhausted. "We have no idea how to live together," I said. "What if we can't stop fighting?"

"I guess I'll leave."

"So you're saying we'd break up?"

"No. Maybe we could keep going out but just live apart."

This hadn't occurred to me. Maybe we couldn't live together—not everybody could. We could live nearby, spend nights at each other's houses. I felt a trickle of relief, and somehow the relief was reassuring, a little window. It took the pressure off just enough for the possibility of not fighting to wedge its way in.

The day before Stephen moved back to Berkeley, I lay on my bed, watching him take down his tapestries, fold them, put them in his black trunk along with his clothes. I stared at the ceiling while he worked around me, separating the things that were his from the things that were mine. I had been so good at taking up the whole bed before, I'd slept diagonally without thinking about it. I felt pathetic. It would be good to have my room to myself again; freedom was good. This had been claustrophobic and muddled and we'd had to make all kinds of stupid concessions.

But I had been happy, and I knew it. This was great and troubling. We were young and we were supposed to be figuring out our separate lives, what we would do with our brains and our time. We were supposed to be setting out. Whatever we did, we were not supposed to compromise for relationships, that had been our parents' generation, and they regretted being tied down so early, marrying at twenty-one and having kids. We had been warned. I had ambitions and the urge to experience all kinds of freedom, and the last thing I wanted to be was a girl following some guy around. But lying here now watching Stephen turn to come sit by me, I couldn't help wanting more of this, wanting to see where it went.

Senior year I'd agonize about it, searching for jobs in the Bay Area, and simultaneously for opportunities of a lifetime elsewhere around the world. But in the end, the illness would call my bluff. I couldn't go live by myself in Alaska, and then come around to being with Stephen. Alaska would be there. In comparison to Stephen, most things would be there. If I wanted him, I had to hurry up.

chapter three

Fillmore street, ten o'clock on a saturday night, headed to a party. I watched the slow parade, people moving in clumps of four and five toward a nightclub on the corner. I'd finished college, and three weeks ago I'd moved out to San Francisco, and in with Stephen. So far so good, the living together, though at the moment in the car he was trying to convince me to like Metallica. He put on their slowest song, which according to him, serious fans derided for being too soft, but which he hoped would be the gateway song for me. For my part, I hoped he wasn't going to go off the deep end, heavy-metal-wise. As it was, we had just enough crossover in our musical tastes to keep us happy in the car. But I had to admit, he knew me; in spite of myself I started humming. Stephen groaned, irritated. "You can't rule out singing along *and* humming," I said.

But then the car veered into a red zone, the tire bumping up against the curb. I turned to see Stephen leaning back against the headrest, eyes closed, tapping around on the right side of his chest with his fingers. "My lung just collapsed," he said.

I'd been right about the groan—he sounded irritated more than anything. Meanwhile, the adrenaline started coursing through me; I gripped the door handle and tried to take deep breaths, which made me cough. He glanced over at me, one eyebrow raised, and then we both smiled in spite of ourselves. For a second, it was funny, the healthy person sputtering while the person with the collapsed lung waited for her to get it together. I tried to think. Somehow I expected disruptions in life to happen one at a time. I'd only been here three weeks, my move was still happening. CF's timing was bad. But I had to ignore that for the moment, I had to figure out what we were supposed to do. The hospital, that's what you did.

"I don't think I can go," Stephen said. It took me a minute to understand that he was still considering the party.

"Don't worry about it. Tell me how to get to the hospital, and I'll drive us."

"It's Saturday night, the emergency room will be packed. I think I'll just head over in the morning."

"But you need to get checked out, see what it is."

"I know what it is, it's a collapsed lung."

I felt like I was talking to a five-year-old, or someone on drugs, all logic out the window. Was I wrong that most people would consider a lung collapse deserving of immediate medical attention? Somehow, he'd turned this around to make me feel like I was nagging, which he knew I'd sworn never to do, as a matter of pride.

"It's not like all the air goes out at once. It's hard to sleep in there. I want to get one night of real rest."

This was how he was, always emitting competence, trusting himself so thoroughly it was hard to wedge yourself in. Usually this just made me argue harder and better; it made me win. But when it came to a collapsed lung, only one of us knew what he was talking about. He was probably wishing he were alone right now, so he could go ahead and do what he wanted.

"You better know what you're doing."

"Trust me. The CF doctors won't even come in till Monday morning."

"I'm driving us home, at least."

We came home to a quiet house. I called our friends to tell them we wouldn't make the party. I mentioned the collapsed lung, and somehow it sounded worse than it had just between Stephen and me. I'm so sorry, our friend Eric said, and I tried to explain that it was reparable; it required a chest tube, but the lung would be okay. Stephen made peanut butter sandwiches and poured himself a glass of milk. I sat at the kitchen table, drinking a beer, listening to him fret about his architecture studio project, which was due next week.

"Just call the professor," I said.

"I guess. I was hoping not to have to go into the whole CF thing."

I sat cross-legged on our bed while he packed. Under the window was an upside-down milk crate, covered with an orange and black Turkish tapestry. On top, Stephen had set his miscellaneous small objects—a round malachite ball, the tiny Crucifixion painting his Catholic cousin had given him, the plastic nun statue, the thin piece of metal with a Jim Morrison decal, the fragments of the bracelet I'd made for him in high school. In the dim light, their composition felt shrine-like. Stephen gathered clothes and books and magazines, the way you might for a vacation that promised lots of lying around.

At the end of the night we lay in bed, our legs intertwined. My mind wandered to a few days ago, biking back over the Golden Gate Bridge. We'd lost track of the day and it was dark by the time we made our way to the on-ramp, all the tourists disappeared. Cars streamed past us, separated from our lane by a shoulder-high metal barrier. They moved in our direction, their lights coming up from behind and illuminating the bridge, then floating away beyond us toward the city. I could not see the water below me but I knew it was there. I tried not to imagine falling in. I watched Stephen just ahead, leaning forward, his legs circling again and again. I loved those legs. It was funny that just the sight of them, in motion, could make me so happy. Now, I found myself memorizing the feeling of his leg over mine. It was something I used to do when we were long-distance. I put my head on his chest and listened. "I can't hear the pop," I said.

"It just happens once. But do you hear a leaking sound? Like air out of a tire?"

"You can hear that?"

"I don't know. I can't. But I always wonder if that's how it sounds, if you can get close enough to hear it."

I pressed my ear against him, getting as close as I could. Maybe I heard it, an extremely subtle hissing, the air escaping bit by bit, creeping into the chest cavity. I kept trying to listen for it, as his breathing got heavier, and I drifted off to sleep.

THE BUS CHUGGED up Haight Street, turning left at the mouth of Golden Gate Park. Out my window I watched high school kids straggle into McDonald's for breakfast. Two girls in hooded sweatshirts stood on the corner, smoking their first cigarettes of the day, backpacks with thin words scrawled on the pockets in Wite-Out. The bus ascended Stanyan, turning right on Parnassus, triple-decker Victorians giving way to eight-story clinic buildings. It wheezed to a stop, and emptied out. The passengers in scrubs hurried away, while the rest of us stood in a clump, squinting around.

The hospital was a city in itself, with a complex pattern of streets and avenues, each wing its own small neighborhood. I wandered through the corridors of 11 Long, feeling nervous, voyeuristic. Every door was open, a curtain drawn around the bed inside. I couldn't help glancing at the end of each bed, the set of feet that stuck out past each curtain, some tucked under sheets, some propped on pillows in beige hospital socks, some with white socks, striped socks from home.

I found Stephen's room, knocked for ceremony. He was sitting cross-legged on his bed reading a comic book, shorts on under his hospital gown. I slid my shoes off and sat down next to him. I leaned as close as I could without bumping the tube, pressed my cheek against his. His cheek felt like his cheek.

"Want to see it?"

"Yeah."

He lifted up his gown. I scrutinized the thick plastic tube, but it was hard to believe it actually went through his chest wall, into his body. The skin around it was covered in gauze so I couldn't see the point of entry; the gruesome part, I had to infer. The tube snaked its way down to a gurgling machine on the floor. The machine was rectangular and clear, displaying all the liquid it was sucking out of the chest cavity. I wished it were at least tinted, I didn't like the yellowish sloshing, but the machine made Stephen happy. He could look down from his bed and measure his progress.

"How's it going in here?"

"A little weird. When I came into this room, I had this feeling the person before me had died. Something was off—the disinfectant smell was too strong."

"Well, you can't tell for sure."

"Jake was on duty last night; I asked."

"Who was the person?"

"A guy in his eighties, with pneumonia. He'd been put on the CF floor because there was an extra bed."

I felt the mattress underneath me. I wondered if they'd turned it over. I wondered whether he'd been asleep, or sitting like we were, the head of the bed raised, blinds open, coffee and newspaper on the rolling bedside table. I wondered whether someone had been sitting where I was, next to him, or maybe one step removed, in the chair. I wondered whether it was true what they said about pneumonia being the old man's friend. Did old men actually see it this way, or was it only younger, healthier people who thought the end of life wasn't worth dragging out?

"The worst thing is, he got a phone call today. A woman asked for Ben."

"What did you say?"

Stephen looked at me helplessly. "I said I didn't know where he was."

I SAT ON his bed, my legs tucked under me, each of us reading a book, the rolling table between us covered in snacks. The hospital menu contained things I'd liked as a kid—vanilla pudding, cranberry juice, chocolate milk, Neapolitan ice cream. When Stephen filled out his menu for the day, he'd order an extra item or two for me. I wasn't sure he should, and he complained that I was too rule-abiding when it came to the hospital. He hated, for instance, that when I was lying down next to him, I hopped up as soon as a nurse stepped into the room. He liked to tease me by pulling me close and holding me there while the door creaked open. I'd struggle, my face turning red, which only made us look guiltier. *Oh, hey,* Stephen would say, pretending to be zipping his pants, *this is my, uh, girlfriend, Liz.* I'd make a point of telling him to shut up, but the nurses always laughed. See, he'd say, you never give people any credit.

It might have been the food or the constant flow of adults in and out of the room, but I felt weirdly young, fifteen instead of twenty-two, sitting on Stephen's bed. We huddled together, deciding whether a particular nurse would notice if he turned up the flow of his IV medications to get them over with sooner. We took dark pleasure in the eerie gurgling of the chest machine and the machine's name itself, "Pleur-evac"—the vacuuming of the lungs. We sat on the bed talking, removed from time, as if we were on an overnight train, or sleeping out to get tickets for a concert—the reason why we were waiting, why we were stuck in this particular place for an indefinite amount of time had been lost to us and we were just hanging out.

And then I stepped out of the revolving door and the fresh air knocked the youth out of me. I walked through the streets, barely seeing people my own age, but watching old people hungrily, seeing how they held their shoulders, plucked coins from their purses, scouring them for information, for how life proceeded when illness was part of it, and how love proceeded, too.

THURSDAY NIGHT I SAT in Stephen's room, watching his favorite doctor, Dr. Stulbarg, listen to his lungs. The tube had been removed that morning, so Stephen was wearing his own clothes, a blue T-shirt and sweats. He was talking a mile a minute, thrilled to no longer be tethered to the wall. Dr. Stulbarg put his stethoscope on Stephen's back and waited. "I hope he doesn't talk this much at home," he said to me.

The lung was emerging shaky but victorious. The chest muscle just needed time to recover. We listened to Dr. Stulbarg as if we were the lung's parents, nervous and proud, wishing there was something we could do to help it along. "We'll watch it for a couple of days," he told us. "By Saturday you should be headed home."

SATURDAY MORNING, the phone rang at seven, and I knew before I answered that we'd messed up by counting on it. Stephen would never be up this early unless something had gone wrong. He was calling to tell me not to come get him. His lung had collapsed again, and later today he'd have to get a second chest tube put in. At first I thought I hadn't heard him right. How could the lung collapse just after it had been fixed? "But the doctors said it would heal," I told him. "I heard them say it, *when* the lung heals, not *if.*"

Stephen didn't bother to answer me. The idea that doctors knew everything, that people expected them to, made him impatient. "Maybe it got another hole."

"How many holes can it get?" I pulled the dark green comforter around me like a sleeping bag.

Stephen sighed. "I don't know. I haven't even seen Dr. Stulbarg yet."

"I'm coming over."

"I'm going back to sleep. Wait at least till ten."

The elevator was crowded but quiet, except for two doctors who were speaking hurriedly about their rounds, referring to patients by their organs—the kidney failure on Ten-Long, the gastrointestinal obstruction down in X-ray. I caught the eye of a man standing behind them, squeezed into a corner, a kid under each arm. The kids were both staring at the elevator buttons, holding balloons. He leaned back against the wall, shifting from foot to foot.

AT BOTH MY JOBS, I found myself not mentioning that my boyfriend was in the hospital. Other people seemed to mention these things, at least at the Wilderness Press, where, ironically, we all hovered in a windowless room under fluorescent lights, me typing Business Return Card (BRC) information into a computer. But I found myself smiling and shrugging when the older people in the office—healthy older people, because this was an outdoorsy place—articulated their imagination of my life: biking to work, time on my hands, not a care in the world. I liked these people, enough that I didn't want to set them straight, and not enough that I needed to, so I'd shrug and smile, until the conversation wound its way back to its permanent home, the politics of the office, and I could relax, the newcomer, ducking out of the crossfire.

At Wah Mei Preschool I could relax completely, because all conversations took place in Chinese. I'd dropped off my résumé with doubts, but the director had been eager to have me; she wanted me to help the kids with their English. I was supposed to help discreetly—the kids had an English teacher already—a friend of the director's, who unfortunately spoke English with a heavy Chinese accent. The English teacher still taught the English classes, but I was supposed to respond with the children, and speak loudly.

The English lesson took up twenty minutes of the day and for the remainder I was lost. The kids ran up to me, speaking in Chinese, first quickly, and then more slowly, and loudly, while I frantically tried to interpret their gestures. Some things were simple—a Band-Aid, a drink of water, a ride on my back. I had to send them to other adults for all conflict resolution, unless I'd seen the altercation take place. I taught them a few games in English so I could give the other teachers a break. We played Captain Midnight and hide-and-seek. This was the great thing about working at a preschool—when you're standing with your back turned calling out "One o'clock, two o'clock . . . Captain Midnight!" at which twenty kids squeal and run, and you give chase, there is nowhere else your thoughts can be.

FRIDAY, A WEEK after the second tube, the lung was still not healing. Dr. Stulbarg sat in a chair next to Stephen's bed. It seemed a bad sign, a doctor sitting down. "We're going to have to try something more," he said.

More than the chest tube? I winced; Stephen nodded. He liked that Dr. Stulbarg had been a philosophy major in college, that he openly admitted the complexity of this, medicine's inability to provide all the answers. At the moment, he was describing pleurodesis. It involved injecting tetracycline into the lung to irritate the lung tissue, to the point where the tissue scarred and stuck to the chest wall. Once the tissue stuck, the lung could not deflate, even if it got another hole in it. The result sounded promising, the method, prehistoric. Was that all they could offer—eviscerate the tissue to the point where it scarred?

"Sounds painful," I said.

"Very painful," Dr. Stulbarg said, and I felt my own affection for him, for the way he looked me in the eye when he said this. "But after this, the lung will never collapse again."

Stephen would be sedated, he wouldn't remember it, but his body would go through the motions of the pain, there would be writhing around.

"I don't want you anywhere near the room," Dr. Stulbarg said to me.

THE PRESCHOOL WAS its own universe, and no part of adult life could infiltrate it. But, as I sat at the computer at Wilderness Press, things started floating in. I could think about ten things at once because the work itself was mindless; I was wasting time. Which hadn't felt problematic before Stephen had gone into the hospital, it had felt fine, I had been happy to have a job at all after a couple of weeks of looking. But wasting time had begun to take on a darker quality, I felt a tugging at the back of my brain, as if my days were numbered, even though it wasn't my life that was visibly shrinking. But, of course, my days were numbered, too, there were just (probably) more of them, and I was viscerally aware that they were finite, and what if they were more finite than I thought, what if I got hit by a bus tomorrow, and I'd spent my last day alive on this earth typing BRCs into a computer? And the computer was unfortunately old and slow, so I could think about all of this between the time I hit "return" and started entering a new BRC. I would have to quit, I wanted to quit tomorrow, but life was chaotic enough as it was.

At home, my housemates were fighting, and construction was going full force on the flat above ours. It was the reason we had cheap rent, but it was spiraling out of control—water poured into my closet, a leg crashed through the bathroom ceiling right over the tub. And the phone was ringing nonstop. My family, Stephen's family, friends from home. The problem was, I didn't know what to say. So, what else is going on? friends would ask, and I hated hearing this, because that was the whole problem, nothing else was going on, and the question seemed unfair, as if I should have been able to keep living my life and doing this at the same time, some kind of dexterous juggling. But this was Stephen's fault. He could juggle; he made a point of juggling, he made juggling look easy.

A FEW DAYS AFTER the pleurodesis, I sat slumped in the chair by Stephen's window, studying the parking ticket in my hands. I had been collecting tickets over the last three weeks—once I was up in Stephen's room I stopped caring about moving the car every two hours. All the cars parked around mine were littered with tickets, too. I needed to write a letter to the *Chronicle* about the way hospital visitors were preyed on. Sure, we were capable of moving our cars like everyone else, but it seemed a little cruel, that the parking police knew where we were and what we were doing. "Oh look, here comes the family with the kid in the ICU, they'll be here for a good six hours."

Stephen sighed deeply as Jake unhooked his blood pressure cuff. He'd surfaced from the pleurodesis surly. The doctors said irritability was a good sign, but they didn't have to live with the irritable person, hear him complain about the texture of his blanket. I wondered if it could count as anything that I was irritable, too.

"We have to get rid of that thing," Stephen muttered. He was eyeing the poster I'd tacked up across from his bed—a woodblock print of Japanese mountains. It had taken some work to find a poster—Stephen wouldn't agree to any of his favorites, on the grounds that they'd carry the aftertaste of the hospital once he got out. This had been mine in Chicago, it had been sitting rolled in a cardboard tube.

"What's wrong with it?"

"I can't deal with seeing the mountains."

"They're not even real mountains," I grumbled. But I untaped the poster from the wall. I stared out the window, down past the hospital buildings, toward the dark green stretch of the park. Cars streamed along its borders. In this room, they could have been part of a video game. And when I returned to the world down there, stepping outside, colors would jump out at me, yellow shirts and deep green street signs, shiny silver cars, the frenetic mix of blue and orange on a bus ad. "When you get out let's go to that arboretum," I said. "I still haven't been there yet."

"Stop," he said, glaring at me, his eyes at half-mast.

"What?"

"The apartment, the park, the fucking arboretum. I can't remember what anything outside looks like. You're making it worse, talking about it."

"What am I supposed to do? My whole day happens out there." Stephen had never even seen the inside of the preschool, I realized. Today at work, the rain had pounded steadily. The humidity had seeped in between the cement walls and the Scotch tape; the kids' paintings kept curling, falling off the walls. The playground was flooded and the kids without rain boots had been cooped up all day, pummeling each other with pillows in the "quiet area." The room had that car-trip smell of apple juice and stale saltines.

Stephen kicked his blanket off and flexed his feet one at a time, stretching out his calves. "All my thoughts are making me itch."

"It's from being in here so long."

"That's the real problem—I'm never getting out."

"Come on, you're getting out."

"Doubtful, honey."

"It's not doubtful. And don't call me honey when you're pissed off." The door to his room was open, my voice was echoing down the quiet hallway.

"First they said a week, then two, today they said three. Wonder what's next."

"People get out of the hospital," I snapped.

"Don't forget Ben."

"Who was eighty."

"You don't get it. They're letting me down easy. Anyway, it doesn't matter."

"What are you talking about?"

"I can't keep doing this. I think I'm done."

Years later, this moment would come back to me, and I'd think, if I'd been able to admit it to myself, I would have known right then how deep I was in. Because instead of kindness, or empathy, or anything that would have involved a sliver of distance between us, I was lit with fight-or-flight. Desperation, fury, giving way to a hardened will. Over my dead body.

"You can't be done," I said.

One day my mother would speak to my father like this.

He'd lose his eyesight in a terrible bike accident and tell her he wasn't sure he wanted to keep living. "Too many people love you," she'd say. He'd tell this story with appreciation; glad he'd decided to live in the end. But still, you would hope a person has a choice. And Stephen and I were only twenty-two, and not the twenty-two of our parents' generation, married with kids, one year into lifetime careers, but the twenty-two of our own generation, which meant a particular kind of freedom. (Your generation decided to have their retirement in their twenties, my dad liked to say.) We still bought separate loaves of bread in the grocery store and cooked our own meals, since he liked meat and I was a vegetarian. We considered ourselves independently happy or unhappy, and we were trying to keep it that way. Everything we were trying for, that I was trying for, felt drowned. Stephen looked at me like I was crazy.

"You don't get it. I mean, what if I'm really dying?"

"But you're not."

"How can you tell?"

"You're not even in the ICU. You're still in the realm of having to try."

"Argh, you are so fucking demanding."

The nurse knocked on the open door, and I realized she was ten minutes late to set up this round of IV antibiotics; she'd probably heard us arguing and stalled. Stephen waved goodbye to me, pretending that I had been about to leave. Fine. I had to meet people anyway. I slunk out of the room, wondering if this nurse would avoid me now, the crazy girl who yelled at her boyfriend while he was stranded in his hospital bed.

I made my way to a bar on Valencia, ordered a beer and fought my way through the crowd to find my friend Chris. She was sitting at our usual table in the corner, her feet up on my seat to save it. She shifted over and I sank down. It was Improv Night. I was hoping one of the comics from last week would return—a woman who'd just had a baby. She'd brought the baby, too, and a friend had watched him while she'd joked about labor, about getting back in shape so her son's teenage friends would want to have sex with her.

Christmas lights skirted the tops of the bar's walls. Sawdust covered its floors. The sawdust seemed sprinkled with a wink and a wry smile, *You get it, don't you? Everyone here* gets *it*. What did we get? That the sawdust was some ironic gesture, harkening to the past, romanticizing and making fun of it at the same time. I wanted to put a ban on all cleverness, to admit the strength and youth of bodies, to stop referring to cigarettes as cancer sticks or smoky treats or anything that pointed to that light lack of caring for the lungs. Each cigarette, Caitlin used to say in high school, was a flirtation with death. We'd smile and inhale, as if the object of our attention were some slightly dangerous guy. But lately death had lost its chill. It was more like the rooms on the eleventh floor, all those machines, the slow deterioration.

A poet leaned into the mike, tilted her head to the side as she began reading. I stared around the black-clad room. The table of regulars next to us, a group of women in their thirties, had always seemed like adults before, their fiercely orchestrated hair, faces slackened by concealer. But tonight they were glowing. I felt like a spy here in the outside world, surrounded by people who felt invincible. Though you never knew who else was here; someone with leukemia could be staring through me right now, that guy two tables away glancing over.

Chris leaned across the table, eyeing my hands. I'd shredded the label off my third beer; my fingers were gummed and twitching. She frowned, pulled me out the door. We walked down Valencia, hands deep in our jacket pockets, heads ducked against the cold. We found the narrow staircase leading up to the women's bathhouse. It was almost ten, we only had an hour, but we had the place to ourselves. We sank into the warm water, each taking a corner of the pool, leaning our heads back against its concrete edge. I closed my eyes and let the water reach my chin.

Woozy, I snuck back to the hospital. I loved San Francisco for this, that the girlfriend could slip back into the patient's room at eleven-thirty at night, as long as the patient was awake. And he was, reading a magazine.

"I'm sorry," I said, because I was. But then I found I couldn't elaborate.

He smiled. "You're drunk."

I shrugged.

"Anyway, you'll be happy to know you guilted me into walking the stairs."

"I didn't guilt you."

"It's the only form of exercise I can deal with in here. I managed three flights."

I lay down next to him on the bed. "How was it?"

"How do you think? It's an internal stairwell."

"Besides aesthetically."

"Not terrible."

AT HOME I ANSWERED the phone without thinking, and of course it was my mom, she always called when there was no way I could hide. How are you? she asked, and I started crying, and when she said she was coming to visit all I could say was thanks.

She stayed for five days, and did everything useful that had never occurred to me. She made vegetarian chili and froze it in portions I could bring to work for lunch. She asked the hospital about VCR use, reserved the VCR on Stephen's floor for several different nights, found out where to rent movies on Haight Street. When friends wanted to visit and Stephen said no, she told me to let our friend Josh through, since he'd been Stephen's best friend growing up. Josh drove up from Santa Cruz, and sure enough my mom was right, Stephen smiled when he walked into the room, launched right into a caustic commentary about hospital life, seeming more himself than he had in days.

My mom took me to meet her friend Missy, who I'd promised to look up but hadn't. Missy's husband was also in the hospital at UCSF, for a brain tumor. Missy, my mom, and I walked out on the wooden docks by Fort Mason. Missy and I talked shop: how it felt to know the patient better than the doctors did, to see little changes that the staff missed; how the sight of an old couple flooded us with jealousy. My mom was quiet. I was uncomfortably old but young with her now, experiencing something she hadn't gone through yet, but also letting her be my mom like I hadn't since I'd been little, or maybe ever, resting my head on her shoulder in the car.

AND THEN, WE were free. The pleurodesis had worked its magic. Stephen's parents arrived the day after he got out of the hospital. I'd overheard him on the phone early on, telling them not to come while he was *in* the hospital, he wouldn't really be able to hang out, suggesting they come afterwards. I'd thought the idea was absurd, but now I saw his point. His parents drove us up the coast to Mendocino, where we had our own tiny cottage with a garden outside. We felt like we'd stumbled into a fairy-tale world, where after a month of grueling days we woke up to find ourselves together again, in a gigantic bed with a white comforter, sunlight streaming through the windows. The four of us met to walk along the cliffs by the beach. Stephen and I were too tired to walk very far. We sat on a log overlooking the ocean, watching his parents wind their way along a dirt path.

"Your parents seem younger than we do," I told him.

"They're always like this on vacation."

"Do you think this is what it feels like to be old?"

"Maybe. I could be ninety, my muscles are so weak."

"They'll come back. You've been in bed for a month."

It was strangely nice, though, to see his parents from this perspective, Fran in her blue coat, Gus next to her, arm around her back, wandering the coast like a young couple.

ON THE DRIVE back from Mendocino, Stephen could tell something was wrong, and the next morning he forced himself to go over to the hospital. And just like that, it snatched him back. A course of IV antibiotics this time. His mom extended her ticket and I set her up in my room. I felt shy and lacking—the apartment had no full-length mirror, the blankets were thin, all the silverware had come from her house. But it turned out she was an easy houseguest; she had mastered the art of being an easy houseguest, which I had not even known was an art. She managed to buy just enough food to keep our household fed without making us feel that she was doing it. *Oh, I just saw these mangoes at the store.* She read the paper, put her feet on the wooden trunk we had for a coffee table. She and I went over to the hospital together, walked through the eucalyptus groves in the Presidio.

"I hate hospitals," she said. " I don't know what to do in there."

I thought, Everybody hates hospitals. I hate hospitals. I'm not going to be the one assigned to the position of liking the hospital.

STEPHEN LAY WITH his eyes closed, waiting to hear back from the doctors. He had seven days left of antibiotics, and had asked if he could finish the course at home. Soon, I knew, he'd begin gearing up for the stairs. He was like someone in the outside world heading to the gym, dreading and resisting, proud when his regimen had been completed. I did not tell him how this got to me, how depressing and weirdly endearing it was, watching him head for the stairs.

A doctor I'd never met walked in briskly. He stood too close to the bed, tapping the chart in his hand as evidence. He had to be somewhere in the middle—not a resident, but not one of the more established doctors. The middle rung seemed to be a painful place in a teaching hospital, or at least there were certain doctors who had a middle-rungness about them, who moved around like mid-sized dogs, needing to make clear at every turn what they considered your relationship to them to be. "The X-ray looks good," he said, "but we want to keep you a few more days."

Stephen sat up. "If I can, I really need to get out of here."

"I understand that," the doctor said.

"Really," I muttered. Stephen shot me a look. We were trying to be diplomatic here, we were bargaining. The person who always accused me of being too polite was guiding me in the tactics of negotiation.

"We can't keep you. But as your medical team, that's our advice."

"So I can go?" Stephen said slowly. The doctor glanced at me and then at him. We all knew what was going to happen.

"Actually, we feel strongly that you should stay."

Stephen started blinking faster, tears escaping out of the corners of his eyes. I wanted to wrap him up in my arms and sneak him home, even for an hour, even if I had to bring him back.

"Like I said, the X-ray looks good." The doctor standing there, as if we were all still capable of talking, watching Stephen lose face.

"Okay, thank you," I said. "If you could leave now, though. And close the door."

He backed out of the room, startled. The door clicked shut. Stephen was crying, there was no tube between us; I hugged him hard. His nose began to bleed, trickling down on his lips and my cheek. The defeating mixture of tears and blood, I started crying, too. "Sorry," I said.

"Why are you sorry?"

"I don't know," I said, because I didn't, I really didn't. It just seemed like you weren't supposed to cry when you visited someone in the hospital.

"You're usually the crier."

"No, I've been crying, just not, you know, in here."

"Where?"

"For some reason it usually happens in the elevator."

"That's awful."

"Only when no one's in there."

"No, I mean, you're in the same building as me and you're

crying alone in another room. In the elevator. That's a terrible thought."

THAT NIGHT, WE told the nurses we were going to walk around the halls for a while, promising to be back for the next round of antibiotics. Stephen led me down a hallway to a wing of research offices. A few nights ago, on his round of the stairs, he'd found something he wanted to show me. We rode a quiet elevator down to the fourth floor and made our way to a back stairwell. Between the third and fourth floors there was an emergency exit door, which Stephen propped open with a newspaper.

"Seems a little sketchy," I said.

"No one's out here at night. Don't worry."

We slipped out the door, and the hospital air gave way to the dense mist of the night. We crept down the fire escape until we reached the nursing school courtyard. The lawn was dark and wet, its wooden benches vacant. Stephen led me silently up a steep driveway. We walked side by side, stopping every few feet so he could catch his breath. I pictured the doctors and nurses peering out the windows to see him trudging along. "We better not get caught," I told him.

He smiled, as if he found that idea darkly entertaining. The driveway took us up along the back of the medical complex, until we were at the rear entrance of an optometry clinic, which was built into the hill. We stepped out onto its balcony, following it around to the west side of the building, which bordered the roof of the adjacent parking garage. Stephen went first, climbing over the balcony's rungs, and stepping onto the ledge of the garage roof, then down a foot to the roof itself. I followed, trying not to look at the tiny gap between the balcony and the

roof, the ground five stories below. I reached out and grabbed
Stephen's arm to steady myself. We had made it; we were on the
roof, in the dark, in the fog and thick outside-world air.

We sat on the wide ledge of the roof, dangling our feet over
Parnassus Avenue. We leaned back, our hands firm on the cold
cement behind us. The streetlights on Parnassus created a dotted path through the air, rising over two hills and descending,
jetting out to Ocean Beach. We listened for the ocean. From
our house we could hear the foghorns, and we thought maybe
we could hear them now, but we could have been imagining it.
We secured our feet on the roof, and lay with our backs arched
over the ledge, looking at the world upside down. The sky was
a deep lake, the houses and stores like docks at its edges. We
stayed like this until we were in danger of headaches and then
lifted our heads.

"Uh-oh, head rush," Stephen said.

"Take it slow."

We crouched down with our backs against the wall of the
ledge, letting the blood move back down into our bodies. We
huddled side by side, pressed close together, our knees near our
chests. We were sheltered from the wind and we were free and
invisible. Come here, he said, even though I was right next to
him. I slipped my hands under the back of his shirt, gripping
him as we kissed. It was freezing. We were on the roof, and
the nurses would be wondering, and a custodian might move
the newspaper from under the exit door, but we couldn't get
ourselves to stop.

chapter four

I WANT TO GIVE YOU A BREAK, THE BREAK WE GOT, AFTER this bleak month. I want you to run around with us in the Technicolor blue of San Francisco September, venturing to the lighthouse, the crumbling bunkers overlooking the ocean, the train tracks leading to the Santa Cruz boardwalk. But I want to give you more than a break; I want to give you post-hospital bliss. Because there's nothing like it, those days after a harrowing hospital stay, when you walk out into the world and every single part of it feels right. It's a cross between the feeling of falling in love and having narrowly escaped being hit by a car. That moment when you glance back at the spot where the car careened, and your good fortune is no longer an idea but a physical sensation. It's that minute, expanded into days. Life on the outside appears as in relief to life on the inside. You see the world the way it looks from a hospital room only you are out there in the world, soaking it up. Maybe it's most like lucid dreaming.

All over the city, people were meditating or practicing yoga to be in the moment, and here we were, the moment slipped into our pockets on the way out of the hospital's revolving door. We smiled a lot for no reason, mundane events were backlit. The traffic lights, our car windows—everything that wasn't broken felt lucky. We sat at the Laundromat, happy enough to be watching our clothes tumble around, eating Oreos from the vending machine.

We took a trip to Colorado for winter break, making the twenty-hour drive in Stephen's two-door Corolla. On our return, with new stretches of ice along Highway 80, the car began to feel flimsy. Late at night on the drive I sank into the passenger seat, my left calf twitching. I took my shoes off, stretched out my toes, and flexed my feet hard against the glove compartment. Leg cramps always came on in places like this, close quarters where it was impossible to stand up—a crowded auditorium during the final act of a play, dinner with a friend who was in the middle of a painful confession. The last time I'd gotten to stretch was four hours ago, the gas station along the side of the road a lone beacon in the dark. I hadn't put on my coat. The snow had come at me sideways, whisking underneath the station's tabletop roof.

I was thankful the leg twitching had come on during Stephen's shift at the wheel. I was itching for us to stop, so much so that when the car slowed underneath me I had the feeling that I might have made it happen. But I didn't want it to stop in this way—Stephen's foot still pressed on the gas, his face leaned close to the dashboard, searching for a clue to the sudden loss of momentum. It felt like we were going up a steep hill, except we were driving flat, the easy highway rolled out in front of us. Had he not filled up the tank? Did the tank have a hole in it? Why did I know so little about cars? The only thing I was good for was changing a tire. Stephen had taken auto shop in high school. He tinkered with his car, paid attention to its chugs and murmurs, but how much he actually knew was unclear to me. He jumped into fixing almost anything.

He muttered about the fuel filter, the alternator. I turned off the heat and the stereo, anything that might be draining power. In minutes the car was cold, wind slipping in around the windows. The car kept slowing; finally Stephen steered over to the side of the road. I thought of the sleeping bags in the backseat. A light snow, but steady, the temperature dropping by the hour.

As soon as he turned off the car we felt the emptiness of the road. We'd liked it only a few minutes ago, jetting through the darkness, music blaring; no one to remind us that this was not our movie. Now we needed those missing drivers, the more of them the better, so we could choose between them, rather than getting stuck with the one lone car that came our way. At midnight, on this long stretch of nothing, who would be in that car? I was relieved there were two of us. Except, if I'd been alone, I wouldn't be driving right now, I wouldn't have tried to make this drive straight through. I was starting a new teaching job Monday morning; we were cutting it close. Why did I agree to pulling this all-nighter? It had been alluring, that one extra day in Colorado, to sleep in after New Year's Eve, go out to Dot's Diner at noon with our friends.

The snow froze against the windshield in tiny disparate smudges. Beyond them, the raised hood of the car. I knew Stephen had set his flashlight in the left corner, flooding the engine.

He'd be poking around with his gloved hands, lifting blackened metal lids, setting them back. I put on my shoes, tied my laces, found my hat. Outside, it was lighter than it had seemed inside the car. I could see the outline of hills in the distance. The car suddenly appeared as a metal carcass, something we could leave behind. The snow was higher than I'd imagined, and my jeans were instantly soaked up to my calves. I walked around to the front of the car. Stephen was leaning over the engine.

"I'll flag somebody down," I told him, walking toward the driver's side.

"A trucker or something—someone who can radio in."

"Anyone who drives by is good enough," I said, walking a few feet in front of the car. "We need a ride."

"We can't leave the car," Stephen called to me. "We need a tow."

I stood out in front of the car, waiting. Steam rose from the highway, which meant it couldn't be as cold as it felt. Our yellow hazard lights streaked across the asphalt, stopped, streaked again. No one. Then, a semi hurtling toward us in the distance. My arms out in the air, barely high enough to intersect its beams. And gone. I thought about the logistics of trying to sleep in the Toyota. Of course we could leave the car. It was a car; no one wanted it out here. Everyone driving by had one already. What was he talking about, not leaving the car?

"If a ride comes, we're taking it," I said to Stephen, though more to the road in front of me since he was behind the hood. Minutes passed. High beams moving toward us. I waved, long sweeps of my arms. The car slowed, skidded to a stop fifty feet ahead of us, backed up on the shoulder. Not hard to do out here, the shoulder giving way to the high plain, crunched snow covering packed dirt. I had never been so happy to see the Nevada

Highway Patrol. I imagined the black interior of the car, warm air blasting from the vents.

The officer walked toward us through the snow, his car almost disappeared behind him now that its lights were off. This would have been a reasonable movie entrance, his brown pants, dark blue parka, approachable smile. The three of us trudged back to his car. Stephen and I squeezed into the passenger seat, even though probably only one of us was supposed to get in. Stephen wanted to be in charge of what happened to the car, and I wanted to be in charge of what happened to us. The officer suggested we get the car towed to Elko. It was fifty miles away, but it was the only town in the area with a big enough garage. He helped us call Triple A. Stephen was thrilled that he could take advantage of his new Triple A upgrade, which allowed him to tow to the destination of his choice, rather than just to the nearest mechanic. "Last year," he was saying, "they'd have towed us back to Wells." I was busy imagining the call I'd have to make tomorrow, to Carol, my new boss. *My car broke down.* She might fire me before I started the job.

Soon we were out of the officer's car, sitting in our own, waiting, this no man's land stretching for miles, remnants of a barbed wire fence curling up through the snow.

We managed to find a room at the Motel 6 in Elko, right across from the garage. Sunday, there was no progress to be made, and it was still snowing. We ate breakfast at eleven-thirty, meandered through the town's small neighborhoods, returned to our den of a motel room. Monday we learned that the alternator we needed had to be obtained from the next town over. More TV and aimless walking, diner meals, conversations about whether either of us would live in a small town, whether we could see doing this together someday, whether we'd end up claustrophobic and stunted, or relaxed and free. We left Elko strangely wistful; looking back at the gas station/diner/motel, where time had been suspended. Too bad we're not retired, we decided, we'd do so well at it, treat the "golden years" with the respect they deserved. In the meantime, we were speeding, trying to make up for the fact that I was four days late for my first day of work.

THE HOSPITAL HAD disappeared from view, the rest of life rushing forward. I biked to the Adda Clevenger School through Golden Gate Park, thirty-five minutes there (forty on the way back with the hill). As soon as I locked up my bike and stepped inside, I was pummeled by the kids, their persistent tugs on my arms. Ilana, five years old, warning me that today her lunch box was filled with grapes. Her mother had slept in, and she'd packed it herself, and she only liked grapes. So. On the back deck at noon, scrounging for lunch scraps, my co-teacher donating part of her burrito, because Ilana would be doubled over in half an hour if all she ate were grapes. Ilana, begrudgingly munching the burrito, talking with Kasha in Russian. Their eyes had lit up when they'd discovered that this world their mothers dove into on the phone, surfaced from and abandoned once they walked out the front door, this *Russian* was comprehensible to another *child*. I had no idea what they were saying, but if they weren't already swearing right in front of me, they would be soon.

My new boss accused me of burning the candle at both ends. Days I hurled myself into teaching, nights I was out late exploring the city with Chris, coming home to stay up even later with Stephen and our housemate Sam, and Sam's new girlfriend

Anna. Sam was over six feet tall, a little Muppet-like—his lanky frame, the fluid ease in his walk, his broad smile. While Stephen was absurd and inappropriate, Sam had a quieter thing going, he'd lean toward you in a noisy room and make the perfect dry observation. He was gifted in the sciences, and his dad, a Korean doctor, was hoping they'd hold his interest. But he saved his studying for his English classes, which was where he'd met Anna. I met Anna when I walked into our kitchen one morning, and found her there, drinking coffee, her long red hair straggling down her back, her eyes puffy from sleep. She was a sophomore in college, double-majoring in English and art, and she painted in thick, dense colors—deep yellows, blues, greens. She was fair-skinned and dissolved into a whining exhausted puddle in the sun. Sam was always taking her places like Joshua Tree and throwing up his hands when she fell apart.

I got caught up in the details of home life, the alliances, the little irritations. Strangely, although she was the visitor, Anna made me feel the most at home. At the end of the night we'd sit on the countertops talking, her in her green sweats, the sound of Sam's guitar flooding in from the living room. Sam and I shared a bathroom, since we felt Stephen's standards of cleanliness were too high, and a certain sensibility, which Sam described as rowing down the river facing backward. Stephen and Anna described it as "Camp Why Talk About the Future," and loved to point out its flaws. Anna was even messier than I was, and when she spent the night at our house, Stephen insisted on making the coffee in the morning so he didn't have to find the grounds embedded in the counter-tile grout. Stephen and Sam had their own annoying habits, having just come from living with fifteen other guys. Stephen was territorial, writing his name with a black Sharpie on his box of Fig Newtons, and Sam kept siphoning off my laundry detergent.

Teaching, while the three of them were on the college schedule, made me feel like I was leading a double life. In the early morning, while the rest of the house slept, I raced to work and assumed the role of a responsible adult, introducing vowel combinations, emptying small shoes of sand. I worried my worlds would collide—some Tuesday at midnight I'd be coming out of a bar, or emerging from the ocean naked, and run into the parents of one of my students.

Stephen had his own doubleness going on. Anna was surprised to find out he'd been in the hospital just before she'd met him. If anything she thought he was too vivacious—his abrasive sense of humor and that wiry skate-rat look. Meanwhile, I came home from work to find him sitting on our futon, fiddling with a small misting machine. "For this drug, DNase," he explained. "I signed up for the trial."

I could tell he liked the idea of being in a study—he would be giving back, playing on the CF team. He set up the machine on the old metal trunk that served as our coffee table. I sat next to him, watching him put the DNase vial in its compartment. The machine stirred and hummed, expelling a thick stream of mist. He held a plastic pipe up to his mouth and inhaled. Twenty minutes, at the beginning and end of every day. The machine made me instantly territorial. We'd have to stay near outlets; we couldn't crash at a friend's house if we didn't feel like driving home. "It's for a whole month?"

"That's the study. Then if it works, I just keep taking it."

I hated this machine. Antibiotics were one thing, they were circumscribed, finite. But this DNase, what was it really doing? It was *supposed to* break up strands of mucus in the lungs, which was *supposed to* make it harder for viruses to grow. It reminded me of vitamins—how did you know if they were working? You never got the chance to see your parallel existence, how you would have felt if you'd never taken them. "What are we going to do about camping?" I asked him.

"I can plug into the car lighter."

"But backpacking."

"We've never even gone together."

"But we said we were going to. We were planning on it."

He held the plastic pipe of DNase away from his mouth. "Want to try it?"

I took a quick inhale. It had the aftertaste of diet soda.

Stephen did the breathing treatment while he read the paper in the morning, while he watched TV or read at the end of the night. When the official study was over, he took some license in the regimen, made his own rules. He never missed more than twice in one week. Mornings he was slow to get up for class, I'd nudge him and he'd stay on his stomach, nestling deeper into the bed.

"I'm skipping. That's twenty extra minutes of sleep."

"You skipped a couple of days ago."

"So now you suddenly love the breathing thing?"

"I don't love it."

"Liz loves the breathing thing," he sang into his pillow, and fell deep asleep.

STEPHEN RAN HEADLONG back into school. Before he'd always been pragmatic, sticking to classes within his architecture major. Now he loosened up. He signed up for photography and poetry, and became invigorated by all the creating. He brought his poems to an open-mike session, drank too much red wine, read a terrible poem about smoking—something about how if his friends didn't appreciate their lungs they could give them to him. He filled three journals with poetry, and on the last page of the third he wrote, "Looks like I'm not a poet, so this will be it."

His photography class had a studio showing, and I wandered through the lobby of Wurster Hall with him, studying the prints. Stephen's series had been discreetly hung on a back wall. In two of the pictures he was naked, staring down at the camera. The pictures were blurred, but if you squinted it wasn't hard to see the shape of him. I remembered when he'd probably taken them. I'd been sitting in my room at my makeshift desk, trying to come up with ideas for a children's book. Every time I'd glanced across the hall into his room, he was still naked, standing near the same spot. "I didn't know you were doing these for school," I said.

"The assignment was self-portraits. What did you think I was doing?"

I studied the first picture. He'd taken it in infrared, his hair sprayed out around his head like a demonic halo, like an old Billy Idol album cover. His face was contorted with a rage I'd never seen. Or, at least, I'd never seen it stilled. In real life, anger surfaced and fled from his face so easily it was casual, the yell from the other room when he'd broken a dish. Something about the expression was private, even with all its theatrics. And then there was the fact that even with the infrared, even blurred, you could see the outline of his naked body. He'd titled the picture "Gnads-o-Fire." It was the part of his sense of humor that could go either way. Later, he'd make the print into a tiny business card, and use the title as his email address until a grad school professor would tell him it made her uncomfortable. I could feel this happening around me already, his classmates giving me sidelong glances as we studied the prints, wondering who would agree to be Gnads-o-Fire's girlfriend.

WHEN STEPHEN FINISHED school, he got a job at the Coastal Conservancy, finding photographs for a book documenting the history of the Coastal Trail. Sometimes I went with him on my day off, hiked around the trails, and wrote in the city libraries. On an overcast Tuesday, we headed across the Richmond Bridge to China Camp State Park. Water spilled over the road, the high tide drenching the small swells of land. We stopped at the ranger station to ask about the history of the place. The ranger offered us coffee, sat us down with a photo album, dates handwritten under pictures and newspaper clippings.

Afterwards we walked outside, stomped through the puddles to reach the abandoned fishing docks. I watched Stephen walk on the rotting wooden boards, his face fresh with the fog, his red raincoat with its blue hood. He paused at the edge of the dock, took the lens cap off his camera. When we'd been in high school he'd said once that he wished he could get a job appreciating the seasons. We'd been hiking in the Gore Range in fall, the aspen leaves turned dark yellow. It seemed to me that this was close to that, he was getting paid to wander around in this weather. He looked more himself out here, maybe we both did. We'd both applied to grad school, but I was thinking, Maybe this is what we were meant for. Forget school, forget indoor jobs. If time really was limited, maybe we should spend as much of it as possible outside. We were talking about this, scraping the mud off our shoes with sticks, when Stephen let out a sharp groan. I knew the groan, and the left lung had been adhered to the chest wall. It had to be the right one this time.

chapter five

THE SKY WAS A METALLIC BLUE, THE WAY IT WAS HERE THE DAY
after a heavy rain. The air had been cleared, the edges of the
buildings clean-shaven. I pulled into the hospital's circular
driveway. Stephen stood outside the entrance, surrounded by
medical gadgets. His lung had healed in less than a week. Aside
from having remnants of the hospital at his feet, he looked like
he belonged in the regular world. His face was still flushed with
color, his calf muscles were intact; he trusted his sense of balance. We packed the backseat with the IV equipment. The most
awkward was the tall metal rolling stand, which we struggled
to fit into our two-door car, finally realizing that it would have
to stick out the passenger window. The base of the pole rested
in the backseat, a medical Christmas tree, surrounded by kits
of gauze, syringes, and plastic scissors.

We jumped in the car, I handed Stephen the keys, and we

were off. At least we were out of the driveway and turning right onto Parnassus. But then the car lurched, revving too high, whining for the next gear. Yes, the same car. Why couldn't he give it up? The clutch was gone. He put on the hazards, and we inched toward the nearest garage, just off the panhandle of Golden Gate Park. The mechanic seemed nice enough, but I knew it was killing Stephen to leave his car with someone he'd never met. We're gonna get jacked, he'd say to me when we got out of earshot. I was thinking about all the equipment, the bags full of expensive liquid medication that had to be refrigerated right away.

Our household had moved over to Berkeley, so there was no quick bus for us to take; we needed to get across the Bay Bridge. We called home, and luckily our new housemate, our friend Hilde, answered. She had just enough time before her shift at the photo lab to come pick us up. We took our wallets, handed over the keys, and crossed the street to the panhandle. It would be a while before Hilde could get here. We lay down in the grass. Apart from the car, we were happy enough to find ourselves here, facing the sun, unrestricted by tubes and cords. I lifted Stephen's T-shirt and ran my fingers over the patch of gauze on the right side of his chest. Beneath the gauze, the incision trickled thin streaks of blood out to the edges of the tape. I moved my fingers from patch to skin, patch to skin.

This time, the eleventh floor had welcomed me back. There was something nice about the hospital—it was the place where illness was ordinary. Once, Stephen and I had run into his favorite nurse, Jake, in Good Guys. Jake had introduced us to his partner while we all stood in line. It had been freeing to think of CF as something that could be discussed in an appliance store.

But our friends had put a dent in the "hospital as normal" idea. This time around, they'd all wanted to visit. Stephen had resisted, uncomfortable with the idea of being seen in a hospital bed. But Jake told me to overrule him; patients always felt that way, and then were happy when their friends showed up. So I did, and Stephen played host, taking them around the eleventh floor, showing them the view of the Golden Gate Bridge from the large corner lounge.

It was a relief to have their company, to drive over with Sam and Anna, to watch a movie in Stephen's room with Hilde. But when I saw the setup through their eyes, it was suddenly less casual. Hilde winced when the nurse put Stephen's IV in, and was quiet on the drive home. Eve had just moved out to San Francisco, and one night after I visited Stephen, I slept over at her house. We huddled under blankets on the couch watching TV. She told me that after she'd seen Stephen with a chest tube in, she'd taken the next day off work. And before I could shut it out, I got a glimpse of what he must have looked like to her, set against the Stephen we'd known in high school.

The next night I lay in bed, his future absence running through me like an electric shock. I thought about calling him, but it seemed cruel to ask him to comfort me about his own death. My sister Catherine had said to call anytime, and even though it was three in the morning in New York, even though as I was dialing I was telling myself not to, I stayed on to hear the rings. She answered, that same voice low with sleep I'd heard my whole childhood, waking her up from sleepwalking or to get ready for school. "Am I stupid?" I asked her. "Have I been stupid this whole time?"

In the dark, under the covers, she told me things you could only hear from your younger sister.

"He can't die, though," I said. "What am I going to do?"

"You'll come live with me."

"I will?"

"I don't know, that's what I always picture."

Now, in the park, Stephen sat up, squinting at something behind me. I turned to see two police officers knocking on the doors of a beat-up station wagon. The driver was slumped over the steering wheel, his curly orange hair splayed out on the dashboard, his friend deep asleep in the passenger seat. Soon they stumbled out of the car, looking seventeen at best. The officers handcuffed them neatly, sent them crouching into the back of the police car. They all pulled away, leaving the station wagon doors swinging open. Within seconds, two scruffy older men crept up to the car and began rifling through its backseat. They lumbered past us carrying armloads of clothes, an old CD player, a duffel bag.

"I can't believe the cops just left the doors open," Stephen said, standing up.

"Do you have to go over there?" I said, but I followed him across the grass, trying to slow our pace a little, this being his first day out. I peered into the car as he rolled up the windows and shut the doors. The backseat was piled with clothes, KFC boxes, old blankets and tapes.

A teenage girl in ripped jeans and a gray hooded sweatshirt crossed the street toward us, scowling, her dark purple lips sucked in, her chin jutting out. I remembered scowling like that when I was her age and I suddenly realized I was the person being scowled at; she thought I was an adult. Which, at twenty-three, I was, but old enough to be scowled at?

"What the hell are you doing in my car?"

Stephen frowned. "This is your car?"

It was not hers exactly, she admitted, it was her parents'. She had borrowed it, or, her sister had borrowed it. Then she'd dropped her sister off at her boyfriend's back in the suburbs and headed to San Francisco with her friends.

"Is one of them a guy with curly orange hair?" I asked.

She laughed. "You thought that was real hair?"

We told her about the police, the handcuffs, the looters. She fished out a cold, greasy bag from the car and offered us tater tots as she grilled us for details. "Shit," she said. "What am I going to do?"

"You could go get the keys," Stephen said. "It wouldn't be hard to figure out where your friends are being held."

"That's the thing, I can't. I don't turn sixteen until June." She started to cry. "My parents are going to kill me."

I thought about her friends, sitting in the police station, probably most worried about what their parents would say. I felt nostalgic for that fear, for the feeling that I was about to be forced to confess, that the game was over. I missed problems that adults could put an end to, or thought they could put an end to, or at least insisted they'd gone through when they'd been my age.

"They won't kill you," I said.

"Yeah, you don't know my parents," the girl said. Then she squinted at Stephen's wrist. "What were you doing in the hospital?"

Stephen gave his usual abbreviated version of a lung collapse, but for every step she had a question. How did it feel when the tube went through? Were you freaked out to wake up attached to a wall? They were questions that people who loved Stephen had too, but as far as I knew, hadn't voiced. When he talked about his illness, his directness had a way of feeling like a dead end. But this girl moved right past that, digging out the details, and he didn't seem to mind.

"Actually it's a relief to wake up with the tube in," Stephen said. "The worst part is lying there all morning, waiting for them to come."

"It is?" I asked. "How come you never say anything?"

"They're coming to drill a hole through my chest wall. What did you think?"

Without warning, the girl turned to me. "You must have been scared," she said between bites of tater tot. I'd been around her age when I met Stephen. If we'd grown up here, we could have been sitting in this park, ditching high school. *You must have been scared*. People said this, and I was always bucking the saddle of it. (Why did it feel like a saddle? Because it wasn't true? Because I didn't want it to be true? Because it wasn't true in the way people thought it was; because the things that scared you weren't the things that were supposed to scare you; because I couldn't explain.) But somehow from this girl, her scowl gone, her imagining my life the way only a stranger could, unhindered by knowing or caring about me, the words came through unfettered.

"Yeah," I said, and I didn't even add, *but not in the way you'd think*. Because who knew, maybe it was exactly the way she thought. And if Stephen was surprised by my answer, he kept it to himself.

Hilde dropped us off and raced to work. We came home to an empty house. What we wanted to do, we couldn't do, because he had to start his IV antibiotics right away, he was already two hours late for the round, and they had to be spaced eight hours apart. The round consisted of two different antibiotics and a saline flush, all in cold, clear plastic bags. He hung the three bags from the IV pole while I put the rest in the fridge. He set up the pump that regulated the flow of the medication from the bag down into the line leading to his arm. I sat down next to him on the bed, and he put his free arm around me. This was torture, sitting next to each other, after eight days apart, alone in our house, on our bed. We started kissing of course, doing our best to be careful of the IV line. The idea of sex seemed twisted and medically unsound, with him attached to the IV tubing. We both shook our heads no, surely we could wait. It turned out, we couldn't wait. Soon the round of antibiotics was long over, it was near dark, and I could hear Sam and Anna walking up to the porch. I searched frantically for my various items of clothing. Usually at these moments Stephen made fun of me for being embarrassed, but this time he started chuckling guiltily.

"Help," he said. "I'm still hooked up."

He was fumbling with the IV line, trying to detach it from his arm. I turned the light on so he could see what he was doing. He gave up for the moment, and got dressed as well as he could. We managed to create a semblance of order by the time Sam and Anna walked in; we were sitting on the bed, working at the IV line. Though it wasn't much of a semblance with Stephen's T-shirt hanging midair, strung up on the tall metal pole.

chapter six

THE WORLD WAS OUR OYSTER THEN, ANNA SAYS TO ME. WE are sitting in the rain outside a bakery drinking coffee, feeling sort of stuck, not in our lives exactly, but in this physical place. Why is it not our oyster now, we wonder, because technically we are in the same city. Why do we find ourselves returning to this bakery, hiking the same three trails in Tilden Park? Why aren't we trekking out to Point Reyes for late-night hikes? Has that traffic changed that much? Is it only a matter of having lived in one place too long? Our oyster, Anna says, and grins. She makes me laugh as we walk down Shattuck, and laughing with her I'm transformed for a minute, I feel young and grubby, a traveler, separate from the people streaming by us, the wet sidewalk catching my eye as it might in a place I didn't know so well.

The oyster time began six months after that last collapse, when Stephen and I were headed to graduate school. The only problem was, we'd gotten into programs on opposite sides of the country. I'd been admitted to the Berkeley School of Education, and Stephen to the Harvard School of Public Health. In the tradition of twenty-three-year-olds, we decided to each do our own thing. I'd stay in Berkeley, and move to a smaller place with Anna and Hilde, while he'd pack his things and move to Boston. It was only a year—not even a year, nine months, and we'd visit over winter break. Though a year for us wasn't the same as a year for other people, and we knew it, and neither of us was doing very well with it, in our different ways. This was the darker stretch from which the oyster time emerged.

There's imagining love in the face of death, and then there's living it out. The imagined version, a favorite storyline of songs and movies, is full of passion and selfless devotion. In life, appreciation comes easy when life is short, but the selfless devotion is trickier. Because there's a difference between imagining this life and living it: in the movies and songs, the final cutaway occurs just after the deathbed scene. As if two young lives have ended, not one. As if one person isn't going to be waking up the next morning, having breakfast, trying to figure out what her life will mean from now on.

Back then, this was my plan to get through Stephen's death: I'd have a life, a self, I wanted to continue after he was gone. But I couldn't invent that on the spot—it would have to already be there, which meant I'd need to live it while he was here, too. I was bent on keeping track of my own ambitions and desires. I knew I wanted to go to school; I didn't want to follow him to another new city without a plan. Pretending otherwise seemed dangerous—the kind of thing that would make me resentful down the road. And it felt even more dangerous to measure a year of my life against a year of Stephen's. Where would this get me? Would I then wait to do everything until after he died? Looking back, there's an immaturity to it, but also an honesty, a fight.

When I think about that time, I remember running in the morning, drinking coffee, sitting down at the low wooden window seat in our bedroom to work on the children's book I was writing. The dark brown branches out the window, the vague sense that our stoned landlady Marla was lurking in the back. Biking to work, to the grocery store. Biking, hiking, running, climbing. Running, running, running. The facts, separate from the feelings: I never considered abandoning my plan to go to school. I urged Stephen to go to Boston without me. I developed a crush on a guy at work. (*Bill,* Stephen would say years later, when we were naming the people the other had had a crush on. *Nah, not really,* I'd say. *Come on,* he'd say, *it was so obvious. Think about it.* I would think about it. *Oh yeah,* I'd say, *you're right.*) I hate to think I was trying to get a break from Stephen, but maybe I was.

Stephen was keeping things from me, too. Recently I reread his "medical history." It's a résumé of sorts, which he created to hand to various people in the hospital—a shortcut past the hour-long talk that began with his diagnosis. In the list, he included only major medical events, with two exceptions: his father's death, and a conversation with Dr. Stulbarg. For March 1993, the medical history states:

Right pneumothorax (lung collapse), resolved with
    chest tube.
First discussion of lung transplant possibility/issues.

Dr. Stulbarg had asked Stephen to think about whether he'd

want to have a lung transplant down the line. When Stephen had asked him what his prediction of "down the line" was, Dr. Stulbarg had said about five years. Stephen had come away from that conversation angry. He'd been so healthy as a kid he'd always hoped he might be an exception, and now Dr. Stulbarg was chaining him to the typical CF course. Knowing this, and knowing the months before and the months afterwards, I can see something I couldn't have seen at the time. A window. The brief period of time between fighting and acceptance, when Stephen could see CF for what it was. Maybe this was why the school decision plagued him, why his conflicting desires were so strong they left him paralyzed—a clear-eyed view. It was right before he got to know CF better, before he read and read, before he had the Single Payer party in our living room, before he developed his take. Maybe he was being honest with himself then.

He must have been lonely in his honesty, because the rest of us were far from that. At least I was far from that, and Stephen let me stay there. I wanted us to be young together; I wanted to get to be young. Except that I *was* young. So maybe for me, too, this was the space between denial and acceptance, the brief window into the darker truth of my own position.

THE OYSTER TIME began three days before Stephen's departure for Harvard. In the span of a shower, he decided to defer. He might have spent a minute of the shower doubting his 180-degree turn, but no more. I was jealous of this ability, the speed and certainty of his decisions. And I realized, when he told me the news and I started jumping around like a little kid, how badly I wanted him to stay.

Anna, Hilde, and I had settled into our new place, and I was surprised that they were happy to have Stephen to move in with us. It made sense in a way. The house would be too crowded, but he was a kind of glue. He and I could have split off on our own, but it didn't occur to us. We were twenty-three, and the only ones of our friends in a long-term relationship, and we went along with the customs of the majority, which suited us anyway. We kept separate hours, took separate trips, each spent hours on the phone with our friends and siblings. We were close, but we had the ethos of an earlier era. Once Stephen came home horrified to report that a woman he worked with had described herself as marrying "her best friend." So awful, he said, I can't imagine a life where you were the only person I felt that close to. Don't worry, you're not my best friend either, I said.

Who knows why our friends were willing to live with us. Maybe the fact that they were friends with each of us offset the annoyances of living with a couple. And maybe Stephen's circumstances had a kind of gravitational pull. We were all just out of college, wandering, exploring the city, figuring out what to do next. Later we'd begin careers and start families. But at the moment we took care of each other, and Stephen and I reaped the benefit of that.

Stephen had a lightness about him—once he'd figured out what he wanted to do, the world felt like itself again, and he ran headlong into it. He went to work with Amani, who'd moved out from Colorado to start up a snowboard clothing company. He was hired on as Twist's controller, his main qualification being his perfectly balanced checkbook. Twist's books were a mess and he jumped right in, getting everything in order. He thrived on the concrete nature of the project, on being with friends all day in a giant warehouse, on the teenage-boyish world of snowboarding. I liked to tease him about it. *Glad you guys are taking on the ski industry,* I'd say, and he'd roll his eyes. Meanwhile, he was glad I had friends at school to talk with about my own current obsession. *Oh no, education,* he'd say, grimacing when I brought it up, covering his ears with his hands.

But the oyster part occurred around the edges of work and school—the late nights talking in the living room, and all those trips. Hiking the section of the freeway that was closed due to earthquake damage. Driving two hours to run around on Limantour Beach in the pouring rain.

During the oyster time, Stephen took to proposing at random, trying to catch me off-guard. "Hey, will you marry me?" both of us slouched at the kitchen table in the morning, before our coffee had kicked in. Sitting on the roof of an abandoned church in Mexico. Watching previews in the movie theater, him withholding the Junior Mints until I answered. It only made me irritated—he knew I wanted to be with him and that I hated the idea of marriage; he was ruining otherwise unruinable moments.

Over winter break I sat in a Mexican restaurant with my high school friends, drunk off margaritas, them trying to convince me. *I'm never getting married,* I told them. *I know, but Stephen, it's different,* my friend Carla said. *What's common law, five years? You might be married already,* my friend Forest said. I wobbled up the winding metal staircase to the bathroom and stared in the mirror, my brain woozy. Married, not married. The person in the mirror could be a married person. I had all these things I wanted to do that didn't sound like the kinds of things married people did. I wanted to go live in a foreign country for a year, even if Stephen didn't want to go with me. Though I'd just brought that up at the table, and gotten rebuffed. *Why can't you do that married?* Carla had said. I went into the stall, sat huddled on the toilet. The person peeing could be a married person.

And then there was Stephen's father. He'd been diagnosed with liver cancer, and the doctors had started speaking in months. If we were ever going to get married, he should be there.

Stephen and I followed a steep, shady path through the evergreens at the base of Mount Tamalpais. It was a different kind of woods than I'd grown up with—the paths damp and dark, sun splattering in here and there, bright green moss on the baseboards used to support the sides of the trail. He wanted to take me to a particular tree, forty feet tall, with branches perpendicular to the ground, so many you could climb them like stairs. He remembered the tree being several miles up the trail, which was about where we were, so he was walking slowly, trying to figure out where we needed to diverge from the trail. I was waiting for him, thinking about Stephen's father, and my father, who'd said, when I brought marriage up, that if I was committed, I was committed, and whether I had a ceremony about it didn't matter very much.

"I'm not trying to get into an argument," I started.

"Mmm, that sounds promising."

"Why do you want to get married?"

He shrugged. "I think it would be great."

"You don't worry about it changing things?"

"Why would it?" He was half with me, half looking for the tree.

"I don't know, we're happy. What if we find out it makes us unhappy?"

Stephen thought for a while. "I guess we'd get divorced and keep going out."

I laughed. Actually, it didn't sound like a bad plan.

Stephen found the tree; its trunk was as wide as four people, and its branches were just as I'd pictured, like a spindle, all the way up. We dropped our backpacks on the ground. I tightened my shoelaces and zipped up my sweatshirt. The branches were thick and sturdy, their rough bark making it easy for me to keep my footing. I bent my knees, trying to keep my legs relaxed so they wouldn't twitch from the height. Sewing-needle leg, we called it rock climbing.

I could feel the wind as we climbed higher, the top of the tree swaying with it. Soon we looked out above all the neighboring trees, over the lumpy green hills that cascaded down to the ocean. We couldn't see the spot where the cliffs met the water, but we could see the water itself stretching to the horizon, a ribbon of light greenish-blue threading the darker water. Low clouds hung out over the ocean, and we were so high that we could see the shapes of the tops of them. I asked Stephen to marry me and he laughed.

"You're kidding, right?"

I shook my head.

"Were you planning this? I mean, it's my favorite landscape, but it feels a little cliché if you planned it."

"You're critiquing my proposal? No I didn't plan it."

He leaned toward me to kiss me, but the tree groaned so we stayed where we were, gripping our separate branches. It was at least ten degrees colder up here, and I wished I were wearing jeans rather than shorts.

On the ground, we put on our backpacks, a little shy now that we were getting married.

"It's unfair that you got to ask," Stephen said as we started to walk.

"You want to ask?"

"Liz, will you marry me?"

"Yes."

"Liz, will you marry me?"

"Yes!"

A few more rounds of this, and then we got out our sandwiches, eating as we walked. Soon the trail began winding down the hillside. We glanced at each other. Neither of us remembered this part of the trail. We retraced our steps. We walked for a long time, the sun beginning to fade. I thought through what we had with us—sandwiches, water, fruit, and cookies. Sweatshirts, but no blankets, no long pants.

The trail opened out onto a meadow. Far below us, we saw a few scattered houses, and a street winding through the hills. We started bushwhacking down through the meadow. Our car could be miles from this little piece of civilization, but maybe we could at least get directions, we'd walk back on clearly marked roads. We cut down through the meadow until we reached a low fence. Beyond the fence, a beautifully landscaped backyard, a deck, where two people sat looking out at the hillside. I froze, realizing we were staring right at them in their own backyard.

"Dr. Stulbarg?" Stephen said.

Sure enough, there he was, on his back porch with his wife, having a glass of wine. He shaded his eyes with his hands and peered out in our direction.

"It's Stephen. Stephen Evans?"

Dr. Stulbarg wandered toward the fence, smiling when he could see us.

"What are you guys doing here?"

I didn't know whether I was more embarrassed or relieved, trespassing into his private life, and on a Saturday evening. He helped us figure out where we'd come from. "That's quite a hike," he said, Stephen's doctor now, impressed. I thought about mentioning the tree but decided against it. He offered to drive us back to our car, which was only fifteen minutes away, but would have taken us until dark to walk to.

"Guess what?" Stephen said, in Dr. Stulbarg's passenger seat. "We're getting married."

"Congratulations," Dr. Stulbarg said. "When's the wedding?"

Stephen glanced back at me. "This summer?"

I nodded. "Probably July."

"Probably?" Dr. Stulbarg said. "You know it's March."

Our mothers would say the same thing that evening, happy to hear about the marriage, but less happy to hear about the date of the wedding, nervous we wouldn't have enough time to plan. Stephen, who was more organized than either of them, would reassure me. "Not enough time for the kind of wedding they'd want," he'd say. "How much could there be to do?"

WE ASKED AMANI to marry us. Stephen found an application for the Universal Life Church ministry in the back of a magazine and Amani sent in his ten dollars and letter of intent. The three of us huddled around the kitchen table, mapping out configurations of people on a stenograph pad, leafing through books for readings. We picked up our pace, began flying through the ceremony until Stephen opened the book that held his favorite poem.

"At least I've got my reading," he said. It was a poem by Pedro Salinas, called "I Wonder, Love." He started to read it out loud.

. . .

Love is the miraculous delay
of its own termination:
it is prolonging the magical fact
that one and one are two, in the face of
the original sentence of life.

I sank deep into my wooden chair. The original sentence of life, at our wedding? In our house, death came up as often as love did—casually, seriously, philosophically, as the subject of a joke, as the subject of a fight. Maybe Stephen had gotten so used to talking about it, he'd lost track of how it sounded to other people.

"It'll be too weird," I told him.

Stephen looked up from his book. "My favorite poem is *weird?*"

Amani got that weary-referee look on his face.

"You know I like the poem. But for the wedding?"

"You're the one who didn't want to get married, and now the whole thing is going to be predictable and boring. You already vetoed my skintight powder blue tux."

"You vetoed tattooed rings."

"That was your all-time worst idea ever."

"Don't you think talking about love as 'a long, clear farewell' might upset people?"

"You care too much about what other people think," Stephen said, which was a low blow, since it was true. Though it was less what they'd think than how they'd feel. There were the people who loved Stephen, the people who loved us both, and the people who loved me. It was the last category that kept appearing in my head—my grandparents, my aunts and uncles. I read the poem again as it lay on the kitchen table.

"*The most certain thing is goodbye?*" I said.

"That's just one line."

"It's the last line."

Stephen studied me with a kind of nonjudgmental distance. It was as if he'd thought we were in this together, and now could see me for what I was, a person without a short life, a person on the other side of the fence. A person he was going to leave behind. "Never mind," he said. "I guess I'll have to write something."

This wasn't the most relaxing thought, either.

We picked up our pace again until we slammed up against the vows. If Stephen was too willing to invite death up on the stage, I was maybe too eager to ban it completely. I announced that I was not going to say, "until death do you part." When most people said they'd be together until death, they were making an expansive, overwhelming promise; it felt like we should get to have something expansive, too. I suggested we say "forever," which seems silly in retrospect, but which felt like a triumph at the time. Stephen was purely skeptical.

"For one thing, it's unrealistic," he said.

After all these years of promoting marriage, of being sure we could last a lifetime, of taking *that* leap of faith without much thought, he was turning practical.

"You can love someone after they die," I argued.

"You can love someone," Stephen said, "but you can't still be married."

It would take years for me to understand the future he was making room for.

———

IN A WEEK, I was graduating from school and we were leaving California behind, driving to Colorado to get married, and then on to Massachusetts so Stephen could go to school. He was doing one final round of antibiotics before we left. Everyone at the hospital was proud and nervous for him, wishing him well, telling him to take good care of himself while he was gone. We enacted our hospital rituals with nostalgia. I brought in my dinner and we ate together, and on Friday night I slept over. The nurses fussed over us while pretending not to. They brought me extra sheets and a pillow and helped me transform the chair into a bed, even though we all knew I could do it myself. Stephen and I lay on his bed, talking late into the night about the move.

We imagined the new hospital in Boston, where we would be anonymous. We listed all the things we took for granted here that we'd probably end up pining for. The nurses were relaxed and generally had senses of humor. A few had particularly great, dark senses of humor. A few were particularly loving, and had been when we hadn't always deserved it. Patients with CF got their own rooms. Girlfriends could spend the night and were never held to visiting hours. Friends could often sneak in, too. We could get sheets, pillows, blankets, ice, and juice without asking. We could get fresh air in the courtyard on the second floor. We could sneak onto the roof, though technically, this was not permitted. Patients only had to stay for four days when doing antibiotics and could finish the rest at home. Patients could write their own items in on the menu, especially grilled cheese sandwiches. Some rooms had a view of Golden Gate Park and the ocean beyond. Each floor had a community room at the end of the hall, with wall-length picture windows, where we could sit and play cards. The doctors here told us what was actually going on. We could always page one of the "real" doctors if one of the doctors in training wasn't telling us the whole picture. Dr. Stulbarg was here. Recently he had handed Stephen a note that read, "Happy Marriage." He'd scrawled the message on a small piece of paper with his name at the top; we realized later that it was a prescription. We could barely imagine a hospital, CF in general, without Dr. Stulbarg weighing in.

We fell asleep to the sound of the machines, still in our clothes. At some point in the night I woke up and changed into sweats, moved into my own bed. In the morning I went across the street to get us coffee and the newspaper. Stephen photographed our breakfast, documented his entire hospital room, took a self-timed photo of us squeezed into the armchair that had recently been my bed.

TWO MONTHS LATER, we hurtled along Highway 80 through Nebraska, Iowa, Illinois, Stephen chewing tobacco and me drinking Dr Pepper, everything we owned packed into the backseat of our car. The plains became greener and gave way to dense, low hills, and soon we were curving through western Massachusetts, along Route 90 and into Cambridge itself. We'd had some crazy idea that our new home would be cooler than the country we'd just driven through, given its proximity to the ocean, and how far north it was on the map. But when we pulled up to our sublet on Mass Ave, the heat was right there with us, the air as humid as Chicago's had been.

We parked outside in a thirty-minute zone and sat in the car for three of those minutes, the thrill of a new life overtaking us. Outside the car, everything we didn't know spread around us.

And inside the car, our oldest possessions, our books and music and clothes and pictures, swelled with potential. Uprooted and set down against a new backdrop, they would be seen as they hadn't in years. And we would pay attention the way we used to, when life had not been a series of routines and escapes from them, but a thick foreign landscape that swallowed us and kept us feeling alive. This was why we were together in the first place, and we had made it back here. All we had to do was get out of the car.

chapter seven

LESS THAN THREE MONTHS LATER, WE FOUND OURSELVES back in Colorado. We lay in North Boulder Park, a field of grass so wide and long you could forget about the houses bordering it on either side. Most Colorado towns had parks like this, expansive and simple, the underlying belief being that kids would be left to their own devices—the younger ones might use the small swing set, but the older ones could figure it out themselves—capture-the-flag, chase, whatever it was, as long as it kept them busy until dinner. Stephen had lived near this park as a kid, but I hadn't been here much before high school, when we'd converge late at night for drunken games of tag, or linger before we made our ways home, lie in the grass and stare at the stars, thinking maybe our parents wouldn't care if we nestled down here and slept till morning.

It was early October, midday, the maple leaves bright red and still pliable after their recent fall. From here the Front Range loomed up into view, the peaks we liked to scramble up in all kinds of weather. Snaking up between those peaks, Canyon Road, which veered off into Four Mile, and then to Gold Hill, where just this summer Stephen and I had stood on a rickety stage in the barbecue yard of the Gold Hill Inn, with a view down into this valley and far beyond, our friends and family dizzy in the 95-degree heat. Stephen's dad, right there in front of me, sitting in his white folding chair, his sunglasses on, twisting his shoelace, his short, appreciative laugh when my sister read a poem by Shel Silverstein. "One sister for sale! One sister for sale!" He'd been too sick to stay long after the ceremony, and maybe that was our fault, having a wedding at 9,000 feet. And we didn't know anything about weddings, so we didn't know you were supposed to take the pictures before the ceremony, and while we'd made all kinds of wedding mistakes, this was the one that would stay with us—his dad, missing from all the pictures. He was in the video, if that mattered—in the footage he hugs Stephen and says, "Nice ceremony," and Stephen murmurs, "We did it for you, Dad," and you can tell they don't know they're being recorded, and it was the kind of thing they'd never want to watch again, the two of them, but now, I didn't know, maybe Stephen would.

"My dad always has terrible timing," Stephen had said to me when we'd gotten the call in Cambridge. It wasn't the thought you were supposed to have about impending death, but it was true. Stephen was five days into his first semester of school, not to mention two days into a ten-day course of IV antibiotics. But somehow we'd gotten here, the blur of the plane, barreling down I-25 in our rental car, pulling up to Boulder Community late Saturday night, rushing through the emergency room entrance to find ourselves in a different kind of time altogether, even thicker than regular hospital time. And the music added to it, the New Age medley of underwater sounds we could hear drifting from Room 317. *What the fuck,* Stephen had muttered outside the door. Gus liked big bands and Dixieland jazz; he never would have tolerated this easing-into-the-world-beyond, death-vigil music had he been conscious. But once we walked into the room, Stephen stopped short of complaining. His mom, his parents' oldest friends, all too tired to complain to, put their arms around us, and told Gus that Stephen was here. And in their voices you could hear the hope—that Gus had been waiting for Stephen, that this cruel purgatory his body was enacting was about to end.

I leaned down and kissed Gus's cheek, even though I wouldn't have done that in normal life; we usually gave each other a sort of sideways hug. But I wasn't sure about putting my arm around his body. Two months ago he'd been gaunt and pale, but he'd been Gus. I wondered whether in his own mind he was still having the same thoughts, even if he couldn't meet my eyes or say "Hi, Lizzie," or give a nod hello. His fingers were so long with their usual flesh gone. I didn't know which was worse; the idea that he was gone but still alive, or that he was here, aware of all this, aware of the music, the baby talk, the fighting to breathe.

We all camped out. Boulder Community had been "the hospital," growing up—I'd come here when my brother was born, when my grandmother took a bad fall in our bathroom, when I severed a tendon in my hand while taking my bike apart. Gus had been a doctor here, and Stephen had visited him, running through the halls as a little kid. But neither of us had ever spent time in the oncology wing of our hometown hospital. It had been upgraded by donations and stood out dramatically, surrounded by its just-making-the-rent neighbors. Its lounge was larger than most Bay Area apartments, with a fully outfitted kitchen. There were small wallpapered rooms for spouses to stay overnight, with alarm clocks poised on wooden dressers. The patient rooms had stereos, and curtains instead of blinds. But the accoutrements were meager concessions: in the entire hospital city, it still felt like the most desolate part of town.

Stephen's brother Clay got a friend to take care of his dogs; his sister Tinka left her sons with her husband. These links to the world set loose, we existed only on that floor. We moved from the waiting room, to Gus's room, and back again. The nurses kept making predictions: no way he can live till morning, should be hours now. But there had been predictions the night before, too. At three in the morning, I went into the empty room next door and crawled in between the thin white sheets. A while later Stephen came in and lay down next to me, and we fell asleep, squeezed onto the narrow hospital bed.

We were startled awake by blinding light—the sun, but it felt more like the high beams of a car. It seemed impossible that the next day could be dawning, that the night had passed and no one had come. We stumbled into our shoes. Gus was exactly as we'd left him. Stephen wet a washcloth, and took the wrapper off a mouth swab. "Sorry about this, Dad," he said as he moved the swab's soft end around in his dad's mouth.

The dying person had outlived the deathwatch. We felt wrong in the bright light of morning, standing around hushed. If it was going to take this long, we'd have to pace ourselves. Clay went home to take his dogs for a run. Fran's friends convinced her to go to church, and stop in at Baby Gap. I dragged Tinka out of the hospital to get bagels across the street while Stephen sat with his dad.

Coming back, seeing Fran in the doorway, something in the way she stood, her shoulders, Tinka and I knew. Stephen came to find me in the hallway. I pulled him close, and wiped the tears off his cheeks. We took the elevator, walked out the hospital's revolving doors. I had no idea where we were going, what a person would need after he'd been with his father as he'd died. Down the sidewalk, across the street, and here we were, North Boulder Park, its warm grass, its backdrop of our mountains.

He lay with his head in my lap. I made him wild promises, the kind you find yourself making when you are cradling someone's head in your arms. I promised him that his dad had heard everything he'd told him even though he'd seemed unconscious. I promised him that even though the last few days were terrible, they were only a few days, that the life itself had been good. I promised him he would not die like this. Years ago, once, when he'd been inconsolable in the hospital, I'd promised him that I would not let him die in a hospital, that he would be somewhere he loved like his own bed or a cabin in the mountains. I couldn't promise that now, after the hospital had become the place we went when things were unclear. Even with him crying and so tired, I couldn't bring myself to promise that. But I did promise that it wouldn't be like this. I promised that if he were between life and death, and lying in pain, I would do something. I wasn't sure what I would do. But we would have a plan. We wouldn't get caught like this again.

THAT NIGHT, WE lay in the dark at his parents' house. I was thinking back to this summer—the day after our wedding, standing in the kitchen, Stephen and me arguing about something stupid, arguing heatedly, comfortably—the way we liked to, the way his dad hated. *Don't start arguing now*, his dad had pleaded. *You just got married.* We'd started laughing. *Come on, Dad*, Stephen had said. *We've been together about nine years.*

"Do you think I'll ever picture him the way he looked before?" Stephen asked me now.

"Probably," I said, even though I had no idea.

chapter eight

THE FIRST TIME I REMEMBER NOTICING THE FEELING WAS
in high school, when Stephen and I were becoming friends,
before we ever went out. It was ten in the morning on a school
day, third period, and I had study hall, a fifty-five-minute
slice of time that was meant to be spent doing homework in
the library. Stephen had study hall, too, and we slipped out of
school, walked up to Pearl Street. It was snowing lightly, but
we had coats and boots and our fifty-five minutes. Our high
school was the same pink stone of the buildings on the nearby
college campus; it was old and beautiful seen from the outside.
Of course it was beautiful mostly because you weren't inside it,
because everyone else was still in there and you'd vanished into
the outside world.

If it was strange that we were high school kids at Rocky

Mountain Joe's Cafe on a Tuesday morning, no one bothered to point it out. A waitress with long black hair nodded in our direction, and the way she nodded, not just letting us know we could find a seat but also giving Stephen some kind of confirmation, it was clear Stephen had come here more than a few times. And it was a little weird, what high school kid went out to breakfast alone during his free period?

We sat by the window, looking down on the brick walkway below, the slick metal statues, a rabbit and a hedgehog with snow at their feet. I ordered pancakes and coffee, he got corned beef hash, and we each took a section of the *Boulder Camera*. I was reading the comics, trying to do the Jumble in my head, and I glanced up at Stephen, who was reading the Sports page, and there was something going on here, this feeling I couldn't explain. It was something about stepping out of the noisy halls and into this quiet, aboveground place, looking down at the world from the second story, the way I could see the mountains as well as the brick walkway, the line of the western slope through the snow. It was something about being out of time, but it was a little different than that, more that time had slowed down, or we'd slowed it down somehow. We'd switched movies or soundtracks, or we were deep inside a single track, the way you could sink into a song, lose awareness of its three-minute life span, live within it for what felt like a while. There was something about this particular ten-fifteen on a Tuesday, we'd crawled inside it, we'd willed it to open up a little, we were stretching it out, the minutes were slowed and they were ours, and we were sitting here in them, like it was what they were meant for, and it was something about the two of us together that was making it happen, or maybe it was just Stephen, maybe this was what minutes felt like to him all the time.

"ISN'T TIME FUNNY," Stephen and Kristie used to say, when
we lived in Chicago together. It was their own version of a Saturday Night Live parody, "Deep Thoughts." Because everyone
knew that time was "funny," that it could be short and long
and nothing like the minutes on the clock, and we made fun
of people pondering that. Meaning we made fun of ourselves,
because the truth was, time *was* funny, and still is, and it's hard
for me to get at exactly how it was funny then. How the length
of Stephen's time here on earth influenced our sense of months,
and years, and minutes, and days. I don't know how to describe
it except to say we were deep in time, and also aware of its passing. Maybe it's most similar to being in love long-distance, when
you finally get to see the person, and you know you only have a
week together, and so you live deep inside that week, refusing
to look out its windows, and your refusal is an acknowledgment
that the windows exist.

Wherever Stephen was, noticing something he hadn't seen
before, the statue of the dog at the cemetery, the hidden bench
in the woods by Fresh Pond, he'd stand there for a while,
absorbing it fully. We were both like that, really, or we were
like that in each other's company. It reminds me of the way,
when we'd go to a hotel, even for a night, we'd unpack completely, filling the drawers and closet and medicine cabinet,
resolutely settling in.

Maybe this is why my feeling about this time in Cambridge
doesn't seem right, given what actually happened. I remember
the upheaval, the health crises, but then what floods in is walking to the video store, the leaves on the ground, the fall air,
the three-story Victorians, the pizza place where Stephen and

the owner had a standing argument about whether pineapple belonged on the menu. It's all mixed in together, everything that was going wrong, and everything that was going right.

IN SAN FRANCISCO I'd felt too serious, in Cambridge I felt too lighthearted. The clothes I wore, nondescript back home, jumped out in the crowd. My jacket, a Twist sample, an oversized mustard yellow coat meant for snowboarders off the slope, suddenly seemed to be making a statement. Of what, I didn't know, but Stephen and I were easy to spot among the gray trench coats as we wandered around Mount Auburn Cemetery.

We walked slowly, reading the headstones, the way we liked to do. We were used to smaller, weedier Western graveyards, the ones we'd stumbled on in Santa Cruz, Elko, Grand Junction. There had been the cemetery in San Francisco's Presidio, with its sweeping view of the Golden Gate Bridge and the ocean beyond, but it still wasn't quite like this, the jolting mixture of names, the local deaths mixed in with the nationally significant, all part of the town's history. It was funny to think of Henry Wadsworth Longfellow as having gone to the bar down the block from here.

It was a Sunday morning, and I'd forced Stephen to take a few hours off from his schoolwork. He'd been studying feverishly, soaking up everything he could about health care policy. This was when managed care had just begun, and everyone at the School of Public Health was scrambling to research roads that might be taken. What if they'd been able to look ahead like this, when health insurance had first come on the scene? Stephen was most concerned about how people without insurance would be managed, or worse, not taken into account at all. He felt indebted to the California state program that covered CF, and he wanted to give back. And I was proud of him, and happy with all this, as long as we also got to hang out together, too.

We'd reversed roles, and now I was the one with the interest in absorbing the day. For the past two years I'd been running nonstop, between school, my research job, student teaching. But when I moved cross-country, I found myself guiltily relieved that Boston and Cambridge Unified had no openings for teachers. An outsider in a new city, the observer in me resurfaced. I found a job as the librarian at a tiny elementary school a few blocks from my house. It was three days a week, and I spent the other two days at our kitchen table, with my notebook and my coffee, working out a novel about a logging camp in Montana.

The cemetery felt full of life, or maybe the life in it was easy to hear and feel, against the deeper quiet. Birds called back and forth, and squirrels chased each other from tree to tree. We stopped to read the headstone of the man who had invented anesthesia. I'd never thought about him before, but I felt grateful to him, imagining all the surgeries before his time. Down the path, surrounded by smaller stones, a giant statue of a man sitting next to his dog.

We climbed the worn spiral staircase of a stone tower and stood out on the balcony, squinting in the sun. It was a relief to be able to get some height here, to see our new city from above. We leaned over the railing, looking for our street. We couldn't make it out through the dense stretch of red and orange treetops, but we could follow the Charles River, and count its bridges to get the lay of the land.

"We should bring Clay here when he comes to visit," Stephen said.

"It's okay, being in a cemetery?" I asked him.

"It feels different. But no more than anything else."

"What does it feel like?"

Stephen was quiet, for so long I thought he hadn't heard me. "Everything looks altered," he said finally. "The world is a physically different place."

WE ATE DINNER on our tiny deck off the back stairwell of our apartment, looking out over our landlord's backyard. We set out a tablecloth and candles on an old card table left by the last tenant. We were tired after Colorado, after school and work, and we didn't say much. I was left-handed and Stephen right, so if I sat to his left, we could eat and hold hands at the same time.

I worked on my black beans and rice, thinking about how lately, throughout the day Stephen had been giving me health updates. He'd say, chest pain's like yesterday, or, a little gurgling in my left lung. I was starting to get frustrated with the play-by-play; I knew most of the patterns by heart. For instance, he didn't feel great when he first woke up. He'd drink his coffee and read the paper, take his inhaled medication, a.k.a the "breathing thing" (as in, "Don't you have to do your breathing thing?" Or, "Fuck, I'll be late for class. Have to skip my breathing thing"). By the time I'd leave for work he'd be looking less sunken into the couch. Minutes later, he'd be out the door to catch the bus, then the T into Boston, hurrying down the two blocks from Longwood Station to the School of Public Health.

And when I wanted to know the particulars of the lungs, I'd ask. He'd be checking his breathing, pausing for a second in the hall or the doorway. I'd say, How's it sound? and he'd usually say, All right, which didn't mean all right in the traditional sense. All right was relative and specific. The "all right" of last year would be great now. Our standards had slipped though we hadn't meant to let them.

It seemed that "all right" had been working, and I didn't know why I was getting more specifics, a few times a day at least. I was already so aware, too aware, sometimes I would have liked to go longer without thinking about the lungs. Just when I was tempted to ask him about it, he brought it up himself.

"I want someone else to know what's going on," he said. "Just in case."

"In case of what?"

"Well, if I collapse and I can't tell the doctors myself when I get to the hospital, what might have led up to it."

"Wait, you feel like you might collapse?"

"There's this new feeling. I'm struggling more to breathe."

AND THEN ONE day it happened. I came home from work to find the door unlocked, and I edged it open nervously, thinking of stealthy burglars. Then I heard the TV—an anthem-like car commercial—". . . new Nissan Sentra, you need this car!" Stephen was lying facedown on the couch, his breathing jagged. I nudged his shoulder. He said he felt queasy, his head was pounding, his body ached; he couldn't get up. He thought maybe he had the flu. I put my hand on his forehead. He had a fever, much higher than his usual low-grade.

"Maybe I should drive you to the hospital," I said.

"Dr. Wohl won't be in till tomorrow morning."

I sank down on the couch next to him.

"Aren't you going running?" he asked me.

"Now?"

"Nothing's going to happen. I've been lying right here all day."

I scrounged around for my running clothes, promising myself that if I got out the door and ran for five minutes I could stop. It was an old trick, but for some reason I was still gullible. I ran down Huron Boulevard, circled Fresh Pond, wishing there were no fence around it. I pretended that the trees extended far into the distance, that the city was gone.

What were we going to do? I made dinner, knowing that Stephen wouldn't eat much but that if I made something he might eat a little out of guilt. We had just gotten some Omaha Steaks in the mail from his mom. Maybe the steaks would help. We couldn't have them tonight, though; I was a vegetarian and had no idea how to cook steak. It was not the time for one of my standard dishes; he needed more calories. I heated up his current standby, frozen Chicken Cordon Bleu, and put my current standby, a Gardenburger, in the toaster. We sat in front of the TV and picked at our food.

And then, the next day, magically, or so it seemed, I came home from work to find him feeling fine. Better than fine— unloading six bags of groceries from a solo trip to the store, teasing me about walking on my toes when I came into the kitchen, suggesting we go out for sushi.

"I think I figured out what's been going on," he said, after we were seated in the corner table he'd requested, me with my plum wine and him with his beer. He looked scared, which gave me a twinge of panic. "It's my pain medication, I'm pretty sure."

"What's wrong with it?"

He sighed. "You're not making this easy."

He'd become addicted to it, he realized. He'd taken too much over the course of the month and run out early. I thought about him lying on the couch, unable to move, shivering, sweating, nauseous. And me, reading stories to the kids at work, setting up the library, expecting at any minute to be interrupted by the school secretary with a call from the hospital.

"All that was withdrawal from *Vicodin*?"

"Well, it's a narcotic, I guess."

"Why didn't you say anything? I've been scared for two days straight."

"I've been trying to tell you."

A memory of Stephen's father came to me, standing in the hallway of UCSF, telling the doctor that Stephen should get off the pain meds as soon as possible post-surgery, he was enjoying them too much. That had been four years ago, right after I'd moved to San Francisco. I tried to remember when the pain meds had joined the rest of the brown prescription pill bottles on his side of the sink. I couldn't remember; it had never occurred to me to think of them at all. This was just before everyone was using them recreationally, before dentists limited the prescription to three days after a root canal, before pharmacies began posting signs—"Sorry, no Oxycontin refills here," before Rush Limbaugh went public.

"How long have you been worried about it?" I asked him.

"Maybe a year."

"A *year*?"

"Maybe not a whole year. You think it's easy to talk about?"

But once he'd unleashed the subject, he wanted to tell me everything. While I'd been oblivious, he'd been all over the map. Thinking it was fine; he needed help with the chest pain, wondering if the pain was even there anymore. In clinic they talked about dependency. It was okay to rely on a drug, as long as you didn't crave more of it. But lately, he'd take six instead of four, and then eight instead of six. It was unnerving, the way he *found* himself doing it. It reminded him of chewing tobacco in high school, but triple the desire.

"It's disturbing, how great I feel after the refill," he said.

"In a weird way, I'm relieved, too."

"You're kidding. You are?"

"To know there's a reason you were so sick. To know it's over."

Later, I'd look back and wish I'd understood. For three days he'd pretended not to know what was wrong. Had gone so far as to suggest the flu. He'd been secretly worried for a year. This, from the person who talked about his early death with strangers, who confessed transgressions with a mischievous smile, who was known for being unembarrassed about anything, for calling attention to things other people found shameful. And now he was telling me, and the depth of his unburdening fell on deaf ears. But that was the great thing, and the dangerous thing, about life-threatening illness—every other problem appeared like a sideshow when cast in its light.

chapter nine

CHILDREN'S HOSPITAL. THE LOBBY WITH THE COFFEE CART. The glass window into each patient's room, blinds pulled back revealing a rectangular rendition of a family's life inside. The window nook by the far wall, where parents curled up to sleep at night. Beyond the nook, outside, across the way, a towering office complex, half-built. The construction workers had taken long pieces of cloth and spray-painted them with messages for the kids who watched them work. *Get well soon. We love you guys.* The messages billowed out from the building in the wind.

A hospital was one thing, a children's hospital another. On every floor of the building, on every hallway of every floor, kids. The kids caught my eye first, but there were also the parents, who had driven or flown from Maine, Canada, Texas. They pulled up chairs to their children's beds and leaned over, rested their heads on the high mattresses and drifted off. Their other children were at home, missing them. It was almost worse than being the kids themselves, being the parents. No, it was worse being the kids. I wasn't sure.

And then there were the people who worked here. Every day, a new sick child, or one they'd seen a few months ago, back again. Every day, these parents, grateful and diminished and ticking like bombs. The nurses, the doctors, the therapists, they were all in the trenches. The trenches were disguised; they were warm and well-funded, quiet, clean. I wondered if they were more alive, working in this trench. I imagined them sitting at the playground, watching their own kids, feeling irritated when another parent made a big deal over a fall off the swings. I wondered if they returned home at night like soldiers, unable to explain where they'd been. I couldn't tell; everyone seemed so calm.

I poked around the gift shop. I'd already been to Harvard Square to search for presents for Stephen. I'd found a three-dimensional puzzle made of wooden pieces that formed a star, a space pen, and the new Chris Ware comic. In the gift shop, I bought two football magazines and a stuffed lion, and then took the elevator up to the CF floor—the only corridor in the hospital with adult patients.

When I got to Stephen's room, he was sitting up in bed, fiddling with his IV line. "I got a pic," he told me. Getting a pic always made him happy. The beauty of the pic line was that it could last an entire course of antibiotics. The regular lines had to be replaced every few days, which hurt a little, and hardened his veins over time. But I wasn't sure about the trade-off. The pic was disturbingly long, and an ordeal to put in. It was a vermicelli-thin line that entered his vein at the elbow, like the regular line, but extended all the way up to the shoulder. At the moment, Stephen was pressing around his vein, moving up his arm, to feel if the line was in right. Be careful with that thing, I told him, though not out loud. I just gave him the look I used for all situations like this, which meant, The way you're messing around with your medical equipment might not be such a great idea. It's fine, he said silently back to me.

He was thrilled with his presents, especially the comic and the space pen. He loved the idea that the pen could, theoretically, be used underwater and in space. He read the pen's description in its entirety while I ate the remnants of his breakfast.

Children's was growing on us. The nurses didn't have the same edge as the UCSF nurses, but then, we were in an institution for children. The walls of the room were painted with brightly colored balloons and fish. The funding was apparently good—new furniture, futuristic medical accoutrements. The rules were more relaxed than we'd imagined. I'd be allowed to stay over and come in late at night, which made sense in a children's hospital. Parents needed to come in and out at odd hours, and I would be among them, though I would get strange looks at the reception desk for a while when I signed in. There weren't many patients here with wives.

We were also excited about Children's head CF physician, Dr. Wohl. We'd been looking forward to meeting her; she'd taught Dr. Stulbarg herself. She was known to be straightforward and smart, almost brusque. She'd been one of very few women in her medical school class, and there was something about this in her manner—her wry sense of humor, the depth of her self-possession. Younger doctors showed her a respect that verged on fear. It was reassuring to have her name in our pockets, to be able to say, to a resident or researcher or anyone else, "Actually, I'd like to talk to Dr. Wohl before you do anything," to know that in the end, they all had to answer to her.

We had to answer to her, too. Already she had her eye on a couple of things Stephen didn't think were big problems. The first was the fact that he was losing weight, and the second, which had landed him here, was his coughing up blood. I was glad Dr. Wohl didn't like this; I didn't like it either. It scared him too, I could tell. Maybe later he'd be relieved that Dr. Wohl insisted on trying to fix it. But at the moment all he cared about was school.

He devised a way to sneak over to his classes. He was allowed to leave his room between antibiotic treatments, and the hospital was only a few doors down from the School of Public Health. Technically, he was supposed to stay in the hospital, because his insurance company insisted that if you were well enough to exit the hospital, you didn't need to be there. But the School of Public Health was connected to the hospital by a series of basement hallways and a very quick jaunt across an outdoor courtyard. He signed himself out to visit the hospital library, and then slipped over to his Monday morning seminar.

"GUESS WHAT," HE SAID, when I came in on Tuesday. "There's a guy here with CF who has a kid. They did artificial insemination."

"With *his* sperm?"

"Yeah."

"You're kidding. Did you ask Dr. Wohl?"

"She says it's possible. I'd have to get my sperm count tested."

We might be able to have a kid. We sat there, the possibility spreading out into the room, taking its various forms. A baby. A young child. Suddenly it sounded great. But crazy. We couldn't do it now, with Stephen's health so precarious. But later, things might be worse. The more time the child could have with both of us alive, the better.

"I can just see it—a little baby Liz," Stephen said.

"I can't believe we're talking about this."

"I can't believe it's appealing."

"Is it?"

"Yeah."

"It is to me too," I said, and we left it there, the theoretical baby nestled between us.

I DROVE THROUGH the dim light of dusk, skirting the river, racing toward Longwood Avenue. Today, while I read *Lizard Music* aloud to the fourth graders, and helped second graders find books on mammals, Stephen had undergone the procedure to stop the bleeding in his lung. A surgeon had inserted particles into a major vein, and guided them through Stephen's body toward their destination. But there had been a risk that a particle could wander off-course, defect from the lungs to, say, the heart. A very small risk, but still.

I found him in his bed, his eyes closed, his hair spread out on the pillow. The room was almost dark, a small light on by the foot of the bed. I leaned down to kiss him. "Six hours," he said, his voice drugged and goofy.

"It took six hours? How'd it go?"

"I can't remember. They told me . . . something. I think good."

He tried to move over so I could sit. "Oh—Oh. Ow."

"What, okay, don't move, what hurts?"

"There's a catheter. Wait, maybe they took it out."

"You can't tell?"

"When d'you get here?"

"Just now. I came from work."

His head lolled, he'd fallen asleep. His bed was propped up at the top, I put my elbow on the edge of the mattress above his head, leaned my head in my hand. I needed a drink, a stop at the bar after work, a few minutes between there and here. And if not that, just a few minutes to talk about work. It felt so paltry, the need to talk about work. Stephen opened his eyes halfway. "Poor sweetie," he said.

"I'm okay," I said, "I'm just, tired."

"Tired," he said, nodding solemnly, his voice still cascading, high.

A nurse poked her head in the door. She was around forty, curly brownish-blond hair pulled back in a ponytail. "You must be Liz," she said. "He was asking about you, I told him you'd be here." And maybe she could see my face because she added, "Don't worry, his sense of time is all screwed up. They've got him pretty doped up."

I moved to the foot of the bed while she checked his temperature, and the IV line in his left arm. "I have to check your site," she said to Stephen. She pulled back his sheet and glanced at me. I nodded casually, trying to make it clear that I was used to this, I had seen nurses with their hands between his legs many times, though actually this was the first. The nurse pulled his leg up and toward her, and then felt around the upper part of his inner thigh. I stepped back, wondering if she felt uncomfortable. Probably not, she'd done this before. I looked away as she explored the region.

"See, Liz," Stephen called down to me, "they shaved my pubic hair."

I glanced up at him.

"You know," he said, "just like you always wanted."

The nurse looked up for a split second, her eyebrows arched, then carefully lowered his leg and put the sheet back on. I blushed in spite of myself, which didn't help my cause. He was so out of it that she probably thought he was incapable of joking. It sounded like something that had just slipped out, which somehow, in his delirious state, he had still known would happen and capitalized on.

"Don't lie," Stephen said. "You don't have to be embarrassed."

chapter ten

I DRESSED SLEEPILY, PUT ON MY BLACK BOOTS IN THE COLD stairwell. It was the first day back to work after winter break, which had caught me off-guard in the way it had worn me out. We'd flown to Colorado desperately needing a vacation, but once we got there I wondered what we'd been thinking, this being our first trip back with Stephen's dad gone. Late the night before, we'd stumbled up our stairs, thrown our bags on the floor, and fallen asleep in our clothes.

Outside, the snow rose to my calves as I walked. The snow had hushed the city, I thought, until I realized that there was no noise to be hushed, so far only three cars on the road. I had yet to cross paths with another person. Cambridge Montessori was dark, its doors locked. A car pulled up into the circular driveway. A woman cracked her window. In the seat next to her, a tiny girl was singing "Twinkle, Twinkle" off-key.

"It wasn't listed on the radio," the woman said. "I was hoping we were on."

A snow day. The old feeling flooded me, seven years old, dancing around in the front yard in a snowsuit to celebrate the day off. I raced home and ran up the stairs, ice and dirt flying from my boots. The alarm was blaring, Stephen lying next to it, asleep. I turned on the radio. Sure enough, Harvard had christened it a snow day, too. I woke Stephen and told him the news. We couldn't believe our luck. Colorado would never have called off school for a foot of snow.

We turned on the TV. Newscasters in trench coats reported from Dorchester, Worchester, Weston, Newton, standing in front of socked-in doors, people gunning snow off their cars with leaf blowers. The storm was expected to last for the next two days. Everybody looked miserable on TV but we were ecstatic. Two free days and a landscape of snow.

We went down the street and found Pentimento's open for breakfast. We sat in one of their purple booths, watching the snow hit the window, eating giant muffins, listening to people discuss the weather and make predictions. A nor'easter, they called the storm. Stephen felt invigorated by his return to sea level and his recent round of antibiotics. We had to get out there. We went home, took our cross-country skis from the stairwell. No one had shoveled, we could ski right from our door. We trekked down our empty street, turned right on Huron and then left into the old, wealthy neighborhood that would empty us out near the river. We slid past two-story brick houses, their grounds magnificent in the snow. By the time we reached the river we were moving smoothly, rhythmically cutting new tracks. We passed a few people, their faces buried in hooded coats. Our path was lit by streetlamps. Their thin black poles, against the cobblestone bridges spanning the river, set us back a hundred years.

We skied into Harvard Square, found the one open coffee shop. We drank our hot chocolate, given to us on the house since we had skied all the way there. We regained our strength and took the short way home, sliding through neighborhood streets. As soon as we stopped moving the shivering began. We barely made it in the door before we made a break for the bed, scrambling under the covers. Stephen announced he was going to brave it and run to the kitchen for grapefruit juice. He brought the whole pitcher back, and we shared it, gulping too fast, feeling a little sick. I hadn't remembered falling asleep, but I woke with my arm crushed between Stephen and me, numb. I shook it free, and looked around our room. I could see from the bedroom through the living room, all the way to the kitchen. Dusk was setting in, the furniture outlined in dim light, the futon couch, the round-back wooden chairs. This was the house in the new year, this was where and how the new year was beginning, in the evening light particular to this kind of day, when the snow absorbed the last of the sun and cast it back up, and light hovered above the ground as the top of the sky grew dark.

chapter eleven

IN CAMBRIDGE, SPRING HAD BEGUN TO APPEAR. THE DAYS felt softer, the difference between inside and outside less severe. I'd been keeping the windows of our second-story flat open at night, and this morning I was woken up by the blare of a voice over a loudspeaker: "Street sweepin', street sweepin', everybody move ya cahs." After the third time the voice spoke I realized it was a recording. Somehow it made me love this city, the fact that the street-sweeping voice had a local accent, the fact that there was a street-sweeping voice, that it told you to move your car, that the point of street sweeping was sweeping the street, not stealthily collecting parking ticket revenue. I lay in bed a few extra minutes, feeling the warm air plunge through my window, stretching out diagonally, since Stephen wasn't home yet.

Dr. Wohl had finally won him over to the idea of a stomach tube. He'd been losing weight steadily for months—no matter how much he ate, he couldn't keep up with the calories he burned, fighting infections and working as hard as he did now to breathe. At first he'd resisted, horrified by the idea. But after he'd dropped to 108 pounds, the idea seemed less horrific. He could tape the tube if he wanted to go swimming, screw aesthetics at this point. Besides he already felt self-conscious, being so thin. Too skinny to be a person, he muttered, whenever he caught his reflection in window glass.

"You must have had some influence in this," Dr. Wohl had whispered, when I'd passed her in the hospital hallway. And I'd nodded, guiltily accepting praise that I didn't deserve. I might have been more horrified than Stephen was, if that was possible.

I loved his stomach. And now, below his belly button and a little to the right, a thin tube emerged from a patch of white gauze, dangling like a strand of cooked spaghetti. Would I ever be alone with his stomach again? It had been my territory, and overnight, while I'd been here, across town, someone had built a Kmart. I imagined Stephen's return tonight, when we'd be grappling with this physical mark of illness, this dependency on a machine.

But it turned out that the difficulties with the tube weren't large and metaphoric; they were small and annoying. That night we didn't grieve; we bickered and negotiated, like two people lost at dusk, fighting over the map. I lay under the covers, watching Stephen pour cans of Ensure into a thick plastic bag that fit into his pump. He reached down and fingered the cap of his stomach tube.

"Wait, wait!" I said. "What are you doing?"

"I have to figure out how to hook it up."

"You're hooking up *first*?"

"You want me to lie with you and then get back *up*?"

Over time we'd slipped into a way of drifting off to sleep. We enacted it casually, but now we had to admit it felt like a given, what the end of the night was meant for. I argued for lying together the way we always had. Already the tube edged between us, we could never be fully naked, there would always be this one little square of clothing. How were we supposed to relax at all with the whole system hooked up, liquid running through, while we tried to avoid squishing any part of it? Stephen argued that if we did what we usually did, he'd be lying there knowing the whole time he'd have to get back up and hook up the tube. How was he supposed to relax, to be finished with the day and free, unless he hooked up first?

"We could switch off nights," I said.

"Then I need my night first. It's going to take me a while to figure this out."

I watched him start to set up, thinking of future annoyances the tube would cause. Falling asleep was a problem. And then what about the times when you thought you were falling asleep, you were exhausted and on the edge of dreams but found yourselves having sex? Would the tube obliterate this altogether? Half-asleep sex with the tube going—was that dangerous, or just disgusting? Could I really overlook the tube leading from his stomach to a machine by the side of the bed? Not to mention him—he'd be feeling the liquid food flow into his stomach. No, he'd have to unhook. But could you unhook mid-meal?

Stephen threaded the cord hanging down from the food bag through a small pump, and held the end of it close to his stomach. He fingered the valve on his stomach tube, getting ready to insert the end of the cord in its opening. Then he'd release the valve on the pump. It reminded me of putting air in a tire. Once both valves were opened, wasn't the cord going to leak?

Or worse, wasn't his stomach going to leak? Something was going to leak. I ran to get paper towels. "Wait to attach it," I said. "I want to see."

"Hurry up then," he called after me.

When I got back Stephen double-checked the valves and turned the pump on. The liquid inched down from the hanging bag, moved through the maze of the pump, and pulsed down the tube into his stomach. He turned the light off and lay down. We shifted around, trying to figure out how not to disturb the tube, and still lie intertwined.

"Fuck," Stephen said.

It was then that the sound registered. A grating churning. It was the worst kind of sound—not constant, not even steady—impossible to tune out.

"Maybe it doesn't really have to go through the pump," I said.

"Trust me, it does. Unless I want to be chugging Ensure. We'll have to sleep with earplugs."

"I hate earplugs."

We lay down together, earplugs in. The sound bled right through. Stephen turned on the light, searching for a way to muffle the pump. He tried putting it under the bed. Then he wrapped it in a sweatshirt and shoved it under the bed. Still, it churned. I found a plastic file box, and we stuffed the pump inside it.

"Wrap a couple of shirts around it," I said. "Really pack it in."

With the final T-shirt, the sound died to a low murmur. Stephen turned the light out, and we lay back down, my head on his chest.

"Are you getting full?" I asked him.

"Pretty full."

"Can we try lying the old way?" I asked.

"Don't call it the old way."

He turned to face me. "I always liked my stomach," he admitted in the dark.

chapter twelve

Double lung transplants appeared in newspapers
and TV shows, on the tips of doctors' tongues. The idea was terrifying: both lungs, replaced. How could it not go wrong? But we
started to have thoughts of what might happen if it went right.

"Everybody at Children's wants me to think about it," Stephen told me.

"Now?" We were on the T, riding home from downtown
Boston, Stephen in the window seat, surreptitiously glancing at
his reflection, so pleased. The G-tube had been a huge success,
and he was like a triumphant dieter only in reverse—eager to get
on the scale every morning, calling out his weight to me across
the apartment, checking himself out in the mirror in the pants
he'd worn a year ago.

"I said I wanted to talk to you. If you don't want me to do
it, I'm not going to."

"If I don't want you to get new lungs?"

"The risk is too big. What if I die after a year, or even in surgery? I'd be cutting our time short."

It was true, we guarded our time jealously, as if whenever we turned our backs someone might come along and steal a few minutes. But still, it was more his time than ours. I thought about Stephen's father, that last operation he'd gotten because his family had begged him to do it. He hadn't wanted the surgery; he'd known he was dying, and he'd gone ahead with it anyway, to make them happy.

The transplant offered the chance of a gloriously normal life. Stephen would have to take drugs to suppress his immune system, but if he could avoid rejection and serious infection, he could live as long as I could, and more, breathe easily the entire time. Since each organ manufactures its own cells, the CF would be gone from his lungs for good. But the surgery was still on the cutting edge of medicine, and researchers had yet to find a fail-safe way to make sure the patient's body wouldn't reject the new lungs. Though the statistics got better every month, right now half of the people who survived the surgery died in the first five years.

"The guy you met in the hospital—with the kid—did he have a transplant?"

"Yeah."

"What did he say?"

"He said to do it. Actually, both. But to wait a while after the transplant before the kid. His wife was agreeing with him in the background."

"Is he scared now, just living?"

"I don't know. Probably. But he said he almost never thinks about breathing—he did at first, and now it's less than once a week."

I remembered a nurse once saying, If you want to know what it's like to have CF, coat your mouth with peanut butter, plug your nose, and breathe through a straw. I could tell she wanted family members to actually try this, but I never did. I'd imagined it, though, and felt frantic. I realized a while ago that Stephen was always thinking about two things at once—breathing, and whatever else was going on. He'd developed a technique for talking, pausing like a singer to take a breath at the least noticeable moments.

"Did talking to him make you want to?"

"Yeah."

"Then you should."

"But what do you think, separately?"

"It seems like if there's something out there, we can't not give it a try."

"If it works we can do whatever we want."

Whatever we want. What would that be? We stayed up late into the night, throwing out possibilities. I thought we should travel around the world, go study Spanish in Mexico. Stephen wanted to move back to Berkeley and get a dog. We got deep into the logistics of this, the bargaining—I agreed we could get a dog if he promised we could still go to Mexico. I felt hopeful, comfortable, the transplant made sense. But then, a few days later, I went to pick Stephen up from a doctor's appointment, and was told that Dr. Wohl wanted me to come back to the exam room.

"I'm glad you're here," she said when she saw me. "Stephen and I were talking about the transplant. I think we should get him on the list within the year."

I stared at her for a second. "*This* year?"

WORK, SCHOOL, THE transplant disappeared. In their place rose Dublin first, and then the ocean between Ireland and Wales, the ship deck lurching beneath us as we leaned over its railing. Everyone else was inside but we couldn't leave the deck; we stood out there in our rain jackets getting sprayed, gulping in the spitting air. We rode the train through Wales and Northern England, hanging out with other travelers on the platforms, young guys with guitars from Manchester who explained to us the grating nature of the American accent on English ears. "You're nice enough," one said. "Don't talk too loud and you'll get on fine."

Stephen's parents had given us this trip for our honeymoon. His doctors were a little nervous about it, but we'd been counting on going. We'd always wanted to see Scotland and Ireland together, and this might be our only chance. We traveled in luxury, renting a car, which seemed like something older, wasteful people did—like trading in a futon for a real bed. But we rented one anyway, a small red Yugo, secured in Edinburgh. We drove north to Inverness, its mix of cobbled streets along the river, old churches, and bleak modern concrete structures. We were both part Scottish; we felt an attachment to Scotland, not one we were about to mention to the people who actually lived there. As we drove through the Lowlands, I could see why my ancestors had gone from Scotland to Montana—the rocky hills, fields of grass, crisp air, the weather harsh to outsiders but feeling right if you came from it.

We drove through the countryside, visiting a wild animal park, Loch Ness, small towns skirting the fogged-in hills. We bought a local literary journal put out by high school students, and all varieties of sweet breads, to which an aisle of the grocery store was devoted. In the afternoon the sky threatened rain. On the roadside, cars had pulled over; an older couple sat in foldout chairs, drinking their afternoon tea from a thermos.

In Ireland we found our way to Annascaul, a three-street town on a hilly road that wound up from the coast. Marie and Anne, who'd come from Dublin to Marie's hometown to start their own bed-and-breakfast, took us in. Anne was in charge of the cooking; Marie was in charge of the hiking. She offered to take us to the start of a ten-mile loop that would lead us back to the inn.

The next morning, she dropped us off by a small path that followed a low stone wall. The wall separated a row of houses from a dry field. We walked on the field side, looking over the backs of the houses, dirt corridors between them. Beyond the field up toward the hills, sheep covered the land. We hiked up through the hills, alongside the sheep farms, into a deep forest that seemed out of place, a cluster of tall pines shooting up in the middle of grazed land.

"This isn't even exercise for you," Stephen complained, when we'd stopped for water.

"A ten-mile hike is exercise."

"Come on, you could run it."

The trail wound through the trees reaching west, until we were overlooking the ocean. We followed the path, now soft under our feet, down to the water. The beach was quiet, a lone food stand surrounded by empty picnic tables at its edge. It hadn't rained once since we'd been in Ireland. Stephen was a little light-headed. He bought two Snickers and wolfed them down. We climbed the path through the outskirts of Annascaul.

A rusty water can and a tin cup, sitting on a tree stump. Piles of sheep manure, formed into giant cubes, set on fire and smoldering. To our right, pastures delineated by small gates. To our left, an occasional home, and then a scattering of homes, their yards backed up against the path. Soon, the back of the Anchor Inn.

The next morning, we set out for the Blasket Islands. We drove the western edge of the Dingle Peninsula and searched the road until we found the turnoff for the ferry. The ferry was a small motorboat, which made one trip out and one back from the islands each day. The crossing was impossible in bad weather, which had made the islands a remote place to live. Their population had dwindled, until in 1953, one of the remaining twenty-three islanders died because no one could cross from the mainland to give him medical attention, and the Irish government decided to evacuate the other islanders for their own safety. We docked at a stone wall, where the deckhand helped us off one by one. "Boat leaves at four," he told us. "Don't get left overnight."

There were no clear paths, only pastures and grooves running through them, tire marks from wagons that still moved sheep around the island. It was hard to tell whether the sheep lived on the island permanently or were taken here to graze. If they lived here, how and where were they shorn? We wandered through what had been a village—abandoned stone cottages, holes for doors and windows, uneven floors. The cottages were built in flat fields, exposed to the elements, the location a terrible choice, but maybe the only choice. People had built these houses and refused to leave them.

We meandered through a grassy field and came out onto an empty beach. We took our shoes off and walked down through the white sand toward the water. Even the ocean seemed quiet;

the beach was protected, facing the coast. Stephen set his camera on a log and ran back to sit down next to me, slightly winded. We stared out into the water long after he rescued the camera from the sand and came back to sit beside me.

He wanted to climb to the top of the island. I wasn't sure we had enough time, but he felt he needed to get up there. There was no path to the top; we hiked up through fields of deep grass. Surprisingly, it was a true summit, we could see down the other side.

"It's three-fifteen," I complained when he started taking all kinds of pictures. We scrambled down the rocky hillside, keeping our steps light so we wouldn't lose our balance. It was the way we ran down trails in the Rockies, all concentration focused on the ground in front of us, the freedom in being nowhere else but here.

chapter thirteen

WE SAT ON A BENCH IN HARVARD SQUARE, EATING FRIED eggplant sandwiches, paper plates in our laps. We'd been yanked out of Ireland too early, and on the plane ride back I'd dreaded Cambridge, but the trip seemed to be continuing here. We found ourselves walking down side streets, struck by details of buildings, faces, weather. We must have still exuded the openness of travelers, because people kept approaching us, which we weren't used to here. A teenager eating pizza nearby heard us mention Ireland and came over to show us his shamrock tattoo. A woman sitting behind us in a movie theater, passing time before the show, told us about her daughter who'd won an essay contest at WordsWorth Books. The man who fixed Stephen's camera told us about his childhood, when the hardware stores in Cambridge outnumbered the coffee shops.

And then, school began and work began, and the illness, as if alerted to the general momentum of fall, picked up its pace, too. Everything started to go wrong at once—even looking back, it's hard to see the details clearly. And maybe it wasn't the details themselves, but the way we dealt with them; maybe we were too tired to be very good at this anymore, to joke about the stomach tube, or the oxygen at night, or the third failed embolization. There was some joking, there was always joking, but it was less frequent and more subdued, and if you knew Stephen, the idea that he was too tired to see the world as funny would worry you more than a trip to the hospital ever could.

The dive in his health made the transplant real, almost visceral. The unknown of it started to throw us all over the place. Some days the transplant loomed sky-like. We could see it from a distance, but we couldn't see where it met with us, we only knew that our bodies were a silhouette against it, seen from anywhere else. Other days it would shift its weight a little and let us slip out from underneath its bulk. We'd walk around full of haphazard tenderness, a nostalgia while events were still in motion. It was overwhelming and addictive. Sometimes it was too much to take. At night our apartment felt like a college dorm, midnight conversations bleeding outward: What did it mean to be here in these bodies, on this earth, what did we want to do with the time? Then we'd crash; sprawl on the couch watching movies.

In the midst of the sudden decline, and maybe because of it, the trouble with the pain medication reared its head. After months of worrying about the craving he felt, Stephen had forced himself to talk to his doctors. They'd switched him from Vicodin to Percocet, thinking that a stronger medication would solve the problem, but it only made the craving worse. Instead of calling them back, he came up with his own plan, involving me.

He'd buy a lockbox with a combination lock from the hardware store. I'd set the lock and dole the pills out twice a day. How could we not have seen what a bad idea this was?

"I don't want to be the gatekeeper," I warned him. "If you ask for more I'm giving it to you."

He nodded reluctantly. "That's fair."

But within a week I began to hate the lockbox, the look of it, its thin unfeeling metal. I began dreading my arrival home from work. "Before when I came home, you were happy to see *me*," I complained as I handed him the pills.

One night, lying in bed, he turned toward me. "I don't want to tell you this."

I closed my eyes. He knew I hated hearing bad news right before I fell asleep. We'd been home all night. There'd been hours full of minutes of better times to tell me whatever he was about to say.

"I picked the lock on the lockbox," he blurted out. "I'm such a loser."

"Wait, what do you mean?"

"While you were at work. The whole time, I couldn't believe I was doing it."

Then it hit me, why he hadn't wanted to bring this up. It wasn't picking the lock, but what had happened afterwards. I'd come home from work, and he'd pretended everything was normal. Which meant, he'd reassembled the box, and locked it back up. He'd asked me for the medication, watched me unlock the box for him, all the while pretending that he couldn't do it himself. I picked up a pill bottle and hurled it past his head.

"You *planned* to lie to me; it wasn't even just lying," I said.

"I did lie, but I did tell you," he said. "I'm telling you."

"I'm supposed to be happy about that?"

In the dark I told myself—One more try, and then, no matter what, I'd make him call the doctor. This was the kind of decision we usually made together, or more, the kind he made on his own. It felt lonely and a little wrong, not including him, and it made me wonder whether either of us could be trusted anymore.

The next day, he came home with a more complicated box. Within a week, he'd dismantled that one and brought home a third. At the end of the month, he told me he was going to call the nurse and say that his backpack had been stolen so he could get an early refill. "Are you crazy?" I said. "Don't you hear how obvious that sounds? Just tell them what's going on. Any other medical problem, you would."

"Yeah, you're right," he said, and then while I was in the shower, he called and said his backpack had been stolen. I caught the tail end of the conversation, lingered in the hallway half cringing, half hoping he'd blown his cover. But nothing happened—the prescription came early, probably mostly because the nurse had more serious CF-related problems on her plate. And so did we. Stephen was headed for a double-lung transplant; he'd just had a third embolization to stop the bleeding in his lungs. Given everything else that was happening, what did the addiction matter? Was it only a backbreaking straw?

I imagine Stephen back then, needing the break the Percocet gave him, that bit of distance, that lens on the world that made it seem like everything was going to turn out fine. I remember him struggling with the opposing urges. I imagine it physically, a tug-of-war, the desire to stop and the desire to keep going pulling at him from either side. And I remember myself, chafing at the tether of the problem, the police-like loneliness of the lockbox, the secrecy, the way we were plotting against each other all of a sudden. The feeling that Stephen was disappearing on me, and thinking he could put a stop to it if he wanted to, if he'd only call the doctors and ask for help.

But he kept not calling, and then he'd go through withdrawal, which rendered him immobile and surly on the couch. And instead of getting him water or a pillow or the newspaper like I would any other time he was sick, I'd leave the house. I'd stomp around Cambridge, resolutely doing my own thing, angry that he hadn't put an end to all this. Thinking, *As if there aren't enough bad-health, miserable days.* And maybe there was a straw in this somewhere, because you might think, what were a few days? But inside that life, every day counted.

And maybe we needed a straw. The transplant, the G-tube, the deterioration—how could we turn on each other about these things? But the addiction, in my mind, was an illness with known cures, which allowed me to hate it. And in Stephen's mind, it had taken over, which allowed him to forget me altogether, to be selfish in a way he'd never been about any other part of being sick. Maybe I needed to stomp around Cambridge, furious, and maybe Stephen needed to let himself off the hook, and maybe the addiction allowed us this, punctured the hole in our marriage and took the pressure off. At the time all I felt was panic. I wanted to somehow break the spell of the problem, the little world held by the two of us.

"What about talking to Amani?" I asked him. "Or your brother?"

But the truth was, I wasn't telling my friends either. I would have had to say, Every morning I unlock a box and take out three pills, hand them to Stephen, make sure the box is locked. He asks me to take the box to work with me, get it out of the house, but I worry he'll show up at work desperate, so I leave it at home. And it had been so long I'd been not telling anyone that it felt impossible now. Why did you ever have to tell anyone anything, in the end? Maybe you could be loved without being known. Though this made me feel more defeated than anything.

For Thanksgiving, my sister Jean took the bus from Hampshire College; Joaquin, Caitlin, and Caitlin's sister Emily took the train from Manhattan; Amani flew out from San Francisco. Thursday morning, we crowded into the kitchen to cook. We threw utensils back and forth, the squash burned in the oven, and turkey juice spilled on the floor. The kitchen was so hot we ended up in tank tops. Stephen took his shirt off without thinking, and Joaquin glanced at his stomach, its round plastic peg. "Jesus!" he said, turning away.

I wanted to kill Joaquin—all the time I'd spent convincing Stephen it wasn't that bad, he could go swimming if he wanted to. More than that, this piece of plastic was an improvement— beautiful compared to the original. The tube had been replaced by a small button with a tiny cap. Yes, it was plastic and alien to his body, but it lay flat against his stomach, nothing dangling from it. Stephen no longer scrutinized himself in the mirror to see if the tube was visible beneath his shirt, or limited himself to the few shirts that hid it best. Still, it was hard to be nonchalant about plastic coming out of your friend's stomach. Stephen pulled his shirt back on.

"Wait," Caitlin said, "I want to see it."

"So you absorb the food, just the same as eating?" Emily asked.

"I've been tempted to pour a beer in there, to see if I'd feel a buzz," Stephen said.

"You haven't done that yet?" Joaquin said.

"Come on, try it," said Amani.

"But wouldn't that spill all over?" Jean said. "You'd need a funnel."

Egged on by all the attention, Stephen couldn't resist. He found a funnel, opened the tiny plastic cap, and poured a beer into his stomach. He burped and we all laughed.

After dinner we fell into the living room, lay on the rug talking for hours. At three in the morning we all drifted off to our separate quarters. Stephen and I were sleeping on a single futon on the floor of his study; it felt like college. I collapsed on top of the covers. Stephen sat down next to me. "Liz . . ." he said, and at the sound in his voice, I bolted up, glanced over at his desk. The lockbox was open. Maybe I had left it open. I hadn't thought about it today, I had gone an entire glorious day without thinking about it. "Let's figure it out after everybody goes home," I told him.

"It's too late. I only have five left."

"Are you sure? Down from . . .?"

"Thirty-five."

"How are you functioning?"

"I didn't know when to tell you. I didn't want to ruin your Thanksgiving."

Withdrawal was going to start in the morning. It was a deal we'd made, after a trip to New York where he'd spent two days skulking around in its throes. No withdrawal while we were with our friends, unless I could tell them what was going on.

"You promised," I said. "Now you're going to make me lie to all of them?"

"It's not a lie. I'll be sick."

"They're your friends, too. Since when do you lie to Amani?"

In the morning, I went into the living room. Emily had made

coffee; everyone was hunched over leftover pie. I sat down on the couch between Caitlin and Jean, my stomach queasy. Jean, who I'd convinced to tell me things she couldn't tell my parents, who trusted me the way only a much younger sister could. Caitlin, who erred on the side of honesty, who'd shown me over time that it was the better way to be. Joaquin and Amani, who could accept the messiest and darkest of truths. I could spill it now, and they'd all hug me, maybe even overlook the fact that I'd been lying by omission for months and just help me figure it all out.

I stared down at my plate. "Stephen's sick," I said, and kept my eyes on my pie for a few long minutes while they waited for me to say more.

He stayed in bed while I figured out a way to get us all out of the house, pushing a trip to Harvard Square. Amani stayed behind with Stephen to watch a football game. I used all my mental powers to telepathically convince Stephen to talk to him, but when we got back, it hadn't happened.

One by one our friends left, I watched them head home, people who felt like strangers now. While Stephen lay on the couch in agony, I wandered through Cambridge, went everywhere but home. I stood in a large park on the top of a hill, staring down through barren trees, trying to figure out what to do.

That night we lay pressed against each other, both lonely. I had decided—I was going to call his doctor myself. He was going to hate me for a while, but I'd get through that, we'd get through that. There were more important things than not being hated. In the long run, years from now, if we had years, he would understand that it was the only thing I could think of to do.

Stephen was grumpy with the young resident in the hospital who had the unfortunate job of unveiling the detox plan. "But

I can't switch *off* the Percocet," he argued. "It's the only thing that helps with the pain."

The resident explained that in order to address the pain they were putting him on methadone. It turned out that Percocet and heroin were not unrelated. Methadone was some calm cousin of both. At first neither of us trusted it, but strangely it worked. For three days, he lay in bed miserable. But then relief began to seep in, he felt a haze lifting. He took two pills a day, and the bottle remained out in the open, holding no allure.

Stephen became interested in the workings of addiction, awed by its powers, humbled by the way it had overtaken him. As always when he changed, he changed completely. He spoke openly with his friends, apologized for having lied, and tried to articulate the mind-set. He became the person to whom others confessed their own habits and weaknesses. I was slower to adjust, to shake off the exhaustion, forgive the fighting, answer my friends honestly when they asked me how I'd been.

"WHAT IF HE quit school?" Eve suggested one night on the phone. She had a knack for solving problems in ways that would never have occurred to me. "You guys could go home, rest up for the transplant."

"Quit?" Stephen said in horror when I floated the idea. I knew he would hate it. We were both terrible quitters.

"At the semester," I said. "We could come back after the transplant."

"I'd feel like such a loser."

I tried to think of something official—a commanding force that would let Stephen off the hook. "What if we ask Dr. Wohl what she thinks?"

Stephen sat thinking for a minute. "The question is, which way would I be kicking myself more?"

Dr. Wohl knew Stephen better than I'd realized. She told him that he shouldn't think of it as quitting, but as giving his health the attention it deserved. *Sometimes it has to be a full-time job,* she said. She told him she was proud that he'd gotten this far, that after the transplant he'd have more energy, and it would be easy to return. *Consider this doctor's orders,* she said. I would have thrown my arms around her if she'd been that kind of person.

chapter fourteen

WE WALKED ALONG NINTH STREET, HEADING TOWARD BOULDER'S outdoor mall. We were in Colorado for winter break, and last night it had snowed six inches. Today the sky was intensely bright, as it was on the coldest winter days. It lifted and opened, the way a sky was supposed to.

"This is going to suck," Stephen told me. "I'm going to see everyone I know."

An oxygen tank rode in his backpack, its tubing threading up over his shoulder to his nose. It was an affront, to no longer be able to breathe in your hometown. He wore his long dark blue coat, walked with his usual long strides, the slower version. I wanted to put my arm in his, but the gesture would expose me as overprotective. I just didn't want him to have to face the mall alone. But how else could he face it? I thought about Heather, Stephen's one friend with CF, and her husband. They'd come to town recently, and we'd all gone out to dinner. She looked deeply tired, her sense of humor so wry, and her husband seemed out of place next to her, glowing with freshly scrubbed health. I could almost see the translucent barrier around her, the way he could not realistically know her at all. Though there he was, hovering, knocking up against the Plexiglas. I held Stephen's hand in spite of myself, and he didn't give me a hard time about it. We walked glove in glove, him inhaling through the plastic tube.

We kicked up slush; Stephen glancing hurriedly around to make sure no one he knew was walking by. At a time like this he was lucky that his default expression made him look skeptical, impatient. His face, unlike mine, buffered him from the peanut gallery. Right now I was trying to tune it out: the apologetic stares, the horrified-shifting-to-kind glances.

A couple around our age walked past; the woman smiled fiercely at Stephen. I had the uncomfortable feeling that the mask made her feel like she had to look at him. *They're just people,* she was saying to herself. *Treat them like normal people.* Which, of course, meant we weren't, and which I'd thought myself, walking by a person with a missing limb. I got glances of a different kind. *Poor girl. What a trooper.* Or, *Thank god I'm not her.* All the relief and fear that's bound up in the pity. For fun, I began to rate people by the way they dealt with the mask.

The bookstore was teeming, lines through the aisles. People moved aside for Stephen even though his tank took no extra room—a sort of disability royalty. Afterwards we sat on the low brick steps at the end of the mall, where we'd sprawled as teenagers on late summer nights, all the stores dark, the mall lit with streetlamps. I imagined sending a friend up ahead of us with a sign: *Young guy wearing oxygen mask approaching: Act normal.* A few months ago, Stephen had met my friend

Joseph for the first time. *"Why didn't you* tell *me he had scars across his face?"* he'd complained, walking home from dinner. *"It's your fault he had to see me flinch."* In this way, I felt bad for the bookstore cashier, for the old high school teacher we'd run into. Only small kids were unfazed by their own surprise, their staring.

WE WERE EASING our way out of Cambridge. At work, I hadn't talked much about Stephen's illness. Now that I was leaving mid-year, though, I had to go public. I put it off for a while, thinking it would reduce the number of awkward weeks, but once it happened, I felt strangely relaxed. The teachers, the accountant, the custodian—everyone came to find me in the library at a quiet moment. The principal sent a letter home with the kids and I felt a little sick to my stomach the next morning when the parents streamed in. Maybe they hadn't read the letter yet, I told myself; they got so many papers from school. But who had, and who hadn't? One mother, who had helped me in the library a few times, came over behind my desk to give me a hug. She apologized for complaining to me about her kids. "All along I thought you were this young woman," she said.

I saw myself through her eyes, appearing on my bike in the morning, sitting cross-legged on the floor reading stories to the kids. I was her younger, freer self—my life didn't look half-bad, through this lens.

The kids wrote me letters and drew me pictures. I hung one picture on the fridge as a transplant omen. It was from Helen, a seven-year-old. She'd drawn a picture of a hospital, and a stick man emerging from it with a smile. Nearby, a stick woman sat in a chair, asking, "So what did the doctor say?" The stick man had no bubble of words. But in the corner, a large pink heart spoke. "Wishes come true, you know," it said.

FRIENDS CAME OVER to help us move. I'd made lasagna; Stephen had bought beer. So many people came to help that the moving took twenty minutes and we spent the rest of the evening hanging out. Generous people were everywhere, they lifted us and carried us toward California so that we barely noticed the work happening underneath us, the boxes shipped, the furniture hauled off, the apartment cleaned. Only we couldn't manage to slip away that easily, because the truth was we'd been a mess here. We'd each been a mess, we'd been a mess together, and maybe we were looking for some way to take it out on each other because two days before we left, we got in a terrible fight. If this were a novel, the fight would go somewhere, it would change the characters, and life would be irrevocably different afterwards. But in real life, we woke up the next morning the same, both hurt and angry, sure that we didn't understand each other, wondering if at some point we would.

It started with something that happened all the time. We were supposed to meet friends for breakfast in a few minutes and Stephen was still in bed.

"I don't think I'm going to make it," he said.

I was standing on one foot, trying to step into my jeans while drying my hair with a towel. We were headed to see friends of mine, who I'd wanted him to meet for a year. Already they'd invited us over for dinner, and he'd been sick at the last minute. I'd gone by myself, and sat next to his place setting. "Seriously? But you have to."

"I feel like shit."

"Because you went to bed at three. I asked you if you wanted to change the time, fuck, it's too late now."

"You can still go."

"Thanks. I wanted *you* to meet them. We're moving in two days."

"Look, I should have gone to bed earlier. What else do you want me to say?"

"I want you to get up and come with me."

He closed his eyes. "Are you listening? I apologized, I feel incredibly sick."

I eyed him. *Incredibly* sick? That was overkill. I knew what incredibly sick looked like. "If these were your friends, you'd be out of bed."

"You have no idea how I feel."

"Likewise."

"Stop."

"No. I'm mad at you. You're saying I shouldn't be mad?"

"I'm saying you shouldn't yell at me while I'm lying here feeling sick."

"Guess I can't be supportive all the time."

"Fuck off."

"Fuck off yourself." My fingers twitched as I tied my shoes.

On the way home I felt hopeful, remembering what Stephen and I had come to when we were twenty-two and sharing a room, and found ourselves fighting late at night after we'd been out drinking. If an argument got to the point where one of us said, "Fuck off," it was no longer a real argument; it was ridiculous. We'd laugh sheepishly about these arguments in the morning, turn them into stories. But when I got home, Stephen would barely look at me. "There was this undercurrent," he said, "like you resent me for being sick. Like I'm a burden."

"I didn't say that."

"Oh—'I can't be supportive all the time'?"

"Well, you were telling me I was a terrible person for getting mad."

"It *was* terrible."

I found myself moving toward the hallway, lacing my boots. "I should be losing it more often. You have no idea how hard I'm trying."

"You know that's not true—wait a second."

I thudded down the stairs, out the door, the cold air hitting hard. I did not want to see anyone I knew. I did not want to see anyone, ever. I wanted to walk through streets until I'd traversed an entire empty city. We'd thought there was room for both of us in all this, but there wasn't. If there had been, and it was a small thing, we would have found a way for him to meet my friends. We would have found a way for me to tell him what it was like to be me, the way we could talk about what it was like to be him. And then one mean thing—yes, it was mean, but one thing and it pierced so deeply that I was a terrible person. I wanted him to step back and imagine my life. And he needed room, too, why couldn't he make a mistake? Was his illness so difficult that it had to be the only difficult thing about him?

I made my way back through the neighborhood and trudged slowly up the stairs. The house was quiet—he was in his study. I knocked on his door, but he didn't answer. I tried the handle; he'd locked the door. I peered through the keyhole. He was not at his desk. The only place he could be was in the closet, which was big enough to sit in.

I sat down on the floor. It was not a part of the apartment I ever spent time in—the square of space bordered by the hallway, his room, the bathroom, and a set of open shelves. The carpet underneath me was gray-blue and needed vacuuming. I pulled my knees to my chest, leaned against the shelves. This was the kind of spot I would have liked as a kid, small and tucked away, a place for a secret club. I could sit here for a long time; I could wait him out.

MY FRIEND SARAH told me that maybe if I expressed my frustration with the illness more often, I could do it without being mean. She was getting a degree in counseling. In her family class, her teacher had talked about a couple that was dealing with the woman's cancer diagnosis. They talked about cancer like it was a separate entity, a third party in their relationship. "Almost like a person," Sarah said.

"Did they talk *to* the cancer?" I asked her.

"Some people even have a pillow, they punch the illness."

"Please don't tell me that."

Trying to explain it to Stephen, I felt like I was back in calculus class. In the presence of the teacher, in the classroom, it all made sense. But at home, the math book seemed written in a foreign language, and all my practice problems came out wrong. "It's like we each have our own relationship to CF," I said.

"Yeah . . ." Stephen said impatiently.

"Well, we could talk about how CF affects each of us."

Stephen frowned. "Don't we do that?"

"I mean, without you taking it personally."

"How can I not take it personally? It's about me."

"It's about CF. I can be mad at the illness without being mad at you."

"How?"

"But I am."

"But it's part of me. So are you saying you hate CF?"

"Sometimes, yeah, I do."

That night, Stephen wrote in his journal: *To get blamed by the person I love most about CF is wrong and hurtful. Any anger Liz has is about fear. It's not fair, I feel that too. No one can get mad at CF and not make me feel bad. Sarah's idea of CF as a 3rd person not going to happen. Bad idea.*

He'd gone beyond accepting CF; he'd come to decide it had given him more than it had taken away. And maybe this was true. But why couldn't the illness be both great and terrible? Maybe this was less about illness and more about Stephen, his tendency to take a side, to love or hate things, to devote himself to the things he loved. Maybe this was about being young.

Youth helped us with illness in some ways—we had the energy for it, the spirit to tackle it or at least try to shape it, to make our own rules. And most of all, we had friends who were willing and able to do this with us, who jumped in to take it on, not only helping out the way people do later in life, but being a part of it, living it through.

But youth worked against us, too. We could have used the sturdiness that comes later on, the knowledge that what we had together wouldn't fall apart if we weren't always happy in it. We could have used some perspective, some stepping back and saying, He's driving me crazy, I think I'll head to New York for the weekend and wait this out. I went to New York, I took my breaks, but I couldn't admit to either of us that this was what they were.

It had taken me two years of unending hospitalizations to throw the kind of fit other people were always recommending. And I threw it, and Stephen locked himself in his room and sat in his closet and cried. I hadn't meant to do that to him, but I'd done it, and I sat outside his door, wishing he'd let me in, but not wishing I could take back what I'd said. Later, Stephen would return to his journal entry about my frustrations with CF and scrawl at the bottom: *Almost 2 months later, 3/13/97. What a loser! Stephen could not hear Liz. What a selfish dolt.*

IN OAKLAND'S TINY airport, Stephen breathed deeply. "Are you noticing the air? I mean, I know you can breathe everywhere, but does it feel better here? Try a deep breath."

I did. The air was thick and cool, Northern California winter, mist promising rain. You could feel the life in it, the hills turning green in a frenzy outside.

Anna picked us up, and I stared out the backseat window as she drove along the freeway. The day had begun to take on fairy-tale dimensions, our white car scuttling through the fog, toward a house with a fireplace and a steep point of a roof. We were tiny characters, having woken up this morning in ordinary lives and then stepped sideways into a fictional landscape, a place where you could exchange your lungs if they were not working. And we were acting a little like the kids in fairy tales, wide-eyed but not as intimidated as we should have been, laughing as we sped along, the feeling that, yes, this was life but it was not entirely real, somehow we'd get a handle on the plot twists and everything would work out.

chapter fifteen

Highway 5, hundreds of windmills, all in motion, which of course they would be, but it still looked like a feat, all the blades turning, windmill after windmill stretched along the grassy hills. We had our music blasting—Stephen had stayed up late the night before making the playlist, all the L.A. songs he could find. He'd conjured this trip yesterday too, because why not, we could, and convincing Anna and Amani.

The transplant was on the horizon, and it could be the end or it could be the new beginning, and we wouldn't know until we got there. So all we had was right now, and we knew it. We'd thought we'd known it before, but that had been a watered-down, ten-years-off knowing. This was something else. We were propelled a thousand miles an hour by the fact that when you could see death, life was yours in an entirely different way. We should get dumb jobs to pay the rent and write that book we'd wanted to write together. We should visit Alix and Carroll in Hawaii. We should hike with our friends in these rainy, green February hills.

chapter sixteen

I WAS IN THE KITCHEN DOING DISHES WHEN THE PHONE RANG. It was past midnight, and I could hear Anna grumbling in her room. My friends were always waking her up. I dried my hands on my jeans, scrambled to get down the hall. The phone stopped. I could hear Stephen's voice from our bedroom, and the absence of the music he'd been playing. I went back to the dishes, thought maybe we needed to make a rule, no calls past eleven. Stephen came into the kitchen.

"That was the hospital," he said. "They have a pair of lungs."

It seemed like panic should set in, like the minute hand on the clock should start catapulting forward, but instead time slowed completely. He'd asked for ten minutes to think about it, and they'd given him five. We were deep inside those five minutes, in the little world of this kitchen. The plate in my hands, the running water, the red cabinets . . . everything appeared in hyperreal detail.

"What do you think?" he asked me.

"It feels right," I admitted. "But I have no idea why."

"I know. I think I'm sure, but I need to be sure I'm sure. Maybe I need to talk to Dr. Stulbarg."

"It's the middle of the night."

"Doctors get woken up. He'd want me to call."

"You have three minutes left."

I SET MY BACKPACK on our bed, started scrounging through my drawers. What did you need for a transplant? Crossword puzzles seemed appealing but I didn't have any. I found a couple of books, a pack of cards, a notebook, and my wallet. I threw in a change of clothes and running shoes and went to wake Anna. She squinted up at me, then put her pillow over her head. "It can't be time," she said. "We're not ready."

We drove down 35th Avenue in Oakland, the street empty, lights blinking red. The entrance to the freeway was slick with rain. I peered out the window of the passenger seat as we drove across the top deck of the Bay Bridge. Dark water churned below us. The bridge was illuminated, its peaks and valleys outlined against the sky. Stephen adhered to the speed limit; it would be bad timing if we got in an accident now.

"Though we could be donors," he said.

"That's not funny."

"It's kind of funny," Anna said from the backseat.

I glanced at Stephen next to me, driving, watching the road. I imagined tonight as our last night. It was Sunday, we'd gone to the sketchy vegetarian diner just the two of us, wandered around Telegraph, losing track of time in Amoeba Records, meeting up in various aisles. It was not a night I'd remember, unless it was the last night, and then it would become something else.

We drove into San Francisco, up the wide lanes of Market Street. Stephen wanted to stop and pick up Amani. Anna accused him of underreacting to the situation. She promised him she'd pick up Amani later. "I always get bulldozed," he sighed, but he turned right on 17th, and we moved steadily up the steep hill toward our destination.

The hospital rose through the fog on Parnassus Street. We began to get giddy as we came close to it, chuckling in spite of ourselves. We stood outside the sliding glass doors to the emergency room and tried to muster some gravity. In the lobby, Anna and I watched Stephen get in the elevator. It felt like we were seeing him off, and I wondered whether he was lonely, preparing for his solo voyage.

Stephen had forbidden me from calling our families until we were sure the transplant was going to go through. I called Amani, who said he'd take a cab right over. Anna called Sam, who also said he'd be right there. We realized that we'd better stop calling people, what if they all came? We were too many as it was, trespassing into the hospital in the middle of the night.

Anna and I crept down the seventh-floor hallway, reading the names on doors. We found Stephen's name next to another patient's. We slipped into his room, passing an older man who was fast asleep, snoring. Next to him, separated by a curtain, Stephen sat on his bed, talking with a doctor, a tall woman in her fifties, who spoke in a whisper. She was the anesthesiologist, here to explain the routine. Stephen would do a round of inhaled meds; he'd shower, and put on a hospital gown. He could wear his boxers until he went into surgery. He would sign the papers giving his consent to the operation. He would wait here until Dr. Keith had checked the lungs thoroughly. If everything went smoothly, surgery would begin in six or seven hours. By the time she was finished explaining, both Amani and Sam had crept into the room and sat by the window listening. Sam apologized for our numbers, but the anesthesiologist smiled.

"No, you've made my night," she said. "You have no idea how many patients I see who are all alone. He's lucky to have you."

"We're young," Sam said. "We've got the time."

"Though unfortunately I'm going to have to kick you out in a minute," she added. "No one can be in the room for the breathing treatment."

Even though Stephen did this treatment at home and we'd all taken in the secondhand mist before, we played by the rules, hoping that this way we'd be allowed to stick around the seventh floor. We retreated to the waiting room. Anna got out dried apricots and chocolate-covered raisins. Amani took bread and cheese out of his backpack. Sam went to the vending machines and got us drinks. We sat huddled together, eating; we could have been on a cross-country car trip, in the tiny world of this room. The windows revealed nothing but darkness. We lay down on the stiff hospital couches and tried to sleep, but we kept whispering to each other, imagining the day ahead.

Later, I snuck past Stephen's snoring roommate. This could be the last night we had, and I wasn't going to spend it in a different room. He was sitting on his bed, a notebook in his lap. He moved over so I could sit close to him. He was making a list of all the people he wanted me to notify. "They're all in my phone," he said.

"You sure you want me to take your phone? That's the kind of thing I lose."

"I put the hospital number in, too, so you can call over during the surgery."

"I won't need to call. I'll probably stick around here."

He eyed me skeptically. "Since when do you do that?"

He was right, it just made me anxious, sitting in a waiting room with other people kneading their hands.

We lay squeezed together on his single bed. I rested my head on his chest and closed my eyes. "This is my last night listening to these lungs," I said.

"I don't want to jinx it but it feels like it's going to be okay."

"I know. But don't say that."

I fell asleep to the sound of his breathing. I woke to the gray light of early morning. A nurse was standing over me, shaking my shoulder lightly. "Sorry, hon," he said, "I have to get his stats."

I lifted Stephen's arm off me, moved out of his way. On the wall below the clock was a day calendar. I ripped off the top sheet to reveal May 5th. "My second birthday," Stephen said.

The nurse led us down the hall to give us a tour of what was to come. He buzzed us through the heavy doors to Intensive Cardiac Care. We were introduced to the night's resident, who shook Stephen's hand, nodded dismissively at me, and launched into the setup, enunciating his words with exaggerated precision. He asked if we had any questions.

"Can I keep my old lungs?" Stephen asked.

The resident laughed. "Uh, no."

"Why not?" Stephen asked. He smiled as he said it, passing the question off lightly, but I could tell he was picturing a glass jar with fluid, the lungs floating inside.

"For one thing, they don't come out whole," the resident explained, forgetting to enunciate, his voice low and irritated.

"They're just pieces of tissue that have been scraped off the chest cavity."

Stephen shrugged. "That's okay."

"No, they get sent to the lab for research."

"They're my lungs," Stephen said.

"Well, yeah, no. They stay here."

"Can I at least take a look at them?"

"Mmm, I don't think it's possible. You'll be under for a while after surgery, and they need to be sent to the lab immediately if they're going to be useful."

Stephen sighed. "I see the point of that."

As the resident hurried down the hall, the nurse gave Stephen a sympathetic pat on the shoulder. "I'd want to see my lungs, too," he confided.

Back in the room, the anesthesiologist was waiting. The lungs looked good, Dr. Keith was ready. I rushed down the corridor like a kid in a school hallway, moving as fast as I could without technically running. I arrived breathlessly in the waiting room. Amani, Sam, and Anna were stretched out on three separate benches, hospital blankets over them. They looked up at me, pale and puffy-eyed. We moved in a clump down the hallway, trying to slip quietly into Stephen's room. The anesthesiologist was still there, waiting while Stephen read through the papers on her clipboard.

He flipped to the last page and handed the clipboard to me. It was a proxy, which gave me decision-making power if he couldn't call his own shots. I'd signed one in Boston and it had made me hope more than ever that nothing would go wrong. I didn't want this job, but I didn't want anyone else to have it either. "You feel the same as you did last time?" I asked.

"About pulling the plug?" Stephen asked.

Sam winced. "There's got to be another way to say that."

"Sorry." Stephen took our copy of the proxy sheet from me and wrote something on the paper. "Just in case," he said, handing it back to me. At the bottom, in small letters, it said, *I told you to pull the plug.* I folded the paper into a tiny square and put it in my pocket.

We packed his clothes, magazines, and papers. I took his wallet and phone. The nurse put the rest in a plastic bag and labeled it "S. Evans" with a black Sharpie. Stephen looked nervously at his belongings as we left the room. We escorted him into the elevator, through a maze of hallways on the second floor, to a small annex connected to the operating room.

"Okay, you guys," the nurse said, and I could see we'd reached the limit of how much we could all be in this together. Stephen sat down on the metal chair in the annex.

"See you this afternoon," he said. "Tonight at the latest."

But he kept me close and kissed me, until the nurse had to ask me to go. I walked down the hall, flanked by friends. Soon, Stephen would take off his socks and boxers, put them on the chair in the room, wonder whether they'd get lost in the chaos. The doors to the operating room would open, and he'd step inside, lifting himself up on the table, swinging his legs around to lie down. The doors would close and Dr. Keith would speak to him as the anesthetic kicked in. *We have to keep you slightly conscious,* he'd say, *but you won't feel anything.* As Stephen drifted off, he'd be saying goodbye to his old lungs. He had spent years taking care of them. It was the end of a relationship, and in a way no one else could understand he felt tender toward them, a little guilty about giving them up. Dr. Keith would keep speaking in that calm, humble way he had that could make you believe this was all just a matter of careful, plodding work.

SAM DROVE US over to Amani's apartment, where I was urged to take the first shower. I stood under the water, trying to pretend I'd just woken from a night's sleep. I wondered whether Stephen was getting any rest right now, if the sedation felt like sleep. I imagined him emerging from the anesthetic, moving through that murky between-worlds state, shifting into silliness. Once after an operation the doctor had asked him if he needed anything else, and he'd asked for pork chops and a foot rub.

Sam lay sprawled on Amani's bed, his giant feet hanging off the edge. I sat next to him, listening to his faint snoring, to Amani rummaging in the kitchen, the rushing water of Anna's shower. Finally I forced myself to get out Stephen's phone. I'd called his family in the dark of early morning. His mom had answered half-asleep. "Oh, Lizzie," she'd said, in a soft whine I'd never heard. I imagined her wandering in a daze in her white bathrobe, too distracted to make coffee, much less look into plane flights. It wasn't fair that Stephen's father wasn't here to do this with her. When I called Stephen's sister, the first thing she said was, "Poor Mom." She was awake and clearheaded, the boys wrestling in the background before breakfast. Clay had simply said, "You're kidding." Then he made me repeat, "Stephen's having the transplant," four times, until he could be sure it had sunk in.

My mom was teaching; I'd need to wait for her break. I tried my dad at work.

"Elizabeth?" he said, unsuspecting.

"Dad?" I heard the speakerphone click off, just him and me now.

"You want us to come out there?" he asked, when I'd explained.

I thought of the plane fares, of work missed, of the way we were killing time around here. "I'm okay," I said. "There's nothing really to do."

My dad laughed. "Of course there's nothing to do. We'll come if you want us."

His voice was breaking me. I pushed back tears. "You think Stephen will be okay?" I asked, like a child.

"I think this was the right thing to do."

"You're not answering the question."

He sighed. "I know, kiddo."

The calls felt like premature birth announcements; all these voices filled with hope and confusion. My brother was the only person who received the news like he expected it, like there was no doubt it would all work out. Eve was mad I hadn't woken her up in the middle of the night. "Hang on," she said. "I'm coming over."

We were strengthening our forces. Eve came, and our friend Forest, who'd just moved out to San Francisco. By the time we went out to breakfast, seven of us sat bleary-eyed in a café on Valencia. We looked just like everyone else here, slackers in our twenties, hungover with time on our hands. I thought of all the people I knew whose fathers or mothers or siblings had died; how you could meet them and never know, how they looked like everyone else, young and wondering what to do with themselves.

Two hours down, six to go. Eve thought we should go back to the hospital, or at least stay nearby, but six hours seemed too long to spend in the waiting room. We decided to hike down to Kirby's Cove. It was Stephen's favorite place, and it seemed like we'd feel closer to him there, even with the physical distance. Eve glanced nervously back at the city as Sam ferried us across the Golden Gate Bridge. Everything seemed imbued with hidden meaning. The air, the landscape, all of us together in one car—these had to be signs from the outside world that the transplant was going well.

We descended the creaky wooden steps to the beach. The wet sand was covered with translucent blue creatures that had washed up in droves. I took my shoes off, rolled up my jeans, and waded calf-deep into the freezing water. San Francisco gleamed across the bay, its white buildings stretching across the hills, a thin green strip running down its center. Beyond the park, I could make out the tall hospital structures. Stephen was in there, somewhere. We were on the outside, like sports fans, unable to do anything but trying anyway. I closed my eyes and pictured him, not in surgery but as himself, looking at me, close-up. Come on, you can do this, I told him silently as I hopped from foot to foot in the water. But if you can't, I added, don't feel bad, don't worry, do what you need to do.

Forest thought we should have a ritual. For once there were no cracks about New Age shit. We stood in a circle on the beach, held hands, and closed our eyes, wishing Stephen well.

As we hiked back up the trail I had the urge to run. Maybe Eve had been right—we should have stayed closer by. When we reached the hospital I rushed into the Intensive Cardiac Care unit and stood near the receptionist's desk, waiting for her to have a free minute. I recognized her from this morning. It seemed like days ago, but she was still freshly made up. Her round bracelets slid back and forth as her hands flew from one stack of papers to the next. She tucked a stray curl behind her ear with quick precision. "I tried to call you," she said.

"Sorry, I was . . ." I looked down. My jeans were wet to the knees; there was a trail of sand behind me on the floor. "How's he doing?"

"So far so good," she said. "His family's in the waiting room."

His family had arrived and I'd been at the beach. How was I going to explain that? I crept into the waiting room. Fran was standing by the window, applying her pink lipstick. She patted my shoulder with her free hand, didn't ask where I'd been. Tinka and Clay came over to hug me. "Lizzie," Tinka said, "you must be so tired."

The waiting room had been taken over. Plates of food lay strewn, backpacks and pillows and cell phone chargers. Celia, the transplant coordinator, came in with a guy named Tim Brooks whom she wanted us to meet. Tim, she said, had recently had a double lung transplant. He smiled shyly at our group as we scoured his body for information. He was on the thin side but not especially frail and seemed to be breathing fine. His face was round, as I'd heard happened with the transplant medications. He had made it through. He now existed with a new pair of lungs in his chest. He spoke with a soft, friendly voice as he tried to answer our endless questions.

"I wasn't too nervous," he said, "but my parents were scared to death. Not to mention they're from a small town in Kentucky, and I hadn't come out to them yet. When I woke up from surgery, they were standing by my bed with my boyfriend."

Celia glanced down at her pager. "First lung is in."

Relief flooded me. I had not known I was afraid, I had kept it from myself, the way I always did. I could feel it now. The first lung was in, he was breathing—halfway, but still. Without thinking, I hugged Tim Brooks. "The first one's the hardest," he said. "Technically, you can breathe with only one lung."

"But what about when they're switching the lungs?" I asked him. "I mean, aren't you between lungs at some point?"

"They put you on the vent. Which I have to tell you, is the worst part. You wake up feeling like you're choking. They tie your arms down so you don't pull it out."

At five o'clock, Dr. Keith walked by the waiting room, and paused at the door. I slipped into the hall. I glanced at his hands—they were clean. "I just wanted to let you know we're finished," he said.

"In a good way?"

He smiled. "The lungs are in, he's doing fine."

I grabbed his hand, forgetting the kind of person he was, so self-effacing. "Thank you," I said, pumping his hand. He looked physically pained.

An hour later, we huddled in a silent clump outside Stephen's room. The fourth wall of his room was a sliding glass door, with a large yellow sign reading *Caution: Immunosuppressed*. The nurse had pulled the curtain back so we could see in. Stephen lay on a high bed, tubes sticking out in all directions. Clay stood next to me, tears leaking down his face. The nurse touched my arm. "Go on in for a sec," she said, handing me gloves and a mask.

The room hummed with the varied pitches of machines. I looked at Stephen, looked away, and looked again. There were more attachments than usual, and I tried to discern the serious from the superficial. The tiny heart monitors on his chest and the oximeter on his finger were harmless. Below the heart monitor, underneath his nipples, a large white bandage stretched across his chest. Four thick chest tubes snaked out from under it, funneling to machines on the floor. The IVs in his arms, I was used to. The one in his neck made me squeamish. And I did not like the head arrangement. His forehead was bandaged with thick white tape. Why, I didn't know. His mouth was taped partway open, the ventilator tube sticking out. His forearms were tied loosely to the sides of the bed. I leaned over him, spoke close into his ear. My voice was muffled in the mask, and he was out, but it didn't matter. He lay there as I rambled, warm and oblivious, his face pinker than it had been for a long time.

AT MIDNIGHT I still could not leave the hospital. I felt like a small child, everyone telling me I had to go to bed when I wasn't tired. The nurse promised me that Stephen would not come out of the sedation until tomorrow. I eyed her suspiciously. She had no idea of his tolerance for drugs. My mom, who'd just arrived from the airport, put her arm around me and guided me toward the elevator. I sulked in the backseat as she drove Anna and me home. We flew along the bottom deck of the Bay Bridge, moving farther and farther away from where we were supposed to be.

At home, I brushed my teeth aimlessly and crawled into bed. My mom stood in the doorway of my room. She had this uncanny ability of knowing exactly when I was about to lose it. I would be fine, as long as I was in the dark soon, as long as she didn't ask me how I was doing. She put her hand on my forehead. "You're warm," she said.

I had been ignoring this, hoping it wasn't true. If I got sick now, I'd be banned from seeing Stephen. I could hear her shuffling through her suitcase in the next room. She returned with bottles and a glass of water. The echinacea came in a vial and tasted horrid. The light off, I lay diagonally in bed and switched my pillow for Stephen's.

"Want me to sing to you?"

"Mom, please, I'm twenty-seven," I said. But I closed my eyes when she sat down. She began "Sweet Afton," which she'd sung when we were little, and I fell into dreamless sleep.

I woke up in the morning with a fever and a sore throat. The ICC staff insisted I go see a doctor before I be allowed to see Stephen. I was glad Stephen didn't hear me admit I had no health insurance at the moment. I was sent to the clinic across the street, where I flipped through magazines, hoping he would sleep until I got back. The nurse had told me he'd woken up in the middle of the night for a second, delirious and disoriented, and pointed to his wedding ring. She'd tried to explain that the doctors had told me to go home.

Finally, I returned to the hospital with a prescription for antibiotics in hand. The morning nurse marched over as soon as she saw me. She handed me a mask and gloves. "The doctors said you can go in, but do *not* touch him."

The medical team didn't have any faith in me. I walked into the room slowly, making an imaginary line on the floor that I couldn't cross. "Stephen?" I said, but through the mask it sounded garbled, more of a throat clearing. He opened his eyes. He tried to say something, but he couldn't talk either, the ventilator down his throat. He motioned with his head toward me.

"I can't come over there," I said. "They won't let me, I have a cold."

He rolled his eyes.

"Seriously. If you get an infection, it could kill you."

He shrugged his shoulders defiantly, pointed as best he could to himself, and then the calendar on the wall.

"Yeah, you made it out of the operation," I conceded.

He gave me a pleading look.

"I can't," I said. "I hate it, too."

He shook his head, seeing right through me. I was trying to be on both sides, too cautious not to play by the rules. *So predictable,* he would have said if he could talk. He motioned toward the ventilator and held up two fingers, then three, then four, raising his eyebrows.

"Anywhere from two days to a week, I think they said."

He moaned.

"Tim's came out in five days."

Who? Stephen asked with his eyes.

"This guy we met who had a transplant."

Stephen's eyes widened, suddenly alert, expectant.

"He looks great. He has CF, and he says he breathes clearly now. He was in a daze for a few days after the surgery. He said the vent was the worst part."

Stephen held up five fingers.

"That was for him, I think it depends on the person."

He sighed, and caught my eye, giving me a long look.

"How do the new lungs feel?" I asked.

He put out his hand, wavering it slowly in a so-so motion.

"Do they feel like the old ones?"

He shook his head.

"Do you feel like yourself?"

He thought for a second and nodded, *More or less.* He pointed to me and raised his eyebrows.

"Do I still feel like myself?" I said.

chapter seventeen

STEPHEN WAS SQUIRMING IN HIS BED, HIS FACE FLUSHED. It had been three days since the surgery, the ventilator had been taken out, and he had an oxygen mask over his nose. A nurse stood at the side of his bed, adjusting the pressure of the oxygen while my sister Catherine and I watched. Stephen looked up at me. "Can't get comfortable," he said hoarsely. He struggled to sit up, waving tubes dangerously in the air.

"Whoa, Steve!" The nurse whirled around. "You have to tell us when you're going to make a move."

"It's Stephen," he muttered darkly. His words were slurring, slipping into each other. "Ready?" he said sarcastically. "I'm gonna sit up now."

Two nurses got on either side of him and moved him to a sitting position.

"Can't do anything on your own around here," Stephen mumbled.

One of the nurses took me aside. "He didn't sleep all night," she said. "He's a mess."

Stephen watched the nurses carefully. As soon as they stepped out of the room for a minute, he looked up at me desperately. "Liz, will you lie down with me?"

"I can't," I said miserably. "They won't let me touch you."

"Liz, just do it," Catherine said.

"Yeah, do it," Stephen said.

I sat down reluctantly on his bed. He worked his legs off the side of the bed to sit next to me. Before I knew it, he'd fallen sideways with a thud, his head in my lap, the tubes sprawled all around us. I sat on my hands, wondered when I'd last washed my jeans. Any minute the doctors were going to come in. Within seconds, he fell into a deep sleep. His head rose and sank against my leg, getting heavier with each exhale. I forced myself to keep sitting on my hands. It was unnatural not to drape one arm over him, to rest a hand on his shoulder, to run my fingers through his hair.

LATER, I CAME into his room to find him choking back tears.

"I got in trouble," he said quietly. "Your mom defended me—moderately."

"What happened?"

"I woke up and there were all these bugs on the end of the bed."

"Bugs?"

"Huge, like tarantulas, but not exactly. They were crawling

up over the blanket toward my feet. I sat up to try to get them off and the nurse yelled at me."

"Because you sat up?"

"Well, and I was kicking at them, and trying to brush them off. I guess I was waving my arms too hard and all the tubes came out and she had to redo everything."

"My mom was there?" I asked.

"She was sitting in here, and she told the nurse I was seeing bugs. That's what I mean, moderately. She didn't think the bugs were really there."

"Were they?"

He looked at me sadly. "I saw them. Both of us felt bad. We said we were sorry."

"You and my mom?"

"Me and the nurse," he said. "But I think she's still mad."

Today he'd become tender and childlike, and no one knew why. Earlier, Anna had asked him if he'd had any dreams about the organ donor. *I've had some dreams that seem like they could have been someone else's,* he'd said.

THOSE FIRST NIGHTS at home, I lay on the futon in the living room with friends, my mom having gone to bed. We had a slumber-party mentality, up late in our sweats telling secrets. The transplant itself had begun to feel a little like a long party. Friends and family in the waiting room, peeling off in twos to see Stephen, to walk in Golden Gate Park, to make phone calls, gathering back in the evening to eat dinner together. Every other time Stephen had been in the hospital, friends had visited, but during the interludes, I'd been there alone. I spoke to doctors, sorted progress from disappointment, and tried to make good judgment calls. Now, I was doing all this with people I loved, who loved Stephen. They, too, rode the elevators full of aching families, charted the recovery, felt tethered to its ups and downs. And the end of the night, they came home with me—my mom and Catherine in the beginning, later Fran and Caitlin. I'd never known I'd wanted this. A few times my parents had insisted on flying out, and I'd told them they didn't need to, then been relieved when they'd shown up. I remembered wanting to ask Clay to come to Boston, but having no clear sense of what he'd do there, what anyone could do when Stephen was sick. Now he was here, and Fran, and Tinka, all doing the only thing there was to do: be here, riding out the days.

Dr. Golden announced that Stephen was ready to move out of Intensive Care. Stephen had been asking for a "real" room, by which he meant a room on a normal hospital floor, with four walls, a little personal space. The rest of us had been eager, too, though for a different reason. The move signified a passage out of immediate danger.

The first morning in his new room, Amani found Stephen making a to-do list in his little green notebook. He was drowsy, his handwriting failing him. "I need to get started on some things," he said. "I need to take the car in, for one. But I'm having trouble with this pen."

"Give me that," Amani said. "I'll make you a list of things to do."

Stephen relinquished the pen and notebook. Amani scrawled out a new list. *1. Breathe. 2. Rest. 3. Heal.* Stephen studied it. "I'm working on the breathing," he said. "But I'm not there yet."

———

THE NURSE CUT the gauze from the bandage on Stephen's chest and peeled off the tape at its edges. She pulled the bandage back, wiped his chest with antiseptic. The scar ran across his chest like a railroad track, its thin line crisscrossed by metal staples. It had a nice curve to it, like a pencil-drawn mustache, or a wishbone. The skin all around it was irritated, and glowed a deep pink.

"Are those *staples* staples?" I asked.

"They're sterilized," the nurse said, "but they're staples."

"How did they get them there?" I asked.

"A medical staple gun."

"It's like you're upholstery," I said to Stephen when the nurse left.

"They'll come out," he said, standing to look in the mirror. "They're not that bad."

I stared in the mirror with him. There was the body I loved, the body that had looked, and continued to look, so good to me. The staples were disturbing. But the scar was strangely beautiful, its severity and magnitude, the curve of its line like a river.

FRAN MOVED OVER to stay with Anna and me. I had never spent time with her when Stephen wasn't around. She came with me to hear Anna's band play at the Stork Club. The bar was a little downtrodden, with bizarre lit-up Christmas décor, people who'd been drinking since late afternoon and weren't intending to stop. We found a small table; I brought us scotch and sodas. Fran leaned back in her chair. All of our friends came over to see her. She was comfortable here, I realized, I was comfortable with her here. We were two exhausted people, lounging, the music flooding through us.

"I'm surprised you haven't taken to drinking, with all this," Fran said to me.

"It hasn't been on purpose," I said.

STEPHEN REFUSED TO take off his oxygen mask. He wasn't convinced that the new lungs were working. Dr. Golden took an X-ray in an attempt to prove to him that his new lungs were fine. The X-ray was even better than expected, and Dr. Golden rushed into the room, waving it in his hand. He held it up to the light. I squinted at a set of white rib bones, against a black background. Stephen drew in a deep breath. "Those are mine?" he ventured tentatively.

"What am I supposed to be seeing?" I asked.

"It's more about what you don't see," Dr. Golden explained. "The area between the ribs, that's the interior of the lungs. It's dark, there are no obstructions, they're healthy and clear."

Stephen was so thrilled that Dr. Golden lent him the X-ray for the rest of his visit. He taped it to the window of his hospital room. With the light coming through the sheet of film, the ribs became luminous. Stephen took deep breaths and nodded privately to the X-ray on the window, as if it were a religious painting.

When he didn't think about breathing, he was fine. But every time he realized he was breathing he panicked. I imagined that it felt like flying in a dream, soaring through the air until the moment you realized you were flying, and knew flying was impossible, waved your arms frantically and plummeted to the ground.

Dr. Stulbarg paid a visit. Stephen started in on his myriad

of questions. How did they know for sure that the lungs were attached correctly? How did his body send signals to foreign organs?

"Let me put it this way," Dr. Stulbarg said. "They're working. If they weren't, the oxygen mask wouldn't be doing a bit of good. You'd be on the vent."

Dr. Stulbarg encouraged Stephen to take off the mask while he was in the room, so he'd feel secure. Stephen lifted the oxygen mask away from his nose, and drew in a quick breath. Finally he freed the mask from behind his ears and let it hang by the side of the bed. He pushed himself up to standing, and then began walking carefully, lifting each foot up and setting it down. He stood by the window, peering at the X-ray, and then to the left of it, down to the world below.

"We could go outside," I said, "try the patio on the second floor."

"I don't know," Stephen said. "Maybe."

"Take an oxygen tank with you," Dr. Stulbarg said. "For moral support."

I ran out to the nurses' station, hoping I could get the oxygen before Stephen changed his mind. When I came back into his room, he was sitting on his bed, leaning over, and tying his shoes. "That fucking seventies station!" he said, cocking his head to the side. "They were playing it all last night."

The room was quiet.

"Ten in a row," he said, "but they keep playing the same loop. The absolute worst songs from the seventies."

"You're hearing things."

"You wouldn't recognize it," he said. "You weren't paying attention in the seventies. I had older siblings, I know all those songs."

"It's the drugs," I said. "Remember the time you heard a symphony coming out of the heating vent?"

"There goes 'Baby I'm-a Want You' *again*! How could I be making up this medley?"

He held my hand as we ambled down the hall. I wished we could go visit all the nurses on the CF floor, show off the new lungs. They'd be so happy. I had run into Jake in the elevator, a few years had gone by since I'd last seen him. When I'd told him Stephen had just had the transplant, he'd come down on his break to say hi, sat in Stephen's room, all of us laughing, rehashing early visits. Stephen wouldn't be staying on Jake's floor again. He was done with CF for the most part; he was a transplant person now.

My hand was small in Stephen's. His sweatshirt hid his incision; its sleeves covered his IV lines. I felt like we were in a movie, the corridor our backdrop as we moved forward, suddenly anonymous, both of us in street clothes. Hospital workers moved around us, streaming through the doors to the courtyard, hurrying across the lawn to the cafeteria. We decided we should go get drinks and sit outside on a bench. The cafeteria was crowded, and I thought I should just go in myself, leave Stephen sitting outside with the oxygen tank.

"I want to get my own Coke," he complained.

"What's wrong with the ones I buy?"

"I've been craving one with the perfect amount of ice."

I rolled the oxygen tank into the cafeteria, trying to stay out of everyone's way. I watched him make his way through the room, taking care not to get too close to anyone, to brush shoulders even. I wondered how much pain he was still in. He did look a little hunched over, as if he was sheltering his chest from the crowd.

Outside, I slouched on a bench next to him, closing my eyes in the warmth of the sun. I listened to rushes of conversation, lunch breaks that had been squeezed in between surgeries, X-rays, ultrasounds, ventilator placements.

Stephen studied the driveway behind us. "I wonder if I could walk up that."

"You don't want to push it."

"From the person who forced me out here."

We trudged up together, with the oxygen tank in tow. People turned to stare at us from their lunches on the grass. I felt like telling them we were trying out new lungs, asking them to cheer us on. We turned toward the steep driveway. It was the same driveway we'd ascended years ago in the dark.

The eucalyptus trees arched wildly over the fence on our left. Stephen began picking up speed, and soon he was striding toward the finish. When he reached the top, I was still several feet below him. I watched him take a 360-degree turn, surveying the land. "Now you can go running with me," I said.

"Except I hate running. Unless it's part of a sport."

The mountains of our hometown came to me, their faces of flat rock jutting against the sky. A winter day with Stephen, lumbering in heavy boots up a narrow trail, climbing out onto a rock overhang, to jump into the deep snowbank below.

"It's weird," Stephen said. "I want to keep my allegiance to CF, but I already feel myself shifting. I keep thinking about my donor card."

I'd been thinking about his donor. All we knew was that he or she was young. Stephen had said he couldn't get away from the feeling this person had been meant to live, and he'd been meant to die. "Do you think the person had signed up?" I asked him.

"Ahead of time?"

"Yeah, or do you think it was the parents' decision?"

"Even if you sign up, you don't really think you're going to die."

I watched a squirrel scale the tree closest to me, make its way out on the electrical wire that ran above our heads.

"I was thinking of writing a letter to the parents," he said, "but I wonder if they'd want it. Their kid's dead, and here I am."

"It's not cause and effect."

"Me being alive doesn't help them. Maybe it makes things worse."

"There's nothing you could do that would make things worse."

"I guess I'd want the letter," he said. "I'd want to know someone was appreciating the lungs."

WE LAY IN our own bed at home. The light was out; the room darkened but not pitch-black. I felt sleepy for the first time in days. We kissed, trying to keep things low-key. I didn't want to be responsible for the first break in the transplant recovery rules. I began to drift, my head on Stephen's chest, his arm tight around me. I could feel him breathing purposefully: deep intakes, jarring exhales. "I'm still not sure how to breathe with these lungs," he said finally.

I slipped my hand under his T-shirt. I could feel the heat of the skin near his incision. "You've been doing it for days."

"I was wearing oxygen at night in the hospital," he admitted.

"Don't worry, you'll wake up if you suddenly can't breathe."

"How comforting."

"Sorry."

"What is it supposed to feel like, with normal lungs?"

I felt my own breathing, trying to pinpoint what I was doing. "It's not on your mind, you don't really have a feeling."

He lay on his back, pushed the sheet to our waists. "Does this look right?"

He breathed a few breaths. I turned on my side, watching, and breathing myself.

"We look the same," I said.

"You're getting deeper breaths, though. Listen when we exhale."

We breathed lying next to each other, me leading the way. I didn't know whether I was really doing anything, but Stephen wanted to keep going with it. "Looks good," I told him. He smiled.

Later, when he'd fallen asleep, I watched him. In deep sleep, at his most relaxed, his body still worked away feverishly, his chest muscles expanding and contracting with force. These mechanisms had kept him going, kept his blood oxygenated, his heart pumping for years. Within less than a week, they'd become obsolete. I wondered how long it would take for his body to catch up. He reminded me of a person who'd lived through the Great Depression, and years later, still stored away food. I drifted off, wondering what I'd be hearing with my head on this chest a month from now.

chapter eighteen

WE WANDERED ALONG THE BEACH IN CARMEL, PUSHING the warm sand through our toes. We had surfaced from a harrowing car chase, having fled a burning house. Our adrenaline drained, we squinted at the sky, at the life that was here now, in which one of us had new lungs. Maybe we should have been calling them used lungs, rare thrift-store-find lungs, out of respect to the previous owner. The lungs had been around, moved through the world for twenty years in someone else's body. Maybe they had been to Carmel, to this beach, taken in this exact composition of air. We put our feet in the water. The beach was deliriously calm. Dogs played in the surf. That was this day, dogs playing in the surf. We watched them play; we were here too, having turned up on the other side.

———

WE CATAPULTED FROM elated to overwhelmed, and back again. Stephen led friends on a hike in Redwood Park, charging up a path through the woods. He and I raced down the trail, because we could. At night we lay in bed kissing endlessly, without the oxygen mask between us. We didn't even care that we weren't allowed to have sex for another week, we just kissed for hours, and no one was out of breath.

THE TACKLE BOX looked like a double-sided suitcase, its orange-tinged lids revealing grids beneath them, meant for varieties of flies. It had been Sam's idea—he'd taken Stephen shopping for a pillbox, but nothing in the drugstore had been big enough. Stephen studied the box as he sat cross-legged on the living room floor. I sat next to him with two UCSF shopping bags full of medication. He was not thrilled that I was here, but Celia had insisted.

The organization of the tackle box felt like a logic puzzle. Twenty-four deep compartments to house a week's worth of medication. Each pill had different requirements: some once a day, some four times a day, one only on Saturdays and Sundays. I took a black marker and wrote the days of the week along the tops of the compartments, and the times of day along the sides of the box. Stephen shot me a look of admiration, which made me wonder what was going on in there. I felt protective of him; I didn't want him to go out alone.

He dumped all the bottles out on the floor and read aloud from the list of medications. "Okay, first one, CellCept." He searched for it in the sea of bottles. Finally he found it, struggled with the cap. He poured a few half-blue, half-orange capsules into his hand, and picked one up. As he tried to examine it, he lost his grip and the capsule popped out of his fingers, flying to the floor. "Fuck," he groaned.

"Just let me take the pills out while you read them off the list," I said.

"I've been dealing with medications my entire life. Now all of a sudden, oooooh, the transplant, dangerous, make sure he knows what he's doing."

"Your coordination's messed up. If you had a broken arm you'd let me open the bottles. You'd thank me for helping, actually."

"It's my coordination?"

"Your hands are shaking. From the drugs."

"But you also want to organize it. You think I'll put the pills in the wrong place."

"That's not true."

"Don't lie."

"Okay, that's true."

"I knew it."

We went through the list, Stephen commenting on the medications as I found them. Mycelex Troche—*pain in the ass.* Prednisone—*get ready for "fat face."* Prilosec—*no one wants an ulcer.* Quinine—*isn't that for malaria? Maybe someone fucked up.*

I dropped seven pills into separate squares. It felt like a game, like playing mancala or resetting Chinese checkers. I entertained myself by trying to find the maximum speed that still allowed for accuracy. I was getting fast, getting good. Finally, we put all the pill bottles back in the shopping bag, and closed the tackle box. A week's work, complete: purple, green, pink, blue, white; tiny, gigantic, round, oblong; capsule, tablet; a concoction to keep the lungs working. We sat on the couch drinking orange juice, admiring our work.

A few hours later, when I returned from the grocery store, Stephen met me at the door, his face flushed. My heart raced; I wasn't supposed to have left him alone, even for an hour; he'd told me it would be fine. "What's wrong?" I said, flashing to the hospital. It was five o'clock, there would be rush-hour traffic, I thought of the surface streets I could take to the bridge. He led me into the living room. There were pills all over the floor. "I picked up the box," he said, choking back tears. "I thought it was latched."

I knelt down on the floor beside the box. One side, empty. All that painstaking work. I started laughing woefully, which made him smile. At least the intact side held the sample day— we could reassemble the pills using it as a model, as soon as we found them all. Were they too dirty now, after rolling around on the floor? We decided to ignore that possibility. "Watch the latch," Stephen said, as I turned the box over slowly.

WE DROVE TO GOLDEN GATE Park for the Heart and Lung Transplant Group picnic. We all felt shy. I kept thinking that half of the people I was meeting had curved scars beneath their shirts. The picnic had been organized by Stacy and Luke, a couple who both had CF. They were in their thirties, both a few years post-transplant by now. He was a contractor; she was a professional clown. I imagined their house, two tackle boxes, two schedules of doctor's appointments tacked on the fridge. I imagined all the ways in which they must have understood each other that Stephen and I did not. And the terrible, inevitable comparison of vital signs. I wondered if they conceived of the illness differently, if one of them was bitter, the other an optimist. In their house, no one could claim territory. In our house, we lorded over our separate domains. There was one way to be with someone who would die young: my way. There was one way to be the person who would die young: his way. This was the freedom we got, and the loneliness.

Sometimes I wished I had a friend in my same situation. This friend and I would, in the same conversation, say things like: "Isn't it annoying when you just feel like he's not listening?" and "How often do you think that he might be dead a few years from now?" This friend and I could discuss our accommodations to this reality, the way most friends talk about accommodations they make in relationships. I might say, "I know this sounds stupid, but I realized that every night before I turn off the light, I look at Stephen and capture his face in my mind like a picture." I'd tell her that he teases me when I do this; he makes an annoying expression, and then turns out the light right afterwards. But he always turns it back on for me after the teasing; he knows I won't go to sleep unless he does. And my friend might say, "You know what I do? I make him wake me up before he leaves in the morning if I sleep in, to say goodbye." And I will know she's talking about those daily goodbyes that might also be real goodbyes, but most likely aren't, so they feel light and lucky. I will know she means the goodbyes you relish.

We tried to mingle. Anna began talking to Tim Brooks' parents. They were here from Kentucky, staying in the Castro, a few doors down from their son. Stephen hit it off with Tim. "I'm fine now," I overheard Tim telling him. "But my parents are too worried to go home. If they stay much longer I'll have to come up with some kind of ultimatum."

I stood at the picnic table, loading my plate up. Two women in their sixties were chatting behind me in line. I remembered them from the support group meeting. They were both married to men who'd had single-lung transplants. The group was divided into emphysema singles, in their fifties and sixties, and CF/pulmonary hypertension doubles, in their twenties and early thirties. The emphysema patients, though older, seemed less worn-out, more gung-ho, more second-lease-on-life about it all. The CFers seemed cautiously happy, maybe a little jaded, or at least a little "let's wait and see how it goes."

"How are you doing, honey?" one of the women asked me.

The other moved towards us conspiratorially. "Is he driving you crazy?"

He had been, and I'd been driving him crazy, too. We were stranded in the house; I had to drive him everywhere. Neither of us could work at the moment, since he needed someone with him at all times. *The transplant's a job at first,* I remembered Celia saying. *It's full-time for the first few months.* But there was something else going on, too.

"He keeps getting upset about the smallest things," I told them.

"The meds make them moody," the first woman said. "Hal started snapping at me all the time for no reason."

The other nodded. "They go from zero to sixty in a second."

I remembered the transplant support group meeting, everyone so angry about the Prednisone, blaming it for all kinds of crazy moods, including anger. It had seemed surreal to me at the time, Stephen just out of the ICU, all these survivors asking when they could get off the drugs that were keeping them alive. Unfortunately, Stephen didn't seem to realize how crazy his moods were. Ironically, he was reading a book called *Coping with Prednisone*, but he was fixated on the physical changes, the fact that his face would get puffy. I did see a pattern of chipmunk cheeks in this group.

"But so, when does it, how does it, stop?" I asked.

"They lower the dosage," the first woman said. "The beginning's the worst."

I WOKE UP in my sister Catherine's narrow apartment. I'd taken the train to New York from Washington, D.C., a one-day detour on my trip to Kristie and Mike's wedding. Back home, friends were taking shifts with Stephen. It had felt like a lot to ask them to cover the days for the wedding itself, and this day was extra. I felt like I was sneaking out of the house as a teenager, so glad to be doing it, hoping I wouldn't be missed.

Cath and her roommate were long gone to work. I lay there for a while, half in the world, then wormed my way to the edge of the bed. Outside, traffic, and the steady banging from a construction project. Liz Phair, *Exile in Guyville*, was in the CD player. I sang with her in my T-shirt and boxers while I figured out my sister's coffee system, boiled water and found the single-cup-sized filter and cone that fit on top of a large mug. I sat on the counter stool, browsing the Village Voice. News was registering, the first time in a couple of months. The world had gone on and I'd missed it, and I needed to catch up. I made toast.

I CAME HOME to learn that while I'd been gone, Sam had been sneaking, letting Stephen drive. Only very slowly, on empty streets, he told me. Where the hell are there empty streets in Oakland? I said. But probably it was fine, and it made Stephen so happy. Every night he recorded how many days were left until he was officially cleared to be back behind the wheel.

STEPHEN WALKED UP hills without noticing, breathed without thinking, gained weight without forcing himself to eat. The tension knob had been turned down to zero and he was cruising, with all the relief that comes with ease. And I relaxed, too, no longer gritting my teeth when he sat up in the morning, ready to see him in pain, or slowing my pace discreetly when we walked. He just was, we just were. Only he was a little different. He wasn't sure if it was the drugs, the anesthetic, or the experience of the transplant, but he felt himself slowing down, days thick as water. He started his usual home projects, but had trouble finishing them. He was like an athlete who hadn't played in years, trying to execute old moves with a changed body. *I feel like I'm at about 85 percent mental capacity*, he kept saying. He listed the post-transplant changes in his journal.

craving for ice cream, taste for coffee, vision seems a little off, no interest in email, can't deal with anyone outside of closest circle, can't express thoughts, becoming a consumer—specifically, compelled to buy Tintin paraphernalia. No explanation other than I enjoy it immensely, but the problem arises when (1) I keep spending, (2) I can't stop, (3) I look like a freak.

In escapist mode. All I want to do is shoot photos, watch The X-Files, hang out with Liz and Amani. I still like the idea of getting a dog—it would help me come

*back to the basics of my philosophy of life—not so
driven and busy.*

He spread out his pictures in the living room, putting
together a photo album from the last two years. From here,
from a time and place in which he could breathe so easily, our
previous homeland appeared stark and treacherous. Sometimes
we felt fond of it, sometimes we felt sorry for ourselves retroac-
tively. Sometimes it appeared as a heroic life-and-death battle,
sometimes it appeared pathetic and measly, threads of a life
compared to what most people were doing. More than anything, it was disturbingly hard to remember. We both had the
urge to grab it as we felt it slipping away. We held it between us
as new immigrants might hold their former home, reminding
each other of places and events. While Stephen flipped through
pictures of our trip to Scotland, we threw moments back and
forth. The time I chucked the pill bottle at his head. The time
he fell asleep at the table during his birthday dinner. His cough.
We strained to re-create the sound of it in our minds. He'd had
it since he was thirteen. It had been how I could find him anywhere.

LIFE EDGED ITS way back to normal. I took a job teaching sixth
grade for the fall. Stephen went back to work, too, only surreptitiously—the way he had as a teenager, sneaking out to cook at
the Wrangler on weeknights against his parents' wishes. Then,
he'd been sure he could handle both work and school. Now, he
was sure he could handle both work and the transplant. He'd
only been home six weeks, and the transplant team had advised
waiting at least six months; most people waited a year. I sug-

gested he see when he felt ready, and then wait a few weeks beyond that. He'd acted like I had a good idea, but then one day he came home smiling guiltily. "So I'm back at Neomorphic," he said.

TIME WAS CREEPING in through the windows, drifting in with the night air. If there was going to be time later, we didn't have to hoard it now. We were hoarders, we were like those cartoon characters who find bags of gold, and dump them out so they can roll around in their money. We lay in bed thinking of all the things we might do. We talked about the future like we had one, trying on the clothes of normal people. We made a list on a scrap of paper. *The next two years: Save for a house, visit Hawaii, BABY??!* It turned out we had mundane ambitions, too. And we'd squander a little time just because we could, work late, take each other for granted, spend a few months in different places.

Eighty-eight, we decided. This was how long we'd imagine that Stephen could live. We would get it in our minds, replace the thirty-five that had been ingrained, stretch out the possibilities. We would not expect it, but we'd point our wills in that direction. Things were more likely to happen if you thought them possible, we theorized. Out of nowhere, one of us would say "Eighty-eight" and the other would smile.

chapter nineteen

AND THEN I CRASHED. NOT IN THE WAY THAT STEPHEN MIGHT have, with none of the magnitude or danger, but in the way of a healthy person, slipping slowly, with the strong sense that it couldn't be happening, I could fix it if I just tried hard enough. Maybe I crashed because I finally could, because Stephen was okay. Maybe it was the buildup of the last few years. Or maybe seeing your husband through a lung transplant paled in comparison to teaching middle school for the first time.

Every day, I walked into my sixth grade classroom feeling like I might throw up. I didn't know what I was doing, and I had to reveal this to a roomful of twelve-year-olds, for seven-hour stretches. Over dinner, I replayed my day for Stephen and Anna and Amani, asking for advice. "Three boys grabbed their crotches, smirking," I told them.

Amani shook his head. "That's completely disrespectful."

"You have to be strict," Stephen said. "They shouldn't feel like they can do that in your class."

"But they did," I said, feeling worse by the second. "So what do I do?"

"The first kid to disrupt, send him out," Amani said. "The rest will get the point."

I didn't want to admit that if I sent the disrupters out, I'd be banishing half my class. The other half hid behind their books, waiting for the day to be over. It had gone wrong before I'd known what was happening. Day one, they'd been quiet, I'd seated them in groups of three, given them homework. Day two they'd returned jumping out of their seats, talking across the room. "It happens to everyone their first year," my friend Gwen, who taught down the hall from me, said. "But you're taking it so hard."

After dinner, I'd sit at my desk trying to lesson-plan my way out of it all. At the end of the night, as I lay in bed, everything I'd done wrong would come to me. I'd never called on Tenisha today. Martin had sat in class, bored, without a clue. He only spoke German, and it was up to me to make different assignments for him, and today it had escaped my mind. Anthony had spit out the window and I'd said I'd hold him five minutes at lunch, then forgotten. Now it was official that I was capable of forgetting; I could expect spitting out the window to increase.

I had this hourly feeling of crisis, without the crisis. I went to bed and woke up with a stomachache. In the morning, my pulse surged in my temples as I drove to school, prepared the room, Xeroxed frantically, stood by the board and tried to breathe.

One night I lay in bed, our new dog, Darby, in his own bed by the foot of ours. Stephen had brought him home after broaching the possibility the previous night at dinner. I'd told him I was okay with a dog as long as I had no responsibility—the last thing I needed was to be in charge of anyone else right now. He'd promised I could be the fun aunt. Our lease was "no pets" but we'd all said maybe he could get a dog in a few months if he checked with the landlady. He'd been thinking sooner—he'd been going to the Humane Society on his lunch break, and there was this dog. Darby, a one-year-old black Lab mix who used his tail like an extra limb: we'd had to tail-proof the house.

Now, hearing me shift around in bed, Darby sat up and rested his chin on my foot. I closed my eyes, trying to relax my mind somehow, avoid the hour-long head-spinning that had come to accompany going to sleep. I turned toward Stephen as he slept, pressed my face into his back. He rolled over and put his arm around me.

"I've never seen you like this," he said. "I think you might be depressed."

I wondered if he could see something I couldn't. He'd gone through depression twice before, but in my memory he'd been the opposite of how I felt now—not frantic and consumed but sluggish, unable to focus. And the misery had run so deep—*I'd take a lung collapse over depression any day,* he'd said. I shook my head in the dark. "I just need to get the teaching down."

"Am I the only one who sees how bad this is?"

"I can fix it."

"It's okay if you're depressed, you know."

WE FLEW TO Colorado for winter break. It was Stephen's first flight in two years that was oxygen-tank-free. And more momentous, landing in the airport, testing his new lungs at 5,000 feet. We got off the plane, his face was pink, and he breathed easily.

Clay was waiting for us at baggage claim, just the way he'd done a year ago, when Stephen had slumped down in a chair, too dizzy to stand.

In the car on the way home, Stephen and Clay talked non-stop, Stephen thrilled to be able to talk again at altitude, Clay so happy to have him back. I sat in the backseat, relieved to be out of the conversation, trying to stop the panic that lurched through me every fifteen minutes or so. I stared out my window at the fields of snow, thinking about how exactly a year ago we'd made this drive, Stephen lying in the backseat, counting the minutes until he could reach the oxygen machine at his mom's house. Now, he was free. We could hike with our friends up to the Flatirons, jump off the boulders into the snow. We could shop at the mall and drink hot chocolate at the bookstore without so much as a glance from the neighboring table. And I wanted more than anything to want to do these things, and I didn't, and I had to admit that I preferred the way I'd felt last year, oxygen tank and all of it, to the way my brain was working now.

Caitlin, Eve, and I lingered on the bridge overlooking Boulder Creek, the water frozen beneath us. High school summers, the water ran so high right here you could convince yourself that the creek would hide you. The three of us used to shed our shoes and shorts and T-shirts and wade in, pretend we weren't right in the middle of town. There were dense trees on either side of the bank, but we probably would have gotten in anyway, our ability to be in our own little world at an all-time teenage high. The water gushed down the canyon from Eldorado Peak—thinly disguised snow. We'd wade to the center and lie in it for as long as we could, trying to outlast each other. A 2 a.m. phone call, a sleepwalking sister—nothing startled you awake like this water. Maybe if it were summer, I could have jumped in, been shaken free.

Caitlin and Eve put their arms around me; I was transparent, and it was kind of a relief.

"Are you sure you can't quit?" Caitlin said.

"This is terrible," Eve said. "You, of all people, you try so hard."

"Tried," I said. "Now I'm just a mess."

"Yeah, you are a mess," Caitlin said. "I'm worried."

"It's almost worse than Stephen said," Eve said.

"When did you talk to him?"

"You know, in his group emails."

"He's been sending group emails? About me?"

They glanced at each other. "Kind of about everything," Caitlin said.

MY FAMILY WANTED me to go see a therapist. I said maybe I would; they said Now. My mom found a Dr. Miller out on South Table Mesa, and I borrowed her car, took the snowy road to his office. Dr. Miller had a kind voice, which immediately made me cry. I felt embarrassed for crying, we'd just met, but he sat and waited, and I cried until I could find a way to stop. He asked me how I was after that, and we both smiled. He asked me about teaching, about Stephen, the transplant. *This last May?* he clarified. He asked me to remember the last time I'd enjoyed something, anything. I had to admit I couldn't.

"Everything you've told me leads me to believe you're in a depression," he said.

It might have begun with the transplant and teaching, he said, but now it was a chemical state. I nodded absentmindedly. I couldn't help feeling that it was less a state than a personal lack—if I could just be a better teacher, be less inept in general, it might disappear. The skepticism must have shown on my face because Dr. Miller added, "If you want to see it more clinically, take a look at this."

He handed me a clipboard and a pencil. I went down a list of yes/no questions. Do you have trouble falling asleep? Do you wake up too early? Have you lost weight? A bunch of physical symptoms I had brushed away since they weren't the real problem, only small annoyances that added to my frustration. But here they were, all on the same piece of paper.

"I never thought of these as symptoms," I said.

"What did you think they were?" Dr. Miller asked.

"I don't know. I thought maybe I was going through a phase."

"Not a very enjoyable phase."

"No, I hate it."

I thought back to that time in Berkeley, Stephen dreading dusk, dreading everything, and me wanting to duck out of the way of it all, turning an eye to sustaining my own decent mood. I hadn't understood. And even though Stephen understood now he'd been ducking a little himself when I thought about it, leaving the house on Saturdays for the flea market or the record store and staying out most of the day.

Dr. Miller recommended therapy, combined with antidepressants. Antidepressants—I wanted to cry, they sounded so good. They might not work, they probably wouldn't, but they offered a tiny, theoretical door.

My brain felt squeezed, churning. I was dizzy when I stood up. It was New Year's, we were at Eve's brother's as always, running through the house, my friends trying not to let me see them smoke. I faded in and out, my mind grasping at teaching, letting it go.

"You look like you used to on Ecstasy," Caitlin said.

That wide-eyed, half-crazy, clench-jawed look. "Really?"

"I didn't mean it badly. It's subtle, just your jaw."

But when I saw pictures from that night, I looked exactly like I had on certain high school nights, my arms draped around my friends, my eyes wild, smiling ferociously. My friends were droopy-eyed from drinking, their heads lolling, arms thrown loosely around each other. I looked out of place, like I was on the wrong drug.

MONDAY MORNING, I stood in the quiet of my classroom. The kids would be coming in ten minutes. I lined up an invisible army behind me—all the family members and friends who'd given me advice over vacation. I was going to make them my bosses, since I hadn't done so well at the helm myself. Run an extra mile a day, Caitlin's mom had said. Put the troublemakers in the hall, my brother had said. Notice the kids who are learning, my sister had said, shift your attention, like the negative and positive space in a picture. Slow down, my grandma had said. It's in the way you walk and the tone of your voice.

The kids tore into the room. They ran up to hug me, telling me everything that had happened since we'd seen each other two weeks earlier.

"I haven't seen you since *last year*," Charysse said, smiling. "Isn't that weird?"

I let out a breath. Here they were, and I was happy to see them.

I STILL HAD the nervousness, my stomach squirmed some, but the pressure began slipping away. I became unfrozen, and this allowed me to find my instincts, to learn from the mistakes I'd made the first months of school. A kid spit out the window and I didn't think too hard about it, I knew what to do. I was both stricter and more relaxed. I laughed more—I found the kids funny. At the end of each day, I read out loud to them, and no matter what else happened, during those twenty minutes we were in sync.

I started playing music in class occasionally, assigning projects that stretched for days at a time. My co-teacher Jennifer and I got the kids building a large pyramid, and the classroom succumbed to the pyramid's needs. Desks were pushed against the back wall. Large pieces of foam core lined the remaining walls. Kids traced tomb paintings onto them, using images cast by overhead projectors. A cluster of desks in the back corner held clay, wire clay cutters, and paint. The room had that chaotic, productive feel of a theater construction site. Strips of papier-mâché lay next to balls of newspaper configured as a small human body, and cardboard for the mummy's-head mask.

The only thing I had to do at night was grade, which I found myself boycotting. Instead I lay on the couch after dinner, reading what I wanted to read, spacing out. Now that I was more relaxed, pieces of my life had begun floating through my mind again. This time last year, we'd been getting ready to leave Cambridge. The transplant hadn't happened. The transplant by itself felt like a year's worth of living, each day a deep blue sky, vivid, intense, and clear. I'd been so sure of myself then. Maybe I was paying for those days now. I thought about some of the kids in my class, how crazy their lives outside of school were, how they felt like they were succeeding, just to be getting by. I could see why they slipped so easily, how much energy it took not to slip.

———

LIFE FELT ENORMOUS, spring was coming. Stephen and I were talking about this one night, ways to be alive, what to do with it all. "It's kicked in," he said.

"What?" I leaned off the couch, petting Darby.

"You're back."

"Are you sure? How can you tell?"

He laughed and then frowned. "How insulting. Like I don't know you."

WE DROVE TO Mendocino for a long weekend. As we came close to the town, I thought maybe we should keep driving, that if we did, other things would fade and we'd be left with what mattered, all of it contained in the green Volvo rumbling through the woods, past mudslides cleared just hours ago.

In the morning I went running on back roads, past old cabins scattered through the pine trees. Afterwards I sat on our balcony, drinking coffee out of a mug decorated with three-dimensional grapes and cherries, looking out at the ragged cliffs, and the ocean beyond. The warm humid air, the dark brown of the cliffs rushed into me, the filter of the last few months gone. It was the way I'd felt as a kid when I'd gotten glasses, and looked up at a tree to see hundreds of distinct leaves where I'd always seen a blur of green. The landscape had woken me up, maybe, the smell of the pine needles bringing me back to the mountains I grew up in. And the antidepressants, though it was funny, I'd expected them to make me feel less, rather than more.

We wandered through town. The day felt slow and vivid, like Sunday in a Catholic country. Before the transplant we'd have headed straight for the paths by the cliffs, but now Stephen was unable to pass up a store, the possibilities beckoning from window displays. He urged me to join in, found books and CDs and little objects he thought I should have. He bought his first pair of binoculars. We took them out to the cliffs. We climbed out on wooden planks and took pictures of each other, balancing on the tops of the planks, arms out to our sides, framed by the sky.

chapter twenty

IT WAS MIDNIGHT, AND AMANI AND I SPRAWLED ON EITHER end of our giant couch while Stephen relayed the names of the twenty-four callers on voicemail. We'd just gotten back from a week in Mexico, and I was still floating the way I'd been there—the humidity, combined with a stretch of time not punctuated by the bell. My mom, Stephen reported, and handed me the phone. She was calling about a bike accident. I couldn't quite understand—something about my dad, but her voice was too efficient, almost upbeat. Stephen offered to call Boulder Community for me. I lay with my eyes closed while he worked his way through two departments and the Intensive Care receptionist, using the word "son-in-law." Finally he found my dad's nurse. He sat on the phone, listening. After a while he tapped me, motioned to the phone. *Can't you just tell me?* I mouthed.

My dad had been riding his bike down a paved mountain road near home. He'd hit gravel on a curve, and skidded off the edge of the mountain, dropping forty feet on his bike. He'd broken his back, his neck, his collarbone, both shoulders, his pelvis, his leg, eleven ribs. His head had been spared by his helmet. Tomorrow, a ten-hour back surgery. Hopefully he wasn't going to be paralyzed. The main thing was that they were pretty sure he was going to live.

Pretty sure? I grabbed the phone from Stephen and called the hospital back. I sat on the dining room floor, leaning against the wall, while the nurse went to get my mom. Her voice was hers. Scared, but hers.

"Where are you going to sleep?" I asked. "You can't get any rest in the ICU."

"They have a little room with a bed and a nightstand," she said.

I should have been worrying about my dad, but all I could think about was her. I wanted to go there and do it for her—the worrying, the conversations with doctors, the sleeping alone, the calls to the insurance company. I wanted to fly her through next week, carry her with her eyes shut out the other side. I felt for my mom, Stephen felt for my dad.

The next morning, I talked to my mom again. She had slept, shaken the vulnerability in her voice, she was back to her message-leaving persona. She assured me that I didn't need to come home. An hour later, my aunt called. "Your mom needs you guys," she said. Sometimes in an emergency, you just needed someone to tell you what to do. I was glad there were four of us. We called each other, decided to take shifts. Stephen offered to come with me for mine. He'd been calling the doctors, making lists of questions, reporting back. My mind slumped over, with him able and willing. It turned me into a child.

We had two weeks in no man's land, while the accident

played itself out. This was how it had been for other people during episodes of Stephen's illness. I had always been at the epicenter; I didn't know how to be on the outskirts. I became spacey and forgot what I was teaching, sank into what I was teaching, remembered the accident, panicked for an unending minute, and forgot again.

The kids at school were making me a list of things I could do to entertain my dad in the hospital. He couldn't turn his head, much less move his hands, which ruled out video games. Also, he'd been unable to see since he'd woken up from surgery. A specialist had said that it was probably swelling in the back of the brain, which was normal after this kind of accident and also after a long back surgery. It would go down soon. My sister Catherine was there for this conversation, she'd heard a forced certainty in the doctor's voice. A week later, my dad's vision still had not returned.

I wondered, as I listened to the kids, why, when I was told this, I did not jump on a plane. Maybe compared to Stephen's dad, or even Stephen, my dad seemed okay. Maybe I was so passive that I responded only to the demands of my immediate environment. I began to see why it had been hard for Clay to think of taking more than a week off for the transplant. Work won't let me, he'd said, and I'd fumed. Now, here I was, flying to Colorado for six days, which seemed a huge hassle for everyone at school.

"Music," the kids agreed on. "Bring him headphones."

"Bring a whole stereo in there," Vince said. "Go big."

"Read him *Roll of Thunder, Hear My Cry*," Zanedra said. Eyes lit up around the room. "Yeah, yeah, read it to him!"

"He can see the story in his mind," said Michelle.

"And don't stop just before the good parts like you do with us," said Julia.

THE DOOR TO my dad's hospital room was open, a blue curtain drawn between the bed and the door. Stephen and I stepped inside. My dad's head was wrapped in white bandages, and he had a giant brace around his neck. The rest of him was under the covers, except for his arms, which were by his sides. He didn't look that bad, I thought, and later I'd realize how strange this was, that my bottom line had sunk so low that "not that bad" was defined by the way Stephen looked, lying in the ICU after the transplant. I squeezed my dad's hand. He squeezed back. He appeared to be growing a beard, and his hair was cropped short.

"Hi, kiddo," my dad said, looking at me. I was flooded with false relief.

"You're looking right in my eyes," I said.

"Am I?" said my dad.

MY BROTHER MOVED home for the summer. I did what I'd criticized Clay for doing just a year ago—I stayed for a week and then returned to work, certain that I didn't have a choice. I'd visited the land of the near-death and was appreciative, but I'd come back to my roots, to the land of the healthy, in which you didn't shape your plans around the crisis, you shaped the crisis around your plans. I told myself, There's nothing to really do here, flew back, promising to return.

My mom assured me it was fine. And I took her at her word, ignoring everything I knew, that the people who loved you helped the most simply by loving you, by showing up, by eating dinner in the cafeteria and riding in the elevator, by reminding you of life before this and after, by including this in life, making it less horrific and singular, an event people pretended to understand but didn't, nodding but getting upset at the wrong parts—the surgery and cries of pain; overlooking the details that got to you—glasses on the nightstand, dirt on the bike tires.

BACK AT SCHOOL, the pyramid was almost complete. Meanwhile, at home, the sewage pipe was leaking again, raccoons were running through the walls, and our lease was up in a month. Stephen picked me up after school for an appointment he'd made with a realtor. I sat in Wendy Louie's air-conditioned office, trying to hide my hands, which were spattered with clay. Wendy had good news—she'd run the credit check, we were in good shape. "Credit check?" I said, when she stepped out of the room. "When did we decide to take that step?"

"You told me I could look into this. She thinks we can do it."

"Of course she does."

Stephen and Wendy had a plan. We were first-time home buyers, we'd qualify for a city program—we'd only need to put 5 percent down. But the monthly payment would be $300 more than our current rent.

"That much money, it's not practical," I argued.

"Unbelievable. You don't see it. It's the most practical thing we can do."

I had the feeling of the ride at the fair picking up speed. I made Stephen promise that if we did this, he'd still switch jobs, get back to public health if he wanted to.

"A house isn't worth being unhappy for," I said. "Life is too short."

"Thanks, I completely forgot life was short."

NINE DAYS LATER we signed our names to an offer on a little white house in central Berkeley, 740 square feet, red cement steps leading up to it, wood floors, a bedroom, and a small room off the living room that could be a study. We got it for the asking price, when everything else was going for more. Wendy guessed this was because of the apartment building behind us, and also the house next door. I peered into the neighbor's yard, which was piled with bags of old newspapers, lamps, and plastic containers. A gigantic pine tree stood at the center of the yard, its branches hovering dangerously close to our roof.

The remarkable part of our house purchase wasn't how quickly it happened, or our timing with the market, or our lack of concern about our neighbors. It was that the obvious issue never arose. Maybe we were sticking to our plan to live like normal people. Maybe I was caught up in the pyramid, final grades, and the push toward summer. But still. Years later I'd wonder if while I was stubbornly living in the present, Stephen was thinking about the future. Maybe he thought I could manage the mortgage without him if he died—the house was small, I could afford it with a roommate. Maybe this even gave him peace of mind about my possible future—something he knew I wasn't thinking much about. It would seem fitting considering the opposing forces within him at the time—his prudent nature, and his crazy post-transplant impulse buys.

We squeezed everything we had into our new place. I'd been thinking we'd move the way we always did, which was to shed half of our belongings, enjoy the lightness afterwards. But Stephen did not want to let go of a single piece of our garage-sale furniture. The yellow curved couch that sat eight, the large blue reclining chair, the five-by-three-foot desk. Amani was coming to live with us for a few months, so there would be three people and a dog navigating the narrow corridor through our living room. When Darby got excited, about every six minutes, his tail whacked the table, the couch, anyone nearby.

We would live here until we decided not to, we would settle in. It was the first time we'd moved into a place without having an estimated date of departure. We were kids in this, seeing the bathtub, exclaiming to each other, a great tub, our tub! The bathroom's sponge-painted walls. The deep kitchen cupboards. It was new for me to notice the parts of a house. Stephen had been like this for as long as I could remember, always getting pleasure from small details of spaces, noticing what needed to be fixed.

LATE SUMMER, I lay in bed in the basement of my parents' house, in the cool of early morning. It had been three months since I'd last visited. I could hear my dad upstairs, trying to learn to play the pennywhistle in his bed. The high thin melodies streamed down through the ceiling vent—"All My Loving" and "Ghost Riders in the Sky."

My dad had emerged from his accident grateful at first. Every day he'd promised he was going to do something nice for the nurses when he left. When he moved to the rehab facility, it wasn't clear whether the quality of care dropped or whether his patience was running out. *These people,* he began muttering. One night his friends came to take him out to dinner. As they wheeled him out, the receptionist stopped them. "You have to check with us," she scolded. "You can't just leave."

He stared up from his wheelchair, his face red. "You have

a fundamental misunderstanding about our relationship," he said. "I can leave anytime I want. You might not let me back in, but that's a different question."

He did sign out, but this began his feeling that he was done. His friends came over to help us set up a temporary bedroom on the first floor, since he couldn't get up the stairs. They'd rented a single bed and we set it up in the TV room. We brought down his dresser and his bedside table. I carried his shaving kit, his shoes. He set his mind on systems—his comb on the upper right corner of the dresser, certain foods on the lowest shelf of the fridge. He begged my mom to put things back where she found them.

My dad was relieved to be home—the freedoms outweighed the constraints. I thought my mom could have used a little more time in the hospital. I suggested we hire someone to help so she could rest up, do the things for him that only she could—love him, and see him through all this.

"They have nurse's aides," I said. "At least until he gets out of the wheelchair."

"Think about the transplant," she said.

"People my age don't hire people," I said. "And that was only a month." But she was right; it was terrible to imagine. Still, I convinced her to make a list of what she did every day, and then look it over for things someone else could do.

I drove my dad down Ninth Street, heading to the rehabilitation clinic. It was the first time I'd driven him anywhere since I was sixteen, lurching in the parking lot of IBM, where he'd taught me to drive. He sat in the passenger seat, feeling the turns of the car and looking in the direction of the window, working to impose his memory of the drive on the vague shadows he saw now. "The cemetery," he said as we passed it. And then, "Arapa-hoe." I was trying to drive as smoothly as I could, but each slight jolt caused him physical pain, upsetting the healing of his bones.

"You don't have to drive this slowly for me," my dad said.

"No, it's the guy in front of us. He's going about fifteen."

"What's wrong with him?"

I peered ahead, at the affronting car's rearview mirror. "He's combing his hair."

My dad gave a grunt of disapproval.

"Now he's changing lanes," I said.

"Finally."

We slowed down for the light.

"Is he right next to me?" my dad asked me.

"Who, the hair comber?"

My dad nodded. I peered past him out his window.

"Yeah," I said. "He's stopped combing his hair."

My dad looked out his window, in the direction of the driver, and slowly mimed the action of combing his own hair.

"Dad," I groaned. "He's right there."

My dad smiled, his eyes lit up. "Does he see me?"

I peeked over at the driver, who was looking right at my dad, probably thinking that my dad could see him. "Yes, he sees you. He's laughing, luckily."

"Good for him," my dad said. "At least he can laugh at himself."

"Not as bad as we thought."

CATHERINE, JOHN AND JEAN and I drove along Highway 36 toward Denver. We'd decided we should go to Water World. We needed a break. We felt guilty, and we were going. I knew, in the pit of my stomach, that this was how my friends felt sometimes, driving away from Stephen and me. I hated the way they saw us in those moments, all illness. But I had to admit it was terrifying to watch people you loved turn into scared animals, hiding their fear from themselves so well that strangers remarked nonstop on their strength, while you saw the tiny changes—my mom edgy, my dad sighing with a deeper exhale, both of them talking about how much they appreciated life now. It was disturbingly familiar. Stephen and I appreciated without meaning to, it just happened all over the place. It was sharp and glorious and not at all relaxing. I'd always thought it was what Stephen got, in exchange for the years he'd lose. But now I wondered if appreciating life wasn't a rare opportunity that crisis gave you, but a coping mechanism. I couldn't even imagine suggesting this to Stephen.

AFTER I FLEW back to Berkeley, I called. The first two calls, my mom hadn't made her list. The third call, my dad got on the phone.

"Your mother tells me you think we need to hire someone," he said.

"She's worn-out," I said. "She doesn't know it yet."

"Who would we hire?"

"A nurse, maybe."

"A *nurse*? To be in the *house*?"

"Maybe not a nurse."

"Jean mentioned a friend of hers," my dad said.

"A friend of Jean's would be great."

chapter twenty-one

NEAR MIDNIGHT, ON SEPTEMBER 15TH, WE SAT ON OUR COUCH, watching the digital clock. Out the window of our bedroom, walnut tree branches appeared and then fell away, lit by the beam of a motion detector. Their leaves flitted in front of the balconies of the building behind us, revealing glimpses of folding chairs, plastic buckets, yellow-handled mops.

In a few minutes, Stephen would be thirty, passing the median life expectancy for someone with CF. He'd been trying to achieve this for years—every time he got close, the life expectancy went up. The urge defied logic—it could only be a good thing that people with CF were living longer. But he wanted to get out in front, to be above average, ahead of the curve. I leaned over him and we stared at the clock together. 12:01. We toasted with our beer bottles.

September 16th, thirty years old, officially in the 51st percentile.

chapter twenty-two

THE COUNTRY OF THE TRANSPLANT WAS A STRANGE, UNDER-water place. The deep relaxation of Stephen being able to breathe mixed with the knowledge that a common cold or the mold in dust could kill him. We crossed the street to pass construction sites, he wore a mask on airplanes to avoid floating germs—these were the things you didn't know about ahead of time. We were learning the transplant together. With CF he'd always been ahead of me—it was territory he understood, and I was always working to catch up. But the transplant was new to both of us. For the first time, he was happy when I offered to go to doctor's appointments with him. He felt overwhelmed by the fact that his immune system was suppressed—that he could be going along fine and then find himself blindsided by something as seemingly harmless as the flu. He had to learn to read his entire body the way he'd learned to read his lungs—and this was complicated by the fact that with CF, enjoying life meant ignoring feeling sick, while with the transplant he was supposed to pay attention to every tiny sick-like feeling. He had to call the clinic when his temperature went over 100, when his blood pressure shifted, or his pulse. He kept track of these things in a little blue book. It was time-consuming and also sort of satisfying, keeping this written record.

There was the new relationship to death, the new relationship to his body, and then there were all the drugs. The drugs were crazy. So many things shifted. He gained fifty pounds. He developed a craving for ice cream and chocolate sauce. His face went from angular to wide and round, and his hair got darker. He looked so different that a childhood friend introduced herself to him as if they'd never met. His handwriting, which had always been neat, became scrawling, almost illegible. His conversational style shifted in the same way, from sharp and pointed to wandering and lengthy. His emails went from one-line quips to three-page ramblings. He began to window shop— it started almost overnight. A month after the transplant, when we visited Carmel with his mom, he'd teased her about wandering into various shops as we walked through town. A year later, I was teasing him about the same thing. We couldn't get down the main street in Mendocino because every single store caught his eye.

Later, a therapist would remark as an aside that Prednisone can lead to impulse shopping. This tiny piece of knowledge could have prevented probably half the arguments Stephen and I had after the transplant. Or at least half the purchases. I was used to his normal, practical self. If I'd understood there were new forces at work I might have been more careful about buying a house with 5 percent down, or made a blanket rule that would have prevented him from coming home with a brand-new truck.

As it happened, I got furious, he felt hurt, and still to this day I own a '98 red Toyota Tacoma.

Like the impulse shopping, the ways he changed could feel benign, intriguing, frustrating, or agonizing, depending on context and degree. The little things he bought at the flea market were endearing—a Magic 8 Ball, a small stool so I could reach all of our cabinets. The truck made me feel done for. Likewise, he was spacey, in his own world, and this could make him more open to suggestion, more willing to see the gray area in things. Movies he would have hated before entertained him. It also meant that he was farther away from me without knowing it. When he gave me a back rub, I could barely feel his fingers on my skin. There was a film between us, between him and other people. He'd always been an organizer, but now he organized group events and then didn't always show up. He was around an hour late to everything, and he could never figure out how it had happened. His thoughts were muddled. I was scared to ask his coworkers how things were going at work.

And I missed him, which felt like a betrayal. But I wanted to be able to talk with him the way I always had. Maybe this was my failing and my strength—I expected to get to have our relationship throughout. It might have been unrealistic, even spoiled. Sometimes I look back and think it was a lot to ask of a person, with everything he was going through. Maybe I should have let him be distant from me, let myself slide into that caretaker role. But when I imagine saying this to Stephen, I see him scowling. *So what would that turn me into,* he'd say, *courageous-disability guy?*

I'd somehow gotten the idea that the film around him was caused by the methadone. Whether this is true, I'll never know. He was on thirty medications, and who knew what happened when you mixed them all together. But I felt desperate to see if there was some way to get him back a little, and the transplant medications were mandatory, while the methadone was not.

I mentioned the idea to Stephen, who at first was insulted to hear that he was spacey, and then annoyed that I thought it might be related to the painkillers. He was planning to get off of them, but he wasn't in any rush. More, he couldn't see how or why his mental state was hard on me. The loneliness of this felt unbearable. His friends and family noticed that he was different, but no one had the heart to tell him. Our last trip to Colorado, his forgetfulness had left his brother frustrated, his sister perplexed, and his mom calling me an angel for dealing with "the changes." I did not want to be an angel; I wanted someone besides me to talk to Stephen. But his friends and family could wait the changes out. They loved him; they could overlook these things for a while. I didn't have any of that distance or patience. I tried to think of someone who could help, who I trusted in situations like this. I picked up the phone and dialed Dr. Stulbarg.

An hour later, he called back. I panicked; I should have let Stephen make the call. But I went ahead and described what I'd been noticing. Dr. Stulbarg suggested Stephen and I come in to see him right away, and I couldn't bring myself to tell him I'd called without telling Stephen, just wanting some confidential advice.

The next morning we sat glumly in Dr. Stulbarg's office. Dr. Stulbarg put his stethoscope to Stephen's back, near his shoulder blades. He asked Stephen about his sleep and suggested that he cut down on the number of Cokes he drank a day. "So," he said, "what else is going on?"

"Liz clearly has a few things she needs to tell you," Stephen said.

I began cautiously, trying to make sure I described the changes the way I had at home. Stephen put his head in his hands as I talked. When I'd finished, Dr. Stulbarg asked him about what I'd said, and to my relief, he said he knew what I meant.

"I lose track of time, I'm more reclusive," he said. "I wouldn't say *spacey*. It's pretty mild. People go through stages. I don't blame her when she changes. But if I change, it's all about the medications. Like I'm a composite of chemicals."

"But these things started when you began taking them," I said.

"You thought the methadone was a great idea. I wish I'd recorded our earlier conversation."

"The one when you said you were eventually going to get off of it?"

We talked for a while longer, too long; Dr. Stulbarg would now be late for the rest of his appointments today. After the receptionist poked her head in the door a second time, he stood up. "I always enjoy seeing you guys," he said. "I think, although this is completely out of my field, that the most important thing to work on is your communication."

Our communication. Out of all the doctors, out of all the people who loved us, in the end it came down to him and me. And apparently the side effects of the drugs were in my head. Was I the only person who thought the people waiting in line at the methadone clinic looked stoned? I was furious with the doctors, I counted on them, and it wasn't a one-way street. I never said, signing up to be a proxy, or the main social support for a double-lung transplant, is out of my field. My field was large and nebulous—I had no idea how to do most of the things in it and all I could do was try anyway. But this was out of my field. It was a medical problem, which no one in the medical world knew how to address: helpful medications had unhelpful effects. They were hard to limit to their intended mission, they ran through the body and brain doing whatever they pleased. This phenomenon, so well known, had to be someone's fucking field.

Stephen was upset for reasons of his own. "The person I respect more than anyone thinks I'm an asshole now."

"No he doesn't."

"I could tell."

"He said we both weren't listening."

"I can't stop thinking about it. You called him behind my back."

"I didn't think I was going to make an appointment."

"So you were going to talk to him without telling me?"

"I was going to tell you," I said, but neither of us believed me. "I didn't know what else to do."

"But why couldn't you just talk to *me*? That's worse than anything."

"I've been talking to you. I've been trying to talk to you."

But he was right. I thought about Dr. Stulbarg, how I'd felt betrayed by him in that office, and in some ways I still thought he was wrong, but there was the chance he was also right. This is one problem, he'd said, and it might be solved by looking at side effects, but there will be other problems to face. He'd been kind enough to say that he'd faced obstacles in his own marriage, and I'd wondered if we were one of them, his willingness to add an extra appointment no matter how busy he was, to come in at seven this morning to help us out. He'd recommended an exercise where each person got to talk for five minutes uninterrupted. Stephen and I had left the office shrugging that off, but then we found ourselves sitting across from each other at the kitchen table with a timer between us.

I talked to him. And he talked to me. Somehow we managed to be honest, which felt like a huge relief but not necessarily momentous, until a month later when I'd be tracing it back, trying to remember exactly what we'd said, and whether I'd said enough.

The next morning, we sat on the couch, drinking coffee and reading the paper. "Happy Valentine's Day," he said. "Too bad it's our last one before the divorce."

"Shut up," I said.

"Dee-vorce," he said. "You know you want it."

I laughed. "Stop it," I said, and he grinned.

chapter twenty-three

STEPHEN LAY DOZING ON THE COUCH, A LITTLE SUNKEN into the cushions. Darby and Luna, a short-haired husky we'd just adopted from the pound, lay on either side of him like bookends. I nudged Luna so I could sit right next to Stephen, have him lie with his head resting on me while I drank my coffee and read the paper. He opened his eyes and frowned at the coffee mug above his head. I held it out away from him, trying to get him to stay in place. It was one of my favorite things—head against leg, paper, coffee. He sat up, though, and wouldn't lie back down until my mug was on the table.

His head was too warm. He was procrastinating, and I let him for a while longer. We procrastinated together; it was Sunday. And then I rested my palm on his forehead, felt my own for comparison. "You're way hotter than me," I said.

He grinned and winced.

"I didn't mean it like that, come on."

"Ooh, baby, you're *way* hotter than me—that's what you said."

We were both giggling. I compared foreheads again. "Maybe over a hundred."

"Fuck." Stephen sat up. His cheek was sweaty, his hair tangled. He wandered into the bedroom and came back with a thermometer. I touched his forehead again. Why hadn't we dealt with this when we first got up? They were going to make us come over to the hospital and we hadn't even walked the dogs.

"One hundred and one. And it's Sunday, it'll be pointless over there."

It was true; the hospital weekend was a slow limbo, none of the regular doctors around. He wanted to put off the call. I was quiet. We both knew he would cave in. I rarely played the "scared" card; I'd kept its value high.

He picked up the phone. I leaned against him, thinking of what we needed to do. Take the dogs out. Get ready for school tomorrow. My grading was probably not going to get done. We both went to our desks, spent too long getting things organized. Finally, I drove us over the Bay Bridge. Stephen sat in the passenger seat, eyes closed, listing things. He wanted me to mail the spare key to our friend Dave, who'd bought our old Corolla. Luna, who had just been spayed, needed to have her stitches taken out. We took the Fell Street exit toward the hospital. "We need to stop for a sec," he said. "I want a Coke."

"I'll get you one when we get there," I said. "We're already late."

"Once I go in, they won't let me have anything to drink."

"Why would they do that?"

"I can't believe I let you drive."

I dropped him off at the emergency room door and went to find parking. I walked the few blocks back to the hospital, stopping at the corner store to get a Coke for him, an Orangina for me. When I got to the ER, I found him in one of the makeshift rooms, with white curtain walls. A nurse stood over him, taking his vitals. She vetoed the Coke.

In the waiting room I graded spelling tests. I attempted to grade biography rough drafts but I wasn't up to it. I read *People*, glanced at the TV, closed my eyes. Hours later, the receptionist called my name. Stephen was on his way to a room, in the seventh-floor Intensive Cardiac Care.

"Intensive?" I asked her.

"Transplant patients always go to the ICC until they're seen by their own doctors," she said. "Don't worry."

On the one hand, this was good, I thought as I carried Stephen's duffel bag over to the elevator. He'd have his own nurse; nothing would go unnoticed. On the other hand, when he was in the regular hospital, I reassured myself by thinking that if it were serious, they'd put him in Intensive Care. There was no place more deserving of worry for him to be sent—no Intensive Intensive Care.

In the ICC, I found Bed 14. The room had a view of the eastern side of the city. I pulled a chair up next to Stephen. He told me I hadn't missed much in the ER. His fever was about the same; he'd see the transplant doctors in the morning.

"Maybe I'll stay and watch *The X-Files*," I told him.

"I'm a little worried about the dogs."

"It's not that late."

"They're used to eating by now, and the house is dark."

"Everything comes back to the dogs these days," I said. But I got up off the bed, put on my shoes, searched around for my keys. Stephen stood to hug me, turned his face sideways so we could rub cheeks.

He was right, the house was dark, the dogs were whimpering as I walked up the front steps. It was 8:45 when I got home. *The X-Files* would be on soon, but I didn't feel like watching alone. I drove over to my friend and co-teacher Beth's house, slipped an orange file folder with my sub plans under her doormat. In the morning, I woke up without an alarm, took the dogs for a run. I was getting in the shower when the phone rang. It was Stephen's nurse. The hospital was not supposed to call me; it was the other way around. She put Dr. Golden on the phone. "Liz," he said, "when are you coming in?"

"I'm about to head over," I said, feeling a little defensive.

He wanted me to know they'd had to put Stephen on a ventilator. They had yet to figure out what was attacking his lungs. They were working as hard as they could, they'd do their best to see if they could get Stephen out of the hospital. I pictured Stephen as I left him, standing up, hugging me, advising me about the dogs. "Page me when you get here," Dr. Golden said. "And drive carefully."

Meaning, the circumstances were such that I should be compelled to speed. Meaning, the vent was not a normal post-transplant thing. What had been wrong with us yesterday? We'd dawdled at our desks, with to-do lists. I sat on the couch and let the dogs nudge me. Dr. Golden had said *if*, not when. But it didn't seem like something he would say.

I poured dog food into the dogs' bowls, milk into my coffee. I grabbed two yogurts, turned a few lights on. I scrounged for change for the hospital phone, and a dollar for bridge fare. Clothes. I was in a towel; I'd been headed for the shower. A shower wouldn't change Stephen's situation, and it would make me feel so much better. Did I need one? Did anyone ever? I was taking one, end of story, two minutes, no washing my hair. Five minutes later, in jeans and a T-shirt, I jumped in the truck and headed for San Francisco.

Stephen's curtain was drawn; he lay in his bed, deep in sleep, his head lolled to the right. I leaned over the bed railing and kissed his forehead. He was pink and sweaty; he looked relaxed. But there were tubes everywhere, tangles of them, hanging from IV poles, the ventilator machine, the feeding pump, the oxygen tank, various monitors, all converging on or into his body. Could I not leave him alone for one night? I could barely reach him with all this equipment, these side gates up, and all kinds of cords looped through them that I was scared to disturb.

I pulled a chair close to the bed, carefully rearranged the tubes so I could lower the side gate in front of me, and put my feet up on his bed. He'd been sedated so they could put the vent in; he wouldn't wake up for a while. I closed my eyes. The room was warm with late-morning sun, and we were on hospital time.

I OPENED MY eyes to Dr. Golden's voice. He motioned me into the hallway and sat down, giving me a chair. We talked about possible sources of infection. I listed everything I could think of—small problems Stephen had mentioned, things he might have been exposed to. Dr. Golden kept diverting his pages. I asked him whether I should tell Stephen's family to come. I knew how to judge with CF. With the transplant, I had no idea. We'd been living with it for two years, and nothing like this had happened.

"You know them," he said. "It's your decision."

"But if it were your family, what would you do?"

"If my son were on a vent, I'd want to know about it," he said.

I went back into Stephen's room. I sat for a while, watching the shudder of the ventilator. Dr. Golden had told me to page him anytime. Dr. Stulbarg had left a message with Stephen's nurse to call him when I got to the hospital. They were trying to take care of me; they expected me to be scared. I slipped out of Stephen's room to make phone calls. I called in for a sub for tomorrow. I needed to run this whole thing by someone else, to see how it sounded from the outside. I called Eve.

"What's up?" she said. "Is it lunch hour over there?"

I told her where I was, what had happened.

"Oh, sweetie," she said. I didn't know if she meant Stephen or me, but I felt tears welling up.

"It'll be okay," I said. "I just wanted to tell someone."

"Should I come over there?"

"I don't know. No, you're all the way in Oakland. I'll call you tonight."

"I think I should come over there."

"Okay."

I went into the bathroom, closed the stall door, put the toilet seat down and sat on it, with my head in my hands. I would have to call our families. If Stephen were awake, he'd probably tell them all not to come. He especially wouldn't want to interrupt Fran and Clay's Hawaii trip. But he'd already left a message for them that he was here, they'd be expecting an update. My family, too, I'd go ahead and call my family. I stood in front of the sink, splashed cold water on my face. I still looked like I'd been crying. I splashed more water, patted it dry with a paper towel.

I ran my fingers through my hair. I looked disheveled, but no more disheveled than I often looked.

Stephen slept and slept. I sat by his bed, reading Lorrie Moore's *Birds of America*, laughing out loud. Stephen's nurse asked me about the book. Eve slipped into the room, told me to keep reading, just sat near me in the extra hospital chair. I procrastinated writing my lesson plans for the next day, finally forcing myself. Eve suggested I go wild; take the rest of the week off. In a fit of organization I rummaged through Stephen's backpack until I found the rubber-banded stack of bills. I paid them his way for once, writing the account numbers in the lower left corners, so tidy.

Stephen kept sleeping. Eve needed to go home and she tried to pull me out with her, but I couldn't go until I'd talked to him. She pointed out that he probably needed to sleep, but after she left I started poking him anyway, telling him to blink his eyes if he could hear me. "I'm going to go call our families," I said, waiting for a sign—a nod, or a grunt. Always, we hashed this out together. I stood up reluctantly, tugging at his shoulder. "Stephen?" Oblivious. I headed for the phone.

Everyone wanted to come. Tomorrow. Clay, Fran, Tinka, Catherine, my parents. They were all worried, and I couldn't tell them not to be. I came back into Stephen's room, hid my candy bar in my pocket in case he woke up. I hated eating in secret, but I had to eat, and he couldn't, so I'd been doing it all day. I sat down next to him, squeezed his hand. He squeezed back. It was seven o'clock, about time. "Can you hear me?" I asked. He squeezed my hand again. It was my window; we talked like this for a while. When I told him that his family was coming tomorrow, he moved his head slightly.

"Are you saying that's good?" I asked.

He moved his head again, but very slightly.

"Squeeze once if you want them to come."

He sighed, and squeezed once.

"Are you worried?"

His shoulders moved up, then down.

"A little bit?"

He nodded.

"Me, too. Dr. Golden thinks it's an infection."

His grip loosened on my hand. He was falling back asleep.

"Do you want some stuff for your lips? They're all dried out."

I sifted through the plastic tub on his side table, found a mini tube of Vaseline, and rubbed some on his lips. He kissed my fingers vaguely. I kissed his cheek, eyes, and forehead. Every kiss I gave him, he made a kissing motion back, the way he did when I kissed him while he was asleep. I held his hand for a while, reading my book as the city grew dark.

ALL TUESDAY, HE slept. His arms had been tied to the bedsides since late the night before, when, according to the nurses, he'd yanked his feeding tube out of his nose. "Very naughty," his nurse remarked to me. "He grabbed it once, and I said, 'Do you promise you won't mess with it again?' Next thing I knew, he was swiping at it."

When she was gone, I loosened the restraints, glancing at his hands every time I turned a page in my book. It seemed only natural, the second you woke up and felt something stuck up your nose, you'd try to get it out. I wondered why he hadn't tried to pull out the ventilator.

Fran and Clay and Tinka arrived, and my parents. My dad,

whose vision had still not returned, came over close to Stephen to say hello, and Stephen answered by squeezing his hand. We all stood around, watching Dr. Golden tinker with the dial on the ventilator.

"What do you think?" Clay asked him.

"Yesterday I was very worried," Dr. Golden said. "Today I'm just worried."

"I guess that's something," Clay said.

"It's most likely a viral infection. We haven't pinpointed what it is. It could be a strain of pneumonia."

"Or the flu," I said.

My dad shook his head. "This is what happens when he gets the *flu*?"

FRIENDS CONVERGED IN the waiting room, a tight gathering. I felt loved and a little self-conscious—we were taking up too much space for one patient. A man walking by made a dark remark about "groupies." There were card games and email exchanges. Everyone wanted to see Stephen; we were supposed to go in two at a time, but people kept breaking the rule. A nurse took me aside, asked me to remind everyone that this was Intensive Care, the rule was there for a reason, Stephen needed to rest. I argued with her childishly. I didn't want to be the enforcer, couldn't people just read the signs? No one was reading them, she pointed out, and she had other things on her plate at the moment. I went into the waiting room, passed the job off to a couple of friends.

Dr. Golden turned the ventilator down to 60 percent; Stephen was doing 40 percent of the work. It was a weaning process. At this rate he'd be breathing on his own in six days. A few more days on the vent to make sure he was okay, a few days of rest, and home. A week and a half. Double that, because things never went as planned. Three weeks. I wondered what to do about my job. Every time I called, my principal told me not to worry; other teachers were writing my lesson plans. One teacher came by the hospital to drop off cards from my class. Folded construction paper, neatly printed notes, drawings of flowers in vases, figures lying in bed, balloons. Separate cards for me and Stephen: Ms. Scarboro and Mr. Scarboro. I taped the cards for Mr. Scarboro to the wall.

I went with Stephen's family to the transplant support group meeting. It was four floors up in the hospital, a large corner waiting room that looked out on Golden Gate Park. We pulled chairs into a circle. It was an open-topic meeting.

"I'll tell you what's on *my* mind," one guy said. I remembered him, a single-lung in his fifties, two years out, ex-smoker. He pointed with his elbow at his wife. "Can't get her to quit the cigarettes. You'd think after seeing me."

His wife shrugged. She was about his age, long tousled brown hair, cowboy boots and jeans. She wasn't having it. "I'm down to a couple a night," she argued. "The hospital, the meds—you try to quit with all this stress."

I could see her point. If I smoked, maybe I'd be doing a lot of it right now. I'd always thought Stephen was the reason I kept myself healthy—I appreciated my lungs and my freedom. But I could see how the reverse might happen—a little escape, a little pick-me-up would be useful.

"His moods are killing me," one woman said. "How long before the Prednisone goes down?"

MY FRIENDS TOOK turns walking the dogs, which was no easy feat. The dogs had figured out that if they pulled in opposite directions, or worse, if they both pulled in one direction, the walker was forced to drop the leash or risk falling over. But I let my friends walk them anyway, pretending it was going fine, because I didn't know what else to do. Friends bought me groceries, put them in the fridge. I lost track of who had a key to my house, and when I'd given them all away I put my own key under a shoe on the front porch, for whoever might be coming next.

FRIDAY, STEPHEN LAY in bed, freshly bathed, hair in a towel, a new hospital gown on. The doctors had told us this morning that his lung was looking better. There was a small part of the lung that had fluid in it, but otherwise he was healing. He looked relaxed to me, his eyes closed, his face soft. Clay and Amani talked quietly with my dad in the corner. My dad was leaving later today, he was getting ready to say goodbye to Stephen. Stephen wriggled, moving his arms up and down, his shoulders back and forth. We all looked down at him.

"What's he doing?" my dad asked.

Stephen stopped, and then started again. He was wriggling exactly when the feeding machine made its noise, stopping when it stopped. Clay and Amani laughed.

"He's dancing in time to the machine," I told my dad. Stephen smiled.

"You're right," Amani said to Stephen. "We should all lighten up."

STEPHEN LAY IN BED, legs splayed, a pillow under his knee. Nothing was private in the hospital. His hair was darker than before the transplant, his ponytail tinged red from the night we experimented with dying our hair. We'd also put on bright blue eye shadow and made ourselves look as ghoulish as possible, but no one in the hospital knew that. He was mad because I'd let them take off his wedding ring. His hands were swelling up; they'd been worried the ring might cut off his circulation. Sometimes this was one humiliation after another. He'd gotten a blood clot, from lying there so long. Where had the blood clot been? I wasn't sure. They'd given him Heparin to thin his blood. His blood, thinner, had streamed out of the IV onto his arm, scaring both of us, I didn't know how to stop it. I'd untied the restraints, tried with a washcloth, afraid to press hard since I knew there was an IV needle in there. A nurse had run in, rescuing us. She took the IV out, bandaged the arm, and sewed an IV line into his foot. She sewed it, I swore, with thread. Gray-blue thread. He didn't seem to feel it, his foot didn't jerk. They had him so doped up. Was the infection painful? A rare form of pneumonia, one they hadn't seen. So much was going on, and so little. Hours here.

MONDAY, HIS EIGHTH DAY in the hospital, construction began next door. It had never occurred to me that there could be construction in the ICU. It was happening right behind the wall at the head of his bed. His bed was vibrating. The power saw screeched arrhythmically. Every so often a loud bang jolted him awake. Tomorrow I'd bring in the sound machine we'd used to drown out the sound of the feeding pump. I looked forward to noon, hoping there would be a lunch break. How did we always end up next to construction? How was he supposed to recuperate when people were jackhammering? I went to complain.

"I know," the receptionist said sympathetically. "It was going on all last month. I guess last week they were just taking a break."

"You mean it's not only today?"

"I think it's a six-month project."

THEY SWITCHED STEPHEN'S meds to sedatives he could handle long-term. Instantly he became more aware, more agitated. I turned up the sound machine. I knew once he tuned into the construction it would drive him crazy. He kept lifting up his arms and legs: he couldn't relax. I offered him a foot massage, which he took me up on. Every hour or so, he spelled "LUNA" into my hand. "I'm taking care of her," I grumbled. But he didn't trust my dog-training capabilities.

WHEN FRAN AND I CAME in Friday morning, Stephen tapped his wrist. He was right; we were later than usual. We were not a good combination when it came to getting out of the house.

"He's full of energy," the nurse said. "I told him you'd be here."

Stephen moved his right hand in a writing motion. The nurse showed me two pieces of paper with scribble marks from earlier this morning. The first page seemed to say *LIZ* and, *MLK M4 DAY*. Apparently he thought I was at work. The second piece of paper was hard to decipher. I could only read *What room are we in?* And *I can't speak.*

"You know you're in the ICU?" I asked him.

He nodded. I handed him the pen, and held a piece of paper down on the table in front of him. He gripped the pen and pressed it onto the paper. Painstakingly, he wrote a *C*. He stopped for a second, lined up the pen next to the *C* and wrote an *O*. He stopped again, lined up the pen and wrote *KE*. Around the *COKE*, he drew a circle with a slash through it, and then a question mark. This was the urgent message he needed to write. It did make sense that he was craving Coke; he averaged five a day.

"You want to know why you can't have one?"

He nodded.

"You have a ventilator in."

He flung his hands open: No shit.

"You can't have anything to drink: you can only suck on ice."

He circled his hands impatiently: Why can't I drink on the vent?

"Maybe they think it'll go down the wrong way."

One side of his mouth went up into a smirk.

"Maybe the ventilator tube doesn't go all the way down to your lungs. No, then air would get in your stomach, I don't know. I'll ask the next time they come in."

He kept writing. I figured out that I could decipher best if I watched him write, so I could see what he was trying to make the pen do. I guessed at each word, and then moved on to the next, like charades. After a lot of work, I read his first thought. *Starting—I remember very little or have only . . . so: fill me in.*

"Remember coming here?" I asked.

He held out his hand, flat, and made it waver: Sort of.

"Remember being at home on the couch and calling the doctor?"

He nodded, without full confidence.

"You know you've been here a week and a half?" I asked. "It's March fifth."

He glanced at the calendar on the wall, and then blinked quickly in horror.

"I paid the bills."

He raised his eyebrows hopefully.

"Yeah, they were in by the first."

He gave me a look I could only interpret as: Why can't you just do things on time in normal life, too? Then he pointed to his paper, to *fill me in*. I told him the story, beginning from the symptoms, to coming to the hospital, to the vent. I told him about the biopsy, how whatever he had, it was something they hadn't seen before, how Dr. Golden wanted me to think of anything strange he might have been exposed to, and I'd brought in a wood chip from the dog park. I told him that each day was a little better; he was down to 50 percent on the ventilator. He held up his fingers, ten plus two, and pointed to his throat: Twelve days on the ventilator?

"I know, it's not good."

He pointed to his chest, held up two fingers. Meaning, after the transplant, he'd only been on the ventilator two days.

"But this is a different thing."

He widened his eyes: *Clearly*. Then he circled his hand: *More?*

"It's your left lung, so it's the one where you'd been feeling the tugging. There's a small part that has liquid in it."

At the mention of liquid he gestured quickly for another piece of paper. He eked out, *When will I see Dr. S & G?* He was surprised to hear they'd both been coming by a few times a day. He started in on a list of questions for them.

1. *What do we know about this set of lungs?*
2. *Any thoughts of time frame?*
3. *White blood cell count?*
4. *Why the feeding tube? I've CLEARLY not had a weight problem! AND I was never consulted so I felt . . .*

"So you felt—"

He glared at me; it was obvious how he felt, how else would someone feel with a feeding tube stuck up his nose? His indignation seemed like a good sign; he was coming back. He pointed to the extra padding on his stomach. I wondered if while he'd been gaining, he'd been imagining future hospitalizations, thinking he could finally relax, eat only when he wanted, not worry if he lost a few pounds.

When Dr. Golden came in half an hour later, Stephen gestured for his paper.

"He has some questions for you," I said.

"Incredible," Dr. Golden said as he studied the paper. He began going down the list. "I'd be wondering about this new set of lungs, too," he said. "As far as we can tell, the lungs were fine. You caught an infection of some kind. You're on the vent because it was ravaging your lungs. They still can't expand and contract on their own yet. You're doing better, though. Liz can tell you, last Monday I was very worried."

Stephen nodded. I knew that if he could talk, he'd be discussing the answers, asking more questions, that we were just skimming the surface of what was on his mind.

When we got to the question about the feeding tube, Dr. Golden looked quizzically at Stephen. "You think you can eat with the vent in?" he asked.

Stephen pointed to his stomach.

"He thinks he could lose a few pounds and still be fine," I said.

Dr. Golden smiled. "Are you kidding? You have to eat. And don't pull that thing out again. It's a lot of work to put another one in."

Stephen pointed to where the tube was coming out and wrinkled his nose.

"He's having trouble with the itching," I said.

"Try some Vaseline," Dr. Golden said. "I don't blame you, I'd be miserable with a tube stuck up my nose, too. Why aren't you complaining about the vent?"

Stephen shrugged and held out his hands in a *What are you going to do?* gesture.

"The vent's not optional," I said.

Dr. Golden looked from me to Stephen. "Can you read her mind, too?"

Stephen shrugged and nodded, pointing to the spot where his wedding ring had been: Old married couple.

"Shut up, we are not," I said before I translated.

"I don't know, "Dr. Golden said. "He could be right."

Stephen frowned at me. What's so bad about that? he was asking.

THAT NIGHT, I'd planned to go to a Dan Bern concert with Eve. I'd gotten the ticket a while ago. It had seemed like a good idea, Stephen was usually asleep anyway, and Fran would be here to keep him company. But it was seven, I was supposed to be at the Great American Music Hall at eight, and he was wide awake, full of energy.

"Go on ahead," Fran said. "I'll be here, keep him entertained."

Stephen flashed me an *I'm fine* look, insulted that we were trying to entertain him. I wavered for a minute, and decided to go, he could be here for weeks; it was better to act like things were slightly normal. I sat down on the bed and hugged him, putting my arms under and around the various impediments so I could get to him. He spelled *D* and *L* into my hand: the dogs.

"Matt walked them and fed them," I said. "I'll be home by eleven."

Stephen must have had some premonition, because when I came home from the concert, Darby and Luna were cowering on the floor. All around them, couch stuffing, shreds of fabric, dilapidated cushions. They followed me around the house, trying to squeeze into the bathroom while I brushed my teeth. They lay on my feet once I settled into bed, weighing down the covers. It had been good to be at the concert, fun even. Dan Bern's pants were so big they were falling off, and Eve had gone up to the stage and loaned him her belt. I fell asleep, drifted deep into my hometown. I was riding in a car with my dad; he had his sight, and he was driving. He pointed out a street corner as we passed it.

"This is right where we were when your brother died," he said.

"What?" I said slowly, trying to understand.

"I turned my head the other way for a second, and he was shot."

Panic flooded me. "But why didn't you call me?" I started to shake.

"There was nothing you could do. We wanted you to go ahead with your life."

I woke up sweating, full of dread. It was dark, I wondered if I should call my brother. I told myself he was fine, tried to shake the dream, the death that hadn't happened. I turned on the light and read, wishing Stephen were lying next to me.

chapter twenty-four

THE NEXT MORNING, WHEN FRAN AND I GOT TO THE HOSPITAL, Stephen was deep asleep. I glanced at the numbers above his bed, inspected the ventilator. It had been cranked up to 80. Who would have made that kind of mistake?

"No one called you?" the nurse said. "He crashed in the middle of the night."

I pulled a chair close to Stephen and rested my head on his legs. It was Saturday, the construction was in hiatus, the whole hospital was in hiatus, and we were in hiatus, too. It was as if his lung had never improved, as if he hadn't woken up, started gesturing emphatically. It had been a mistake to get excited, to go to the concert, to call work and say I might be back next week.

Fran and I were tired, everyone was tired, the nurses strangely distant and business-like. Maybe they thought I was selfish for coming in at ten, for leaving at seven last night. Maybe they'd outrun the normal course of friendliness for a hospital stay. But something felt weird. Stephen was doing badly, and they were not looking at me, like we'd passed the point of being people they could relate to. He was too sick for that, they just needed to do their jobs. We had a life too, I felt like saying, a home, dogs, an existence outside this room. The same people who'd lingered over the cards on Stephen's wall slipped in and out of the room, like they were bussing our table. I did not want Stephen to wake up to this.

Eve came in to see us just as Dr. Golden was arriving.

"What happened?" I asked him.

"The infection is incredibly strong. But there are still some things we can try."

He studied the ventilator and the scoreboard, shaking his head.

"I guess this isn't the kind of job you can do drunk," Eve said.

Dr. Golden smiled. "I like that. I'll have to remember that."

"I can't believe this," I said. "Last night he looked ready to leave."

"And those questions," Dr. Golden said. "A little scary how coherent he is, on all these drugs."

"Stephen's personality doesn't seem like the suppressible type," Eve said.

"Do you think he can hear us?" I asked Dr. Golden.

"I think patients probably hear more than we give them credit for."

How had we gotten here? Stephen was working so hard. So were we, so were all the doctors and the nurses; everyone was working so hard. "I wish I was religious right now," I said. "Then I could question my faith."

Dr. Golden smiled. "I'll have to remember that, too."

THAT NIGHT, I stood outside in our tiny backyard. I looked up through the walnut tree branches, into the small area of sky sandwiched between the balcony of the apartment building and our next-door-neighbor Rivka's second story. Rivka's lights were out, no radio or TV to be heard from the apartments. I imagined myself walking across deserts, mountains. Willing to do anything, and nothing to do. I thought about the transplant, how so many people had been pulling for Stephen that night, and how I'd thought maybe this had had something to do with the operation's success. All the same people, thinking of him now, while his lungs careened. Still, I looked up at the few stars and wished like a child.

STEPHEN'S KIDNEYS BEGAN to fail. They could get him through this, but they'd have to put him on dialysis. He'd be on it from here on out. It was up to me. My friend Wanda's brother was on dialysis; he went to the hospital twice a week to get hooked up to machines. I pictured driving Stephen to the hospital, him talking to me in the car. That would be better than fine.

Gary, the dialysis nurse, came to set up the machine. He was in his fifties, with a walrus mustache, heavyset. He was cheerful and relaxed, illuminating the tenor of the rest of us, fast-paced, wound tight. When he finished putting everything in place, he patted Stephen's arm. "Looking good, buddy," he said. "See you tomorrow."

DR. STULBARG CAME by in the evening. "Do you have a minute?" he asked me.

I smiled. It was always the other way around. He brought me into his office. It was seven; he should have been home by now. We sat in metal chairs. The room was dingy, lit by a fluorescent strip. It seemed strange that this was the headquarters for all of his research. It had never occurred to me that doctors would have the same kinds of offices my college professors had—small unkempt nooks tucked away from the public; measly, compared to what they deserved. Dr. Stulbarg relaxed into his chair. We were removed from the hospital world; it was quiet in here, the door shut behind us.

"I've known you guys for a long time," Dr. Stulbarg said. "And I know you'd want to know."

I waited, winding my feet around the legs of my chair.

"The doctors aren't optimistic."

The doctors, who'd joked with me earlier today, told me there were things still left to do. Trying to make the best of things, maybe. And maybe I hadn't been listening. There had been some comment about the *Titanic*. "They told me they could pull out the big guns," I said.

"They could try Vancomycin. But it's rarely used because it knocks out the rest of your system. In the best case Stephen would need to go live in a rehab center for quite a while to recover."

We could handle a rehab center. I'd go live with him there, I didn't care. I imagined a cluster of buildings similar to those in my grandparents' nursing home, like the rehab center for the blind I'd driven around once, thinking of possibilities for my dad. There were woods nearby; maybe there would be places I could run. I didn't know what we'd do about the dogs.

Dr. Stulbarg shook his head. "It's hard, even for doctors, to step back, see what's going on. His organs are failing. His kidneys have failed, his heart's having trouble."

I thought about Stephen, all our conversations about no life support. Was dialysis life support? I'd agreed hungrily. How easy it was to become this person. Stephen should have been in charge. I forced myself to ask the question I knew he'd want answered. "What are the chances he'll live through this?"

"Very slim," Dr. Stulbarg said.

A piece of thread, twisting, spiraling. This was Stephen's chance now. It struck me that you could hope more than you ever thought possible and still not make a dent.

"How long has it been like this?"

"Didn't he have a really bad night this weekend?"

"Friday."

"I think his system started to crash then."

"No one will look at me." I blinked back tears.

"They feel terrible," he said. "They feel like they should be able to save him."

"Nobody's that powerful. I'd never assume they could save him."

"People do this job to save people."

"It's a little arrogant," I said. "I mean, not you. But it's seemed pretty clear from the beginning, this whole thing is a mystery, people are just helping, chipping away."

"It's especially hard when patients are young."

We were quiet. It had been two days, no one had told me.

Maybe they didn't want me to give up hope. As if I could. Here I was, sitting in this office, hoping. Dr. Stulbarg sat next to me, his eyes soft, his dinner cold, his family probably irritated at home. Did he tell his family about Stephen, about his days at work? He'd done this before; he'd have to do it over and over, all of his patients died young. This office had been occupied by other people, all crumbling in the chair I sat in now. I couldn't hold back my tears. Dr. Stulbarg squeezed my hand.

If Stephen were in this meeting, he'd gather information. The doctors weren't optimistic. This was what we knew. Did it matter how they'd come to this conclusion? Did we need to know anything more than "the big guns"? We already knew they probably wouldn't work. My only real question came to me. "Are we talking about weeks, or days, or hours?" I asked.

"I would say days," he said. "Probably a few days."

The last few days. In the hospital, with construction going on. Was I supposed to tell him? Would it make him lose hope if I told him now? Would I be denying him if I didn't tell him? He'd want to get the hell out of here and go home, and that was impossible because of the vent. The first time he'd been in here, he'd told me he didn't want to die in the hospital. I'd promised him that I wouldn't let it happen. I was twenty-one then, I'd envisioned sneaking him out, bringing him to the mountains, an open field surrounded by aspens.

"You can think about how you'd like this to go," Dr. Stulbarg said.

I took a deep breath and tried to think of what we could do with what we had. "I want to sleep next to him on his last night," I said finally. "And I want to talk to him one last time. I know you can't take the vent out. But if you could lower the sedation enough so he can hear me."

Dr. Stulbarg nodded. "We can figure that out."

"Thank you for telling me," I said.

We sat in the quiet dusk of the office.

I WALKED THROUGH the ICC doors, past the reception desk, making my way to Stephen's room. He was alone, sleeping deeply under his white woven blanket. It had all seemed imaginable in Dr. Stulbarg's office. Terrible, but clear. But seeing Stephen, I realized it couldn't happen, because I was incapable of it. I pushed the tubes out of the way, climbed up on his bed, and collapsed, the way I collapsed with him and no one else. This was how we did things—we made it through the hospital and then went home, collapsed together. If he wasn't coming home, was I just supposed to collapse on my own? I lay next to him, saying all the wrong things. "Please," I said, "maybe your body has some extra reserves. If there's anything else you can do."

I'd thought I knew how much I loved him. Nobody knew. They didn't know. I was only beginning to feel the size of it, knowing he'd be gone. I probably shouldn't have loved him so much; you probably shouldn't love people past the point where you can let them do what they need to do. But it was too late, it had happened.

"I'm not going anywhere," I told him, and then realized I had to find a way to make this happen. I begged the nurse to let me stay overnight in one of those foldout chairs. She reminded me that no one was allowed to stay in the ICC—the rooms were small, the doctors needed to be able to get to the patient quickly. I argued that I was small; I'd only fold the chair out partway. She tried to bargain me down to the waiting room. As she spoke, I began to feel clearheaded. I hadn't felt this lucid since the transplant, the room appearing in hyper-detail. "They told me he's dying," I said. "Who cares what the doctors need."

She stepped back. I was becoming a person who made people nervous. It was not such a bad thing. "I guess we'll have to borrow a chair from another floor," she said.

"If the doctors get mad, just say I dragged the chair in here myself."

"It's all right," she said. "I'd probably be like this, too."

I WALKED DOWN the hallway to the bathroom, changed into Stephen's sweats and T-shirt. The waiting room still had its lights on, two men sat slumped on a small couch, watching TV. When I came out of the bathroom, I passed them again. They had not changed position. I made my way back to Stephen's room, sat next to him for a minute, kissed his forehead and his cheek. It occurred to me that I had probably heard his voice for the last time. I conjured it in my head, I wished I could tape-record my brain in case it started to fade. "Wake me up if you wake up," I told him.

I lay in my own bed and closed my eyes. It was bright in the ICC; I rolled over to face the window, and pulled the blankets over my head. The nurse slipped in and out. I woke to the feeling of being tucked in. An X-ray technician stood over me, draping me in an X-ray-proof gown. "It's okay, keep sleeping," he said. The gown was luxuriously heavy, covers in winter; I drifted off thinking of snow.

In the morning, the construction began full force. I made my way down the hall to the bathroom, put my contacts in, changed into jeans and a T-shirt, washed my face, brushed my hair. I always looked terrible when I first woke up, and it was sort of a relief to look in the mirror and see that today was no exception—my face was puffy, my eyes sunken in. Before I could make any phone calls, I needed coffee. I took the stairs down to the cafeteria, like old times. I felt nostalgic for the other nights I'd spent here, for the bagels and orange juice and weak coffee, for the dark red trays I'd take up to Stephen's room. I wasn't hungry, but I bought food anyway.

When I got back to the room, Gary was there. "The dialysis will take a couple of hours," he said. "After that he might feel a little better, we could lighten the pain meds for a bit. His doctor told me you wanted a chance to talk with him."

I sat down in the chair by Stephen's bed, drinking my coffee. When the dialysis ended, Gary patted Stephen on the arm, and closed the curtain behind him. I pulled my chair next to Stephen's bed, lowered his armrest, untied the arm restraint and held his hand. "Hey," I said. He opened his eyes half-mast. I pulled the lever on the side of the bed and raised the bed until he was partly sitting up.

"How do you feel?" I asked him.

He grimaced and shook his head.

I tried not to cry. He'd been trying to tell us. Last week he'd pointed to himself, then out the door. *Out? You want to go out? Not yet, but we'll be home soon.* He'd rolled his eyes, tried again and again. We'd been hopeless, not ready at all.

"Remember going to see Alix and Carroll in Hawaii?"

His lips moved slightly.

"And how we drove on that one-lane highway to Hana, over all the bridges, and we kept letting local people pass because we were so slow?"

Stephen raised his eyebrows—*We weren't slow, they were fast.*

"And all those huge flowers, and waterfalls, how we surprised Alix and Carroll by jumping in the river with our clothes on? And staying up playing Spite and Malice, and you and Carroll called me Queenie."

He smiled, it was their joke, not mine.

I kept going, so desperate to get us out of here. "Remember the path through the grass that went down to that one pool, it was freshwater but right next to the ocean? And we jumped from the rocks way above."

He nodded.

"And we climbed out on those black rocks, and watched the ocean shoot up right next to us. And then we walked a strange way back—"

He squeezed, interrupting me.

"Something else happened?"

He moved his hand in a small circle: *Try to remember, guess.*

"Oh yeah, we got in an argument. About . . ."

He shrugged.

"Something stupid. But it seemed important at the time."

He shook his head.

"You thought it was stupid then?"

He nodded.

"What was it?"

He shrugged emphatically.

"Something so stupid you can't remember?"

He nodded.

"Me neither," I said. "Sounds like something I started."

He moved his head from side to side. And then he smiled. *Probably.*

I leaned down and kissed him, we kissed the best we could, given the tube.

"Are you scared?" I asked him.

He thought for a long minute, and then he shook his head.

"Me neither," I said.

He squeezed my hand hard. *Don't lie.*

"Fine, I guess I am. Actually, I don't know what I am. I don't know how to be."

He squinted, thinking about this. Then he reached up with his hand and stroked my check.

TUESDAY NIGHT, I was so exhausted that no one would let me stay at the hospital. Tinka and Fran were staying at a hotel down the street from UCSF. They invited me to share their room. Early in the morning, Stephen's cell phone rang. It was his nurse. We all stumbled into our clothes, walked up the hill to the hospital, took the elevator to the seventh floor. In Stephen's room, a ring of doctors circled his bed, all quiet, watching. I peered between them. Stephen was thrashing, his legs and arms shaking, his face contorted in pain. I squeezed past the doctors to get to him, put my hands on his forehead, massaged his temples. I leaned down close to him, ignoring everyone else in the room. He shook violently. Then he relaxed. When I looked up, none of the doctors had moved. After a few minutes, they slipped out of the room.

"What's happening?" Tinka asked Dr. Golden in the hallway.

"His heart's having trouble." He took us to the chairs in the nurses' station, cleared his throat. "We're not there yet," he said, "but you should think about what you want to do. I don't think Stephen has anything in writing."

I looked at Fran and Tinka, so quiet. Tinka had brought her

dad candy right up until he died, when he lay in the bed unconscious. And Fran. How had she ended up here again? "What do
you think?" I asked them.

"You all talked about it, Lizzie," Fran said.

That morning after his dad died, his head in my lap in North
Boulder Park. I'd promised the end would be different for him.
He'd wanted me to say I'd slip him the morphine myself, but I
hadn't gone that far. "He said no machines," I told them.

"How do you feel about that?" Dr. Golden asked.

"I want to do what he wants. He can't talk or he'd make it
happen himself."

That night, I went with my family to their hotel across the
street. Again, Stephen's cell phone rang, my favorite nurse. If
I wanted to spend the night with him, this was the night, she
said. My family walked back over to the hospital with me. The
waiting room was still full. No one could bear to leave. I headed
down the hall, through the doors of the ICC, into Stephen's
room. It was nine-thirty at night, early for us. I pulled up a chair
and talked to him. He made no sign that he could hear me. His
hand was relaxed, limp. I squeezed anyway, just in case. He
was in there somewhere, I thought, so I kept talking. Or maybe
he wasn't, maybe he'd left his body, if that was possible, if that
was what happened.

I walked down the hall to the bathroom, changed into
Stephen's T-shirt and boxers. On my way back to his room, I
peered into the lobby. John and Jean were playing cards. My
mom was curled up on a couch, a blanket wrapped around her.
My dad was talking with Amani, Joaquin, and Josh. Cath and
Tinka were sitting under the window together, not saying much.
It had to be eleven o'clock.

The nurse had moved Stephen over a little, made room for

me on the left side of the bed. She'd brought in an extra pillow. I took off my shoes, pulled Stephen's covers back, climbed
over the armrest that was supposed to keep him from rolling
off the bed. I lifted up the two large plastic tubes coming from
the ventilator and eased myself underneath them. I curled into
Stephen and lay with my head on his chest, my arm around him.
His breathing was made percussive by the vent, but I could hear
the murkiness, the sound of whatever it was in there, ruining
my life. We had a special blanket—extremely light, filled with
warm air. I slept deeply for the first time in days.

Early in the morning, the nurse woke me. She needed twenty
minutes to adjust the machines. I climbed out of the bed and
got my sweatshirt, put on Stephen's sweats and my shoes. It was
five-thirty. I walked out of the ICC, down the hall. I wished I
could have brought Stephen with me. The lobby was dark, the
rectangles of the windows delineated by early morning gray.
My parents lay on couches, hospital blankets drawn over them,
curled on their sides. Amani and Joaquin were asleep on the
floor. My sisters were in overstuffed chairs, sleeping restlessly.
My brother sprawled on a bench under one window. The room
had that slumber-party look, everyone too exhausted to notice
their own discomfort, stale food scattered around.

I kept going down the hall. It had been years since I'd done
this, and Stephen had always led the way, but somehow I managed to find the right door. I propped it open with a newspaper
and stepped outside, snuck down the fire escape, made my way
around the top of the clinic building that was set in the hill. It
was an easy step from the building's walkway to the roof of the
parking garage. It was not even six; this part of the hospital
was dormant.

I belonged out here, on the roof. I walked to its edge and

looked over. Parnassus Street stretched out below me, empty in early morning, becoming Judah Street as it headed south, and running to the sea. And straight ahead, the woods of Golden Gate Park, beyond them city neighborhoods, and the bridge, and the mouth of the ocean. The air was thick and cold. I leaned back over the wall and looked at the world upside down. I felt closer to Stephen than I did down there in that room. This was the kind of thing we liked to do. The first time he'd snuck out of his room, we'd thought things were terrible, we'd come out here and kissed in the face of it all. And now things actually were terrible, and it still felt good out here, looking down, letting time stand still.

I ATE BREAKFAST flagrantly, no chance that Stephen would wake up and see. The construction picked up where it had left off. It seemed wrong that the last sound Stephen would hear would be the jackhammer. Somehow we always seemed to live next door to some big loud mess. Anna snuck in as I was finishing my bagel. "Can I talk to you?" she whispered. She had heard about a woman who'd had her husband's sperm frozen; it was something you had to do before he died. "You don't have to use it," she said. "It would be there, just in case."

It had never occurred to me. It seemed absurd, inappropriately funny, maybe even like an act of revenge against death. Our kid. A kid who might hate me for knowingly bringing him or her into the world with a dead father. But the other option would be not coming into the world at all, which at a later age the kid would hopefully figure out. Our kid. I didn't know if I could handle a kid. But it would be later, the sperm would be frozen, it could be in the distant future when I was okay, if that ever happened. It was sort of weird and distasteful, but who was going to criticize me today? I leaned over Stephen. "What do you think?" I asked. I imagined him grinning. Then I imagined him wincing. It was true; they'd have to cut.

Dr. Golden called a friend, the only doctor at the hospital who did the procedure. The friend was headed for the golf course—his long-awaited day off. "She's one in a million," Dr. Golden said into the phone, smiling at me. He was asking a favor, so willing to do anything that might help.

He took Fran, my parents, and me to meet with the hospital lawyers. We sat around a long conference table while the lawyers explained that this procedure was classic lawsuit material—they couldn't get the patient's consent, and later, family members sometimes objected to the widow having the sperm. It was important that we think seriously about Stephen's wishes, they warned me. In the middle of their explanation, Dr. Golden asked me if I was cold. Before I could answer he put his coat over my shoulders. The lawyers softened their tone as I sat, so tired, with the stethoscope dangling from my pocket.

I crawled back into bed with Stephen. Death thought it was going to come out of the game with everything. I squeezed him tight, and woke to a doctor tapping my shoulder. Dr. Turek, ready for the procedure. I climbed out of bed, went into the waiting room. The mood had lifted slightly because of the sperm aspiration; it had given everyone something to talk about. He'd better be heavily sedated, the guys were saying.

FRIENDS STREAMED INTO Stephen's room. It seemed unruly but only right that everyone got to see him. He'd always said the people he loved were more important to him than anything else, and here they were. He was deep in his own world, but maybe some part of him knew. Still, all these people running around the Intensive Care. It wasn't standard procedure, they were being kind to us, or maybe they were too worn down to say no. Either way, I was grateful.

Fran went in, then Clay, and then Tinka, then me. I climbed clumsily onto Stephen's bed, bumping his leg, the IV in his arm. I heard the curtains close behind me. I lay on him, hugging him, telling him anything and everything and nothing important. "I'll be here," I said. "If you ever get scared, come find me."

Celia gathered us in Stephen's room. Fran stood at the foot of his bed, holding his toes through the blanket. Clay held Stephen's hand. I rubbed his forehead. His eyebrows were thick and unfurrowed, his cheeks rounder than he liked, his lips chapped and open. His eyes were closed, the eyelids I loved to kiss, which made him squint in protest. His hair, a tangled mess on the pillow behind him. I smoothed the hair near his forehead with my fingers, pushed it back. His forehead was warm and damp with sweat. This would kill him, turning off the vent. Did he really want it, like he'd said he would? How did he feel about it now, so close? "We're right here," Fran told him.

Celia took the tape off his upper lip and pulled the feeding tube out of his nose. Maybe in some distant way, he sensed its removal and felt triumphant, finally comfortable. Amani and Joaquin slipped into the room, stood near Fran as Celia asked us about the vent. Some families wanted it taken out, while others just wanted it turned off.

"I think Stephen would want it out," Clay said.

"Will he die right away?" I asked.

"It usually takes a little while," Celia said.

She turned off the ventilator. I pressed my palm against Ste-

phen's head, silently telling him not to worry. Celia took the
tube out of his mouth and slipped out of the room. I could see
his entire face for the first time in weeks, the dark mustache he'd
grown recently, and beard to match. He was becoming swarthy
after the transplant; now that he could actually grow a beard
he'd been giving it a shot. His face stayed relaxed when the ventilator went off; he looked like he always looked when he slept
deeply, his skin soft and smooth. He was so relaxed that in spite
of ourselves we began to relax; we sank into the stillness of the
room. His chest jolted, and it seemed like something escaped,
like *he'd* escaped, into the room, in fact it seemed like he was
floating over near Clay, just above him. His chest jolted a second
time, and his body became heavy in the way of a sleeping child's.

His skin was becoming blotched with gray. We all held on
to him. I smoothed his hair, squeezed his puffy hand. His chest
was colder now. I rested my head on it. I knew he wasn't in
there but I couldn't help it. All those years when I'd measured
everything from right here, heard small tugs, and thickness, and
longed to hear less.

I had the uncomfortable feeling that Stephen was there. I
swore I could feel him sort of dancing, trying to get our attention, wondering why we were all looking at the body. He might
have been laughing, and I couldn't say this to anyone because it
was the wrong way to be feeling, he was being inappropriate as
usual. He was going to want me to live and I didn't feel like it.

Amani had run from the room sobbing. The rest of us
walked out slowly. I felt light and in slow motion, everything
around me saturated with color and sound. I was supposed to
be a mess, I would be soon, I had been, but in this moment I felt
strangely calm, like I could see death for what it was, the phase
of life we forgot to talk about. Stephen had worked so hard on

his body, tended to it, altered it, and willed it to keep going. It had allowed him to be here and that was everything, and it had also had its limitations. I had no idea where he was or if he was, and I'd never know. Out in the lobby, friends gathered blankets and pillows, looked aimlessly out the window. The action was elsewhere and we lingered, waiting for someone to tell us to go home.

THAT NIGHT I slept across the street from the hospital, in my family's hotel room. I slept in a bed with my sister, who pulled me close to her as she fell asleep. It was midnight. Stephen had died at seven-thirty. I had ripped the piece of paper with the date off the hospital room wall calendar, like Stephen had asked me to do the day of the transplant. This one read March 11, 1999. I knew Stephen would have appreciated the fact that I was keeping a souvenir of the day. His body was gone from the room by now. I had agreed to the autopsy, it had been what he'd wanted; medical research had saved his life again and again. But I did not like to think of the body I loved being taken apart.

I woke up early, listened to the sounds of sleeping in the room. Light came in through the windows. I put on my clothes, slipped out, walked downstairs to the sidewalk. The hospital was still across the street, but it had no urgency to it, though I was tempted to go in and just double-check that Stephen wasn't there. The sky was a deep blue, and it was hot out, very weird to not be engulfed in fog.

chapter twenty-five

I RODE WITH MY FAMILY ACROSS THE BAY BRIDGE, INTO BERKELEY. Inside my house, Darby and Luna lowered their heads, came scooting toward my feet. They'd torn up more of the couch; the long seat cushions had jagged rips in their yellow fabric. Clay had piled the stuffing neatly in the corner.

My family filtered in. Fran and two of her friends had gotten here ahead of us, and one of them had put an old Broncos tape on TV. I watched Elway throw the football. I knew this video—some Super Bowl remembrance, a series of highlights. The sportscaster's voice was making me claustrophobic. I had done a lot of this with people around, but this part, the coming back to the house, felt private. I had not known it would be; I had not known it would be anything. But I could tell now because I was about to lose it.

Everyone filed out, my family and Stephen's, so tired, probably also wanting to lie around this living room. I just needed
a couple of hours. I opened the fridge. People from school had
filled it with food—the kitchen staff had devoted a day to it,
making soups and a huge pasta dish, all kinds of vegetables.
I got out the pasta. Behind it, a jar of mayonnaise loomed, so
obviously Stephen's. I hated mayonnaise; I needed to throw it
out, but one thing at time. I microwaved a dish of pasta and ate
on the couch, looking out on the view of our bookcase, of the
dark wood shelves full of small objects. A green stone pyramid, a wooden kaleidoscope, a box painted with frogs. All these
little objects, put together, did not add up to a person, which
it seemed like they should have, given how much Stephen had
liked them. They reminded me of him, but where did reminding get me? Whatever people wanted to take to remember him
by, they could have. I'd open up the house, let everyone rifle
through it all. If nothing remained, I'd have exactly what I had
right now. I thought about Stephen, scrawling indignantly about
the feeding tube. *AND I was never consulted!*

I opened his closet, pulled a sweatshirt from the high shelf,
turned it inside out, and buried my face in it. I tried to put it
back but I couldn't reach, so I put it on instead. I looked at his
desk. A pile of cards with a list of names on top: thank-yous
he'd meant to write. A note to me, an accidental last letter, on a
square yellow stickie. "Liz—This is the ONLY copy of the Cres-
sida key in existence—please put it back here after moving car
for street cleaning. Thanks. I love you.—S." His computer sat
front and center, all the late-night games. I'd tried Riven with
him once but I couldn't get into it—there were only so many
interests you could adopt from another person. But thinking

about it now, I crumbled, all the ways, small and large, I'd hurt his feelings.

My brother and I drove the red truck through Oakland. I let him drive; I opened the window and felt the warm air come in. I sank into the passenger seat, my body loose from exhaustion, my mind set on cruise control. It was the heat, or the depletion of the last weeks, that kept me from what was happening, buffered me in the way a state of shock buffered the body. It was not, as Stephen would have put it, entirely unpleasant.

We drove out to the crematorium, in a sprawling cemetery just below the Oakland hills. The cemetery was sun-filled, neat and spacious, of another town or world. Its streets were wide and there were no other cars. We wound our way past the gated entrance, through meandering grave villages, to a large building that housed the cremation offices. The lawns were majestic and the gravestones timeless in a way that made me think Stephen had been wrong—he'd always said cremation but I could see him buried in a place like this. But then he'd be in California and his family would be in Colorado, and what if I moved, it would be weird if he were here all by himself. It would be better, in the long run, to just visit the ocean or the mountains. Or would it? It was hard to be sure.

John and I walked into the building. I tried on the word *widow* in my head, smiled because it was the kind of thing that Stephen would laugh about inappropriately. I thought about *dust* and *toast*, and all the synonyms he had for "dead." And the way he used to tease me about *wife*, repeating it over and over, wife, wifey-poo, lucky little lady.

Linda, a woman in her fifties, led us into her office. We sat down across from her, and she lifted a file from the pile on the right side of her desk. Stephen already had a file. We began filling out the death certificate. It was less awkward than I thought it would be, though Linda did look up at me for a second when we reached the age box. I had never thought about who filled in a death certificate. It seemed strange that I was declaring it all—his date of birth, father's hometown, his years of education. When it came to Stephen's occupation, I paused. I realized that I could tell Linda to type in whatever I liked. I knew what Stephen had planned to be, and it wasn't his fault that he hadn't had time to get there. "Public health," I said. "Advocate for the uninsured." It would be how he'd want to go down in the books.

Linda frowned. "I can't fit that."

"Okay, I guess just public health."

We filled in his parents' names, first, middle, last, and where they'd been born. Clayton Anthony Evans, New Mexico. Frances Berry Bonnyman, Tennessee. It was heartening that I could remember. I could still see the picture he had of his dad as a baby, bathing in a metal bucket on the front porch of the wooden house in Albuquerque. I'd find it and give it back to Fran.

Linda handed me a clipboard with the itemized bill. This place was like a wedding hall, everything overpriced. They knew you wouldn't quibble—you were supposed to want the best on this day. It was once in a lifetime, they did have that. In honor of Stephen, who thought the whole thing was a racket, I got the cheapest urn possible, though I felt a moment of shame in front of Linda. "We're not keeping the container," I told her. "He wanted to be spread around."

Linda brought us a gold-colored box, a tin, lined in plastic. I held the tin in my lap while my brother drove. It was counterintuitive that a body could be reduced so significantly, that his whole body was inside this thing.

"Maybe he'd want to be out at Kirby's Cove," I said. "But then there's Colorado."

"You don't have to put them all in one place," John said. "That's one advantage over burying."

"It seemed like we talked about everything," I said. "And then there are all these things we missed."

"Maybe he's communicating," John said. You never know."

"The other problem is, I have this feeling he's coming back."

My brother sighed and put his arm around me.

SUNDAY, THE DAY of the memorial, we woke to steady rain. Catherine lay next to me—my sisters had been taking turns, I had yet to fall asleep alone since Stephen died. All kinds of plans were in place. We'd spent yesterday choosing things of Stephen's to put up at the memorial, Tintin prints, photographs he'd taken. A couple of people had made picture boards, which seemed like a good idea, but I couldn't help thinking how horrified Stephen would have been, watching helplessly as his pictures escaped from their albums. We gathered small things to give away. I knew Stephen would have liked this, everybody who loved him having a little piece—a Tintin magnet on their fridge, a Ray Bradbury book, an REM T-shirt, a tiny CU buffalo, an obsidian sphere for the bureau.

The entryway filled with people, wet from the rain. It felt eerily like our wedding, so many of the same people, only four years ago. Amani had made a program. Clay spoke first, about Stephen and him as kids, picking Stephen up from preschool, when Stephen liked to dress as a cowboy, his hat and chaps. When I got up I found myself describing the devil mask Stephen had nailed to the apex of our roof recently. Forest and

Carla sang "Desperado." Stories and more stories. And laughing—it would have sounded like a party if the windows had been open.

Afterwards, we drove through heavy rain out to the Marin Headlands, hiked down to Kirby's Cove. I wore Stephen's red raincoat, walked with my sisters down the dirt trail. To our left the green hillside careened down to the bay. This place had always seemed fixed to me, and I noticed now that it wasn't, that most of the world I lived in would look physically different from now on. We climbed the bunkers, descended the steep wooden steps down to the beach. It was early evening, the sky gray and deepening. I couldn't tell who started it, but suddenly there were five naked bodies running for the water, then more. Within minutes the sand was littered with jackets and shoes, the water dotted with people leaping around. People who on any other day would have balked at the idea of this raced into the ocean for Stephen. *Come on,* he said. *You know you want to.* I shook my head. *I'm cold,* I told him. *When I was here, you always forced me in,* he said. *But were you tired like I'm tired?* I asked, huddled in my raincoat. *You're just worried about what my mom will think,* he said. I glanced over at Fran, who had turned discreetly toward the bunkers. My sisters nudged me and we pulled off our clothes, left them in a heap on the sand. We ran in as fast as we could, pushing through the instant deep pain of the freezing water. I yelped, and dove under.

EVERYONE HAD GONE HOME. I stood in the bathroom at the end of the night, opening and closing the bottom drawer of the medicine cabinet absentmindedly. I'd given all the unopened transplant meds to Tim Brooks at the memorial and the unused medical supplies to a local clinic. But there were still half-empty bottles of enzymes, inhalers, and vitamins. Little substances that had fit into my life in particular ways, trips to the pharmacy, filling the tackle box, seeing them lined up on hotel bureaus. I felt fond of them, especially the inhalers, remembering the soothing air-sucking sound they made. I brushed my teeth, decided against flossing. Maybe I was done with flossing permanently, flossing was about the long haul and I was not. Life already seemed too long. I was not about to shorten it artificially, but I was not going to go out of my way to prolong it. *Sorry,* I told Stephen, because it seemed a slap in his face, to not care about the length of life. *Then give a few years to me,* I could hear him say, mainly angry because if he were here he could push the flossing.

I lay in bed with the dogs by my feet, listening to REM in the dark. I had the CD player by the bed, hit the third track over and over because it seemed like a great thing, that you could want to go backward, and actually be able to do it. Outside, just beyond the flimsy back fence, my neighbors in the second-story apartment were at it again. They had two loud modes, fighting and singing, and tonight they were crooning to love songs. I wanted them to keep singing; I lay in bed and pretended I had what they had.

Where was he? Before he'd died I hadn't needed to wonder about life after death. Now it wasn't enough to think maybe the soul lived on and maybe it didn't. Did it, or didn't it? Was Stephen somewhere, or not? If, as people of many religions believed, he was journeying somewhere, or becoming something else, was I getting in the way by wishing he was here? Did I have an effect on him? If he existed, was he okay, was he aware? Did he know I was a mess? If so, was he removed enough from life to see it with distance, to feel for me but know whether, eventually,

I was going to be okay? And if so, could he somehow communicate with me and let me know how long it was going to take until I'd feel like myself, or, forget that, just feel that life might be interesting again? I doubted he knew all of that, if he knew anything. He'd only been dead a few days.

chapter twenty-six

TUESDAY I WOKE UP AND GOT READY FOR WORK. IT HAD only been a week and a half since Stephen had died. But the kids had had different subs for over a month, and I felt the pull. And more, I didn't know what else to do with myself. I got dressed thinking that I didn't have much of a lesson plan. I pulled up to school, gulping my coffee and eating the last of my toast. Two of my students, Miriam and Jessica, leaned in my window before I could get out of the car. On the sidewalk, they hugged me, thrust a stuffed Chihuahua and balloon strings in my hand. "You made it," Miriam said. "Did you miss us?"

I nodded, realizing I had. Miriam and Jessica had broken the ice of coolness; kids who would normally not do so hugged me hard, and by the time we got to the classroom I was weighed down by enough of them that I couldn't move forward.

"Let's go, let's go," Kendra commanded. "She's hardly standing up."

I accumulated cookies, flowers, snack bar candy, face powder, Minnie and Mickey Mouse. The kids put their backpacks down and ran to sit in a circle on the rug, beginning a day in which they would lead me through all of our routines, which I'd established but couldn't remember. They fought to sit next to me. I wondered if I'd have an entire day before they went back to taking me for granted. I looked around the circle. Here they were, alive and healthy, and so direct. I loved them, I was grateful for them, for the fact that in their presence I could not be anywhere else. We went around, each person telling me one thing that had happened since I'd left. Michelle's sister had had a baby named Desiree, who had to stay in the hospital for a week. Peter confessed that one substitute had caught him cheating. Jordan complained that there had been no free time for weeks. Adilene's grandparents were here from Mexico. Edgar had gotten into a fight, which Fernando had broken up. Ms. Sonnenberg had cried one day while I was gone, and when this happened they'd known my husband had died. They'd made pancakes in the kitchen.

By the time we came full circle, the kids who'd gone first were restless; the tall boys were beginning to get leg cramps from sitting cross-legged for too long. But when I told them they could go back to their seats, no one moved. Michelle, who was sitting next to me, touched my leg. "You skipped yourself," she said.

They looked at me uneasily. Jack nudged Michelle. "She doesn't have to *say* it."

I thought about a discussion we'd had in the fall, about times they heard their parents speak in low voices. Sometimes you pretend you don't know anything's wrong, they told me. When I asked why, they looked at each other; I was missing the obvious. So you don't make your parents feel bad, one said. Your parents feel bad when you worry, so if they're pretending nothing's wrong, you have to pretend not to worry. I'd failed at my job as the designated stable person during their day; the least I owed them was a direct conversation.

When they were at their desks, I sat down on my stool. I rarely sat in class, but I was tired, I was leveling with them today. I told them some of what happened, the stories of it, Stephen dancing to the machines, trying to sneak and pull out the feeding tube. I told them I'd put their cards up in the hospital, and that everybody loved the food their parents had made. I told them I was tired. I passed out pieces of scratch paper, so they could write down anonymous questions. It was a method I'd learned from Beth, who used it when she taught sex ed.

They began writing quietly, some writing three questions, some writing one, a few asking if they could just write me a private note. I collected the notes and read the questions out loud, answering them as I went. They were good questions, questions that adults never voiced. What did your husband look like when he died? Does it sometimes all feel like a dream? Did the hospital kill your husband? What was the last thing you said to each other? What did they feed him through the tube? Did he want to know about the dogs? Were lots of people at your house? Were they all crying? Could you eat while this was going on? Did he know he was going to die? Did they bury him with his wedding ring? Did they have to stop machines to let him die? The final note said: *Please don't read out loud: Ms. Scarboro, Your husband will always be with you. Love, Adilene.*

They began telling their own stories, deaths they'd gone

through, grandparents, uncles, pets. "I still think about my cat," Aram said.

"This is a weird question," Dominic said, "but my mom knows people who've lost their loved ones, and she says they usually go crazy, you know, start doing drugs, or kill themselves. You're not going to do any of that, are you?"

I shook my head, though I wasn't entirely sure. But I was pretty sure; I didn't have the energy to do anything dramatic.

"But one day," Pamela said, "I think it was right when your husband died, someone told us you weren't coming back. And everyone started crying."

"Not everyone," Xavier said. "I mean, the boys weren't crying."

"Some boys were," Jenny said.

"We don't need to get into all that," I said. "I'm sorry it was all such a mess."

SOMEHOW, I TAUGHT. I helped them organize their notes for their biography project, I introduced a novel, we deciphered Latin roots. We signed up for the computer lab, and they typed up their biography reports, which we'd been in the middle of when I'd left. Consciously or unconsciously, they gave me a break for a week. They pushed no limits, did their homework for the most part, and kept their arguing to the playground. They weren't awkward, they came up and told me all kinds of things out of the blue, the way kids will, but they watched out for me. Anytime we left the room as a group, they checked to see that I had my keys, and someone took charge of the papers we needed to bring with us. They reminded me to collect the homework, which would have been unthinkable before.

At the end of one day, I knew there were three kids I had to keep after, for writing on their desks. The deal was, if you wrote on the desks, you cleaned them. I tried to stick to it, mainly so I didn't have to clean the desks or hear outcries when they changed seats. "I have three people staying for desks," I said. "Edgar, Jordan, and . . ." I looked around the room. My memory was gone.

Ashley raised her hand. She looked at me with sympathy and affection, as if she were the adult. "Uh, Ms. Scarboro, it was me."

I was being taken care of by twelve-year-olds. It was humbling, but I didn't have another option. I thanked her, and Edgar got the sponges.

I FELT A STRANGE nostalgia for the hospital, that second home that was no longer mine. I wished I could go there and lie down on one of the beds. The hospital was probably not worth it because I was receiving far better care at home. I didn't know how my friends knew what to do, and I was overwhelmed with all the debt adding up. They'd been helping for years and at this rate I'd never be able to pay them back. But I let them anyway. They walked the dogs, brought me groceries, and made me extra keys when I lost mine. They distracted me with visits to used clothing stores, canceled Stephen's plethora of credit cards. They called, and when I didn't answer, came over anyway and rented movies since I couldn't hold a conversation. Beth forbade anyone at school from making me attend lunchtime meetings. Instead she and I swam in the pool, sat out for a minute in the sun, and then downed food before the bell rang, teaching our afternoon classes with wet hair.

Mornings I got up, made coffee, poured a bowl of Grape-Nuts, and gave the dogs their food. I was half glad and half disappointed that my body could just keep going. It wasn't what I'd imagined. Somewhere I'd had this picture of death, where the person in mourning fell apart completely, and then one day, rose, recovered. So far it was nothing like that. I didn't know what it was yet, but it was not that. It was more like moving through water, each hour stretching to the length of an afternoon. I'd been thrown back into a child's perception of time. It wouldn't have been bad if I'd been learning something specific, something I wanted to learn, how to speak Spanish or fly a plane. But I didn't know what I was learning; things were at work in the basement of me.

I hadn't expected to die when Stephen died, but I must have expected something, because being here felt strangely uncalled for. I was the news anchor who didn't know the tape was still running, sitting at her desk, purposeless and a little disheveled. I did not know if I would ever feel like myself again. All along, I'd thought that we were two people going through this together, grabbing life while we had it. Not true. Stephen had grabbed life, since his was short or since he was who he was, and the feeling had been contagious. Alone my abilities were paltry, like singing along with a friend who has a great voice and she stops and you hear your own, thin, wavering, off-tune.

On the other hand, Stephen had said he'd kill himself if I died. I'd gotten furious when he said it, made him take it back, told him that he had the luxury of feeling like that because *he* didn't really have to consider living without *me*. I was in that future now, getting up and around. I thought about Stephen, how there was never a little break from having CF, never just a little vacation. I wondered if he ever felt like I did now, like I just needed ten minutes to lie down in my former life.

During the day, the dogs and work propelled me forward. Work had the added benefit of making me eat—if I got too hungry in the middle of the morning I'd crash, which was a mistake, being in charge of thirty twelve-year-olds. But the nights spread out like fields of snow, sleep at the very edge of the horizon. I tried to think about things but my brain was heavy and slow and drifting. Even a newspaper article required too much concentration. For a quick second, I'd surface, remember something tiny, like his voice, and then slide back underwater, my mind protected and numb. It was going to be like thawing out, I could tell. I had never expected losing someone to be so physical. I thought about something Stephen said when we were long-distance in college: "I'd pay five hundred dollars to see you walk off a plane." Back then I'd missed him and known he'd come back, which was bearable missing, great missing, really. This new missing was a weed that grew crazily. I wondered if grief was going to be like falling in love—so consuming, and tiresome to other people.

THE SERVICE IN COLORADO was held at Fran's church, where Gus's service had been. Stephen had never gone to church; it was funny to think of him here. Clay put together a mixed tape of REM for the end of the service and brought up the fact, when he spoke, that Stephen would have wanted people of all religions and no religion to feel comfortable at his memorial. I didn't mean to be stoic, but I couldn't feel anything. I mostly thought of Fran through the service, how her whole town was here and she had to face them, this second time, and no matter how badly people felt or how much they cared about her, she'd be dreading seeing them face-to-face when the service was out, over punch and cookies.

Afterwards in the basement, unintentionally, a receiving line formed. Clay and Tinka slipped out, so it was Fran and me, and for a while just me, being hugged by all these people who loved Stephen. Our high school teachers, Stephen's first girlfriend, his dad's sister. I felt young and indebted, taken into their arms.

That night, Clay and Tinka and I snuck out onto the golf course. There was a small stone bench where they'd stood with Stephen four years ago, doing shots of Jack Daniel's and flinging their dad's ashes out onto the wet grass. The three of us sat on the bench. I held the Tupperware container filled with Stephen's ashes that I'd brought with me on the plane. Clay handed us each a Coke. We snapped them open in unison. We were just going to put some of the ashes here—Stephen had so many places he loved to be, the spot with his dad was only part of the plan. The plan hadn't been solidified, but involved the Rocky Mountains and the Pacific Ocean.

I opened the Tupperware, releasing gray dust into the air. The plane had caused some kind of compression. We took turns dipping our hands in. For their dad, they'd told a story for each bit they threw. For Stephen, we decided that we had to think of one thing he liked to repeat over and over for each toss.

"*Je suis une baguette,*" Clay said, flinging his handful of ashes into the darkness.

"Wakey, wakey, eggs and bakey," Tinka said.

"Teenie Weenie, you better git in here," I said, in Stephen's cowboy voice.

By now we could all hear him, the way he'd drive those

things into your head and you couldn't get them out. Tomorrow we'd climb up Red Rocks, carrying the Tupperware container. Tinka would be nervous with the footing but we'd convince her, we'd sit on the rock ridge overlooking town, stick his ashes in the crevices. We'd be quiet, missing him. But tonight we had him with us, we were cackling and devilish, choking on mouthfuls of Coke until the sprinklers drove us out.

chapter twenty-seven

Here was the problem with navigating cystic fibro-sis: no one we knew had been there, no one could tell us what to do. And here was the great thing: no one had been there, no one could tell us what to do. The territory was unmarked, it was wilderness; we were hacking our way through, making all kinds of mistakes. No one judged us openly, except the occasional nurse who made it clear she thought I should come to the hospital more often, or that Stephen should keep himself away from the pain meds and stop with the dark, inappropriate jokes. And these nurses were easy to dismiss, because at the end of the day they left, no lung collapses, no boyfriends in the hospital, so how could they know? We created the guidelines together, until we reached a point where even that wasn't possible. I had no idea what I'd do or who I'd be if my life were short. And

Stephen had no idea what it was like to love the person with the short life, everything it brought and took away.

Maybe grief is the happy medium, when it comes to an experience other people can or can't share. It's particular enough that no one dares to tell you how to go about it, but it's not so rare that *no one* you know has been there. In your twenties, not many people your age have been there, but others emerge. I remember the bookstore I wandered into a few months after Stephen died. It was a small store in a small town in Vermont, and it turned out that its owner, a woman in her sixties, had lost her husband five years back. We began talking, she giving me trail markers, though not quite a road map, me looking at her and gleaning the answer to the only question I really had: Was it possible to make it through the first year? That was my goal then; I'd told myself that I just had to live through the first year, and after that I could decide if I wanted to keep going. This was the way I got myself to do things. I'd put on my running clothes, telling myself I only had to put them on and walk out the door, and after five minutes I could go back inside if I wanted to. This was how I took up running, and now this was how I was taking up staying alive.

You imagine that if your spouse died you'd change everything—new city, new job, a solo trek through the Himalayas. But in this imagining what you don't realize is that the death makes these changes for you—you find yourself a foreigner in your own kitchen. You hate mayonnaise, and now the jar in your fridge appears as an artifact, knife marks still intact. You can listen to music you know or music you don't know—it all sounds entirely different. You are set free and lonely, you are weightless and wandering the globe.

I remember thinking that if I had any guts, any energy, I'd get in my car and keep driving, end up in some small town somewhere, sit in a diner eating pancakes, and take it from there. I remember thinking that it took energy to grieve in some kind of original way, and that I didn't have that energy; it was all I could do to get through a day full of hours, of minutes, of tiny surprise attacks: Stephen's handwriting jumping out at me from the phone message pad, a song he vehemently hated springing up on the radio as I drove to work. "Heaven" by Eric Clapton, which Stephen thought was too sentimental, and it had seemed harsh, criticizing a song about the death of a child. Now, as if to spite Stephen, the song was getting to me, making me think about the person who'd derided it with tears in my eyes.

I remember the way my mind let the truth in slowly. A phone conversation with my mom a month after Stephen died, about a family trip to Alaska. "There'll be a great surprise at the airport in Juneau," she said. I could think of only one great surprise. Maybe it was possible, maybe my mom had actually figured out a way to turn this all around. "Stephen?" I asked hopefully. "Oh, sweetheart," she said. "No. Your cousins."

DURING THAT TRIP I wrote Stephen letters, sitting on rocks at our campsite along the Tatshenshini River. I was delusional, though not delusional enough to mail the letters. I told him that the river, the glaciers, mirrored life right now, expansive and wild, endless in scope. I was coming to feel marked, the way he'd always been. People ran into me at the grocery store and stared at their feet. The distance made me lonely, but it also gave me a certain kind of freedom. I felt apart from the working of things. He'd died at thirty and he'd had a real life; from this angle everything after thirty was a surplus; all years from here on out were extra.

On that trip, we hiked to the top of a hill on a glacier. It was a giant snowslide, and in our rubber suits we had no need of sleds. When it was my turn I lay on my back, and my sister gave me a push. I began sliding, the snow under my back cold and hard, rough at first and then suddenly smooth, shooting me down the hill. I was flying, the air wet and fierce against my face. Life rushed into me, I was awake after three months of sleep, here I was landed in Alaska; it was me, jetting down the hill! By the time I landed, the feeling was gone; I'd disappeared.

BACK HOME, MY friends converged to take care of me, like incredibly skilled dancers, hiding the work of it, moving so seamlessly that I barely noticed the details, I just felt, underneath me, a solid floor. But the things I needed to take care of myself slipped by the wayside. Bills. Appointments. The dogs. I understood why Stephen had been spelling Luna's name into my hand those last two weeks. She was unpredictable, and getting more so, and she and Darby had formed a little pack.

I sat on top of the wooden picnic table at the dog park, watching them warily. Darby lay down on the ground with a tennis ball in his mouth, methodically shredding it into tiny green pieces. Luna bounded toward me, coming to say hi. The guy sitting next to me held his hand out to her. He had large black boots and a Mohawk. "She's not always friendly," I warned him.

He moved several feet away from me, and put out his hand. Luna licked it. "She's just protective of you," he said. He had his own dog, a huge animal on a choke chain, that kept its ears pricked in a constant state of alert, and could have killed Luna without much effort.

"He's friendly," the guy said. "It's part of his training, to be here on leash."

I told him about Darby and Luna, the way they'd started ganging up on other dogs, the general mayhem they caused. "I'm thinking of doing some training," I said.

It turned out he was a dog trainer, and I hired him to help me. At the end of the third session, he asked me out. I should have seen it coming; Anna had told me he'd been undercharging me. We were walking through Berkeley High's campus and I panicked—my usual answer was no longer true. I was being asked out and I was single. It had been ten years. I felt like a movie character, a woman in her fifties just divorced, fumbling around for what to say. "I really like you," I stammered. "I, I don't think I'm ready to go out with anybody yet. I just, it's only been a few months, and . . ."

He smiled. "It's okay," he said. "I can take no."

Right. Twenty-nine was far from nineteen. By now everyone but me had learned how to have this conversation. In minutes I had gone from thinking that no one would ever ask me out, to being terrified that people would.

MY YOUNGER BROTHER John moved out from New York to live with me, and we ordered pizza late at night and sat on my banana-shaped couch with our feet up, watching TV. When the phone rang he answered it, and all my friends loved him for this; I was finally reachable. He sat me down at the table with a pile of random bills I'd been ignoring. Usually he was as disorganized as I was, but now he organized me, keeping Captain Crunch and milk and Dr Pepper in the house. I kept thinking, He's twenty-three, too young to be doing this, but then I was twenty-nine, too young to be a widow, so what were we going to do?

My youngest sister Jean moved out, too, to finish college, and I relaxed with the two of them around. No amount of crying fazed them. They were also accepting about other emotions, so I could tell them things I hadn't told most people—the feeling I had that Stephen was around and helping me through this, the way I crossed the street when I saw an old couple coming, how I'd felt personally affronted when a friend reached for her husband's hand across the table.

"It'll take a while," John said.

"A while," I said. "Like how long?"

THE SCHOOL YEAR BEGAN, and I was sucked right into its frenetic flow. I woke up with a sharp emptiness, stumbled to school, and escaped into a seven-hour break from my life. When I arrived the kids would converge, telling me something urgent before the first bell rang. Greg's hat had been broken, he was crying; the hat *mattered*. His dad had given it to him, and his dad had recently moved to Texas. They'd been playing keep-away with the hat, but they hadn't meant for it to break. Did I have a way to fix it? I'd begin class with the baseball hat in my hand, my own problems long vanished, no time for an extraneous thought as I got the kids working, tried to make life easy for Greg as he emerged from the bathroom, taught a history lesson while intermittently trying to fix his hat.

That fall, a girl with CF entered my sixth-grade class. Rosy, smart and funny, asked me on day one about my husband and how long he'd lived, and smiled in awe when I said thirty. She liked and did not like the fact that I knew something about what she was going through. On the one hand, she could talk to me about anything. When the rest of the kids were at P.E. she'd stay in and draw, and our conversation roamed the CF landscape, from whether she wanted to get a transplant to being frustrated about the new hospital rules, that kids with CF could no longer share rooms. On the other hand, I cramped her style. When she told me that she hadn't come to school because she was on a round of Tobramycin, I pointed out that it was an every-eight-hour drug, and told her to get up earlier, do her first round, and get herself to class. When she said she needed to go home for oxygen, I got her aide to set up a tank in a back reading room, because I knew she was going home so none of the other kids would see her with the tube hooked up to her nose.

Most important to Rosy was that she be normal, that she be treated like everyone else. This I understood. When her aide insisted that she needed to be at Rosy's side every minute because she was scared Rosy would die in one of her coughing fits, I promised the aide that I wouldn't let Rosy cough alone and then broke my promise. What twelve-year-old wants to hack away in class, in front of all her friends? She'd leave the room, cough in the hallway or the bathroom, sneak back in and smile at me. We were both pretending to be normal, really. I'd been doing it while Stephen was alive, and I continued now, except now I was exposed, practically naked; everyone knew my husband had just died and it was probably the first thought they had when they saw me walking through the halls, carrying my coffee and my stacks of Xeroxes, imagining I passed as one of them.

I KEPT UP at work that fall, but on the home front I faltered. Even with my brother on my case, I managed to misplace a lot of mail. One day a representative from Triple A called to tell me that my car insurance had expired in spite of repeated letters I'd received. I would need to reinstate in person, and pay the year in full.

I drove, uninsured, down to Triple A. I'd been there a few months before to make a last-minute payment. I hoped I would not end up speaking to the same agent. I signed my name on the waiting list and sat down in a white plastic chair. Soon, an agent named Lou Peterson called me into his cubicle. He was in his mid-fifties, well dressed and handsome, a disarming smile. I sat down across from him at his desk while he looked me up on the computer. He read the screen and shook his head. I glanced at the pictures above his desk: a young couple, not quite a prom picture, but a studio picture, and two elementary school photos—a boy and a girl, both grinning.

"Well, Elizabeth," Mr. Peterson said, "looks like you need to reinstate."

"I know," I said guiltily. I wanted to explain how it had happened. The Widow Card, my brother called it. I wished there actually was one, I could flash it to get on a crowded bus, to ward off movie-rental fines. I wondered when it would expire. I glanced up at Lou. Everyone had an excuse, I was pretty sure.

"There are also late fees on here," he said, sliding the papers toward me on his desk. I studied them. The policy was in Stephen's name.

"I guess while I'm here, I should switch this into my name," I said. "Stephen Evans, my husband, he . . . died. I've been meaning to take care of it."

Mr. Peterson looked up at me slowly. "I'm sorry to hear that," he said.

"I know it's not an excuse," I said, "but I've been forgetful."

"When did your husband pass away?" he asked.

"Eight months ago," I admitted. "That probably sounds like a long time."

He smiled slightly, shook his head. "My son died April first."

I met his eyes, both of us open books. "How old was he?" I asked.

"Twenty-three." He closed his eyes for a second. "How about your husband?"

"Thirty."

"What happened?"

"He had this illness, cystic fibrosis—just, over time."

"That's terrible," he said. "Look at you. You're so young."

"What about your son?"

"That's him, there," he said, nodding toward the wall. I could see the resemblance now, the young man a vibrant version of Mr. Peterson, chiseled jaw, warm eyes. "He'd just joined the Richmond police. He was shot off-duty."

"I'm so sorry," I said.

We sat quietly for a minute.

"Do you think about him all the time?" I asked.

"From the time I get up to the time I fall asleep," he said.

"Me, too," I said. "Work is the only vacation."

"I've been staying almost until seven," he said. "Most days I feel like there's nothing to get up for, but somehow I get up anyway."

"And then you feel bad for being able to get up."

He gave a short laugh. "Can I ask you a strange question? Do you ever find yourself talking to your husband?"

I nodded. It wasn't something I'd been telling people.

"I mean, I would've thought that was crazy. Talking to a dead person. And I'm not even that religious."

"For some reason," I said, "it's usually when I'm driving. It's weird. I guess I'm alone, facing forward. But then it makes me wonder, when I see people singing along to the radio or whatever, how many of them are doing the same thing."

Lou shrugged. "Who knows. There are a lot of dead people out there, a lot of people missing them."

IN MARCH OF THAT school year, I drove to Mendocino, sat on the bed in my hotel room, looking around me at one of everything. One water glass overturned. One washcloth used. One toothbrush. One year since Stephen had died, which was why I'd come here. Rain hit my windows. I put on my tennis shoes and Stephen's red raincoat, and snuck out into the night. The main street was quiet, except for one strain of music, drifting out of the local bar. I walked away from the bar, deeper into the stillness. I rolled up my jeans, made my way through the wet grass as far as I could go, out toward the ocean. The rain picked up fiercely and receded. I traced a narrow path that ran around the edges of the cliffs. Below, the ocean jetted up through holes in the rocks.

Life felt all over the place, or I felt all over the place; while my friends were settling down, I felt light and reckless, self-absorbed, not of the world. Though last week I'd been brought back for a split second. Sunday, walking with my brother to a pick up soccer game, passing the soccer ball between us, my brother with a pair of cleats slung over his shoulder. The cleats had bounced a little as he'd walked, he'd bounced a little, he'd walked like that since he was a kid, like there might be something interesting around the corner.

It was early Northern California spring, the air cleared by a morning rain, wide orange leaves, dilapidated palm fronds. We'd climbed the chain-link fence of the high school and hopped down to the springy surface of the track. As we'd walked toward our group, I'd noticed a stranger, a guy with black hair in a maroon sweatshirt. As we'd gotten closer, I'd had the urge to make sure he knew that my brother was my brother. We'd been placed on opposite teams. Within minutes he'd come barreling down the field on a pass from my brother, and I'd scrambled to get the ball, checked him with my hip the way I would someone I knew, only he'd been over a foot taller than me, and the check hadn't worked at all; we'd collided, scraping our knees on the AstroTurf, me feeling shy as he'd helped me to my feet.

"There was something about that guy," I'd said to my brother on the way home. "I just felt strange."

My brother laughed. "It's called being attracted to someone," he said. "Has it been that long?"

"No, more than that; I mean *really strange*."

"Attracted to someone, and it could actually go somewhere."

That night I'd lay in bed, feeling great, and terrible.

Now, in Mendocino, I found the wooden beam Stephen and I used to climb out on. I walked along it as if it were a tightrope, or a log serving to bridge a stream, and lowered myself until I could sit securely. I talked to Stephen in my head as I dangled my legs over the churning water. *It's not fair,* I said. *I don't know what to do in this world without you in it.*

Do all the things we never got to do, I imagined him saying.

I surveyed the coast, the dark patches of brush, the fingers of land stretching down to the water. I imagined hiking along it, walking on the hard sand by the water when I could, scrambling back up to Highway 1 when the beaches got too narrow. I realized this sounded appealing, and I was elated—I'd thought of one concrete thing I wanted to do. *I think I'll hike the coast,* I told Stephen. *Start all the way in Oregon and hike down it until I reach San Francisco.*

Alone? he said. *That's a little terrifying.*

It'll be fine, I said. *Maybe I'll bring the dogs. I'm restless.*

That's a good sign, Stephen said. *Remember? That's what they used to say in the hospital.*

It was true. Irritable and restless. *There are so many things I'm sorry for,* I said. *For not staying with you every night that last week, for criticizing you too much, for never taking a second trip to Hawaii. For brushing off your ideas sometimes. For not getting you a Coke on the way to the hospital that last time. For still being here, getting to live. For getting to flirt with someone else, for hoping it leads somewhere.*

I imagined him, and what he'd be sorry for. For dying and leaving me. For spending so much time on the computer when it turned out it was our last year. For running up the credit card bill, not realizing it would be transferred immediately to me. For the fact that I had to deal with everything alone now.

I stood up slowly, holding my arms out for balance, and walked back along the wet wooden plank. I hopped down to the ground and followed the narrow path back toward the town's main street, feeling the soft dirt beneath my shoes, how the more I knew I was here, the more I knew Stephen was not. All the things we didn't do. I thought about my new plan, to walk the coast. Tomorrow I'd peruse the hiking guides in the bookstore. I'd get a bagel and a cup of coffee at the bakery, and drive down the coast, returning to the strange country I lived in now, having come from this overcast home.

A LETTER FROM THE UROLOGY DEPARTMENT AT UCSF HAS been sitting on my desk for months. The department is moving, and in the process of sorting and cataloguing what they need to take to their new site, they've found something that belongs to me. Or, fifty million things that belong to me. It doesn't seem right that they're mine, but they are mine more than they're anyone else's. The letter reads: "It has come to our attention that we are storing a frozen sample belonging to your deceased husband."

The letter sits five feet away from my sleeping three-year-old son, who lies in his bed, oblivious to the life that was mine before he was. Though all that will come, and maybe soon. Recently he saw a picture of me with my high school friends, and asked me to point out who everyone was. When I came to Stephen, he squinted closely. He's heard the name in the way you hear certain family names that float around in the household air. And just yesterday, he overheard a piece of conversation and his head whirled around. "*Two* husbands?" he said.

If Stephen could look in on my life now, I think he'd understand what I need to do about the letter. He'd see me, with a family, in deep. *There is room*, my second husband said early on, before he was my husband, and maybe if he hadn't said this, if he'd been more possessive and less self-possessed, I would have had to forget my old life completely. But I was grieving when I met him, and he probably understood better than I did that it was all of me or none.

Still, he has his limits. We'd only been together a few months when the frozen sample came up somehow. "I think you should know, I'm not up for that," he said. And in a way it was a relief. I wasn't up for it either.

But I'm having trouble checking the "donate to science" box and mailing the letter in. When it comes to Stephen's belongings, the closer something is to having been part of him, the harder it is to give away. The definition of "part of him" narrows with time—books and clothes were hard at first, but became easier. The little Post-it notes inscribed with his handwriting are gone, but I still have letters, and the photographs he took. And this is as close to being him as something could be. Though I can hear him laughing at that. "You're kidding," he'd say. "You feel bad for the frozen *sample*?"

But I can't help feeling like I'm in charge of part of his life, and it's a fragment of the way I felt all those years ago when Dr. Golden sat me down in that hospital hallway. I knew what Stephen wanted, but I still had the feeling I have now—like I'm in the emergency exit row of an airplane, and I'm not sure I'll be good at the job, but I don't trust anyone else to do it better.

If we'd lived fifty years ago, there would have been nothing for me to decide—no machines to keep him alive, no procedure to take his sperm. His body would have been able to die on its own terms. But we never would have met, he'd have died long before high school.

I watch my son sleeping, thinking about that between-worlds place where I used to live, how far I am from it now. Though I carry where I've been with me in the deep way we all do, so deeply that carrying is the wrong word—it implies too much separation, the possibility that you can see the shape of it, like a suitcase, set it down. It runs through me, unnoticed until someone points it out. The fact that my kids play "hospital"—that when I needed to think of a fun, expansive game that could include both a one-year-old and a three-year-old, I didn't think restaurant or office or house. ("I can see 'doctor,' " a friend said, "but 'hospital'?") The fact that in this game the hospital teems with busy life, with a cafeteria, and a lounge, with beds that move up and down, and repeat customers who seem happy enough to be there.

The fact that I still can't convince myself that the future exists. I want it to and hope it does, but there's no part of my brain that feels comfortable thinking twenty years out. The fact that if my second husband, Cullen, is out late and I've expected him earlier, I don't imagine an accident or an affair the way some people might. My mind jumps past worry; it's all over—I loved this person dearly, and now he's been taken away.

Ironically, as soon as Stephen died, because he died, I understood him better. I feel now, about the people I love, the way Stephen felt, then, about me. My innocence about death is gone, and it's better than it sounds. I don't wake up at night trembling; I don't have interfering thoughts about potential disasters.

Maybe I'm an optimist at heart. I'm an optimist who knows her days are numbered, who thinks of life as a sidewalk, that easy to step off of, that fast. I don't imagine the plane crashing when I fly, but I also don't imagine myself at seventy without inserting the word "if" or "hope" into the equation. Weirdly it doesn't bother me that much. In fact, if anything, I like it. I think about death, and I feel deeply alive, and I must have inherited this from Stephen.

The fact that I think of Stephen as having lived fully, even though I'm older now and should be able to see everything he didn't get to have. But the life felt full when it was happening, and it's still hard for me to think of it any other way. From the outside you'd expect that sadness dominated it, but we were happy. The happiness ran the way happiness does, underneath the exhilarations and the disappointments, the fights. It was separate from time and emotion, maybe more of a truth we held between us than a feeling. The truth being that this was what we wanted, to live out being together for as long as we could. It's hard to explain—the life was difficult but not lacking. I remember it as a great life, really, and no matter how much time I spend back in a more normal existence, that doesn't seem to change.

The fact that I can't just mail in this letter. It seems like there must be something better, more specific, to do with the sperm than donate it to "science." I don't know what area of science the urology department has in mind, and it occurs to me that if the sample would be useful to anyone, it would be CF researchers. There may be researchers out there who want to examine sperm with DNA encoded for CF, and if so, they're hard-pressed for material. Men with CF have no vas deferens, so the only way to extract their sperm is through aspiration, which involves a long needle to the testicles. It's hard to imagine anyone signing up for that study. So I call the CF clinic and leave a message, letting them know I have the sample, and asking if they know of a research team who might want it. It's sort of a weird thing to do, but the doctors have known me for years over there, I'm not too embarrassed. Besides, the whole situation is weird. Stephen lived on the frontier of modern medicine, which is a weird place to live, and this is the kind of death that follows that kind of life, messy and strange and terrible and lucky.

WHEN I WAS ABOUT to get married again, Stephen's brother Clay told me he was jealous—I got to have another husband, and he could never have another brother. I was furious when he said it—caught up in all the implications, that I was replacing Stephen, that once you remarry, your previous life is magically erased. But years later, I hear it differently. Here I am, in love with someone else, fully in this world.

You'd expect that someone else to want you to shed the first life completely. Strangely, my second husband doesn't feel this way, even when other people do. I have friends who are impatient with me for writing about Stephen, disturbed to see his baby picture up on our wall. When I told Cullen maybe we should take it down, he said it was up to me, but he was fine with keeping it there.

It might have been different if I'd fallen in love when I'd imagined I would—years after Stephen's death, if at all. But then I crashed into Cullen on the soccer field, which is pretty much the way it feels to fall in love while grieving—viscerally thrilling and painful, and embarrassing. And humbling, most of all—an overwhelming mixture of reckoning and urgency—life has handed you a rare chance, and after what's happened, you'd be ignoring everything you learned not to take it.

Cullen and I talked at soccer a few times, and then he showed up at the bar where I went on Fridays with my friends. I could barely look at him, and I couldn't look away either, and when I got home I told my brother that it was too bad. I'm not ready, I said. Maybe in a couple of years I could go out with him. John shook his head. In a couple of years you can go out with someone, he said. But it won't be him. You think he's going to magically be free two years from now?

It was my brother who pushed me forward. It has to be you, he said as we were walking to soccer. How would a decent guy know when to ask a widow out? I shook my head; it was unimaginable. At the water break, John leaned close to me. That girl in the purple shirt is flirting with him, he said. I glanced discreetly in her direction. It was true; she was stretching right next to Cullen, giving him that look. After the game, my brother shoved me toward Cullen's car. Come on, go now! he said, and before I could think, Cullen was rolling down his window.

A few nights later, he was on his way to pick me up for dinner, and I was staring around my living room, imagining it through his eyes. Pictures of me and Stephen, all kinds of little objects related to us. There wasn't time to take them down. Would he shy away, after seeing all this? Wouldn't anyone? It wasn't fair, the widowness. It stuck out from the start, making it impossible to proceed as most people got to, revealing themselves little by little. Think of it as a litmus test, my brother told me. The doorbell rang. I opened the door, and Darby lunged at Cullen, barking ferociously.

That first year was full of euphoria and guilt. Clay told me not to worry; Stephen would be okay with this, and I wished

I felt as sure as he did. I knew Stephen wouldn't want me to be alone, but it still felt like a betrayal. He always said I was the love of his life, and now I could tell I was going to have two loves of my life, and the second would last longer than the first, in the best-case scenario. Then the betrayal began shifting in the other direction. I'd hear a song on the radio, think of Stephen, and feel guilty toward Cullen. Gradually, this feeling lessened, too.

My friend Wanda told me that at some point, maybe after five years or so, you find yourself thinking about the person who has died and feeling the way you did when they were alive. They are whole and real, no longer reduced to your own missing, and this allows the thoughts to come and go more easily. I don't know if it's exactly like this, but I do know my dreams have shifted over time. My dream life always takes a while to catch up with my waking life. It's been years since my dad's accident, and for most of those years, when he appeared in my dreams, he could still see. After Stephen died, I had dreams of all kinds—nightmares in which I'd find out he was lying in a hospital bed somewhere and I'd been neglecting him, and after I'd gotten remarried, dreams in which he'd reappear and I'd panic, because how was I going to tell him? More recently there are dreams that remind me of who he was when he was here; casual dreams in which he gets to be himself and not his absence.

Two nights ago, I dreamt that he called me on the phone. After a few minutes he told me he needed to get going. "You?" I said, a little insulted. It seemed that of the two of us, I should have the time constraints. "I'm in the middle of a big project," he said. He told me he was involved in music production, that there was a whole afterlife segment of the music industry. "Who's the artist?" I asked. "I can't tell you," he said, "but when it's released, you'll know." "That's so annoying," I said. "Fine," he said, "one guess." "Kurt Cobain?" "Nope. I really have to go."

I might not have remembered this dream, except that last night turned out to be the night of Darby's death. Two years ago, the vet had told Cullen and me that Darby had a brain tumor. We cried a lot around then. I wasn't ready, and I realized that you're never ready, which I'd known, but hadn't remembered, which seems like a general truth, but it turned out was very specific—you learned it about each person, each being you loved, the particular absence you weren't ready for. That night, Cullen and I lay in bed, each missing Darby in our own particular ways. You'd think Darby would have been mine, since I was with him longest, but when it came to devotion, he saved it for men; he was Stephen's, and he was Cullen's. And though it might sound ridiculous to compare myself to a dog, it occurred to me that Darby was the only other living being that had loved these two people the way I had—first, most, completely. And how for both of us there was no contradiction in that, because there couldn't be, because that was what life had made possible. And how lucky we both were for it, and how it might make other people uncomfortable.

OUTSIDE, IT'S SNOWING. I am running around my parents' house, searching for mittens and boots and wool socks, telling myself that getting out of the house is always the worst part, that if I can get the kids in the clothes, the rest will be easy. And at least in this weather, the clothes have a payoff—we get to run around in the snow. I love snow more than most adults I know, more than an adult should, given the work it requires. But that's what happens now that I visit Colorado for a week in December. I can't wait to get out there in it, to help my kids learn to love it, to make sure they do not become people who limit where they travel or live based on the California fear of being cold. My daughter, who's not quite two, is thwarting my efforts. She doesn't understand the point of mittens, or maybe she does, but she still refuses to wear them. She's torturing me, actually, by wearing a single mitten, both inside and outside the house.

I scrape the windshield of the rental car, shovel snow from beneath its tires, and we're off, in that slow-then-suddenly-skidding snow way. We are headed to visit Fran. As I'm driving out 49th Street, with Cullen in the passenger seat and our kids in the back, with the three cornerposts of my life here in the car, my old life drifts through me. Driving this road with Stephen, going to stay at his parents', having come from my parents', the car containing the tiny family that resided within larger families, just as it does right now. My life is thick with human entanglements, and yet when I drive and no one's talking, when "Free Falling" comes on the radio, I'm Tom Petty, and not the good girl waiting at home. Maybe everyone is. And I think about how I've always loved songs about leaving, about heading down a road alone, about venturing to the middle of nowhere, and how I've always considered myself to be the kind of person who does these things. I somehow maintain that sense of myself, and yet it has nothing to do with the way I've lived my life.

In my mind I am following the snowy road as far as I can see and then some, heading to Wyoming, but then I take a left turn, and there we are, pulling up at Fran's, which feels like home, or one of my homes. My kids instinctively grasp this. I haven't turned off the car before I hear them start to work on their seat belts, getting ready to race up the front walk.

———————

YOU'D THINK IT would have been easy to tell my kids about Stephen, given the visits to his family, the openness of their dad, the pictures around the house. But in the end, my son brought it up himself. We were on a camping trip, setting up our tent in a grassy field. The kids were trying to get their sleeping bags out, with limited success. My son paused for a second, and then studied his sleeping bag's case. I glanced over. It was Stephen's childhood sleeping bag, which had held up over the years, and had been saved for practical rather than sentimental reasons. Stephen had printed his name on it in large capital letters.

"Who's Stephen?" my son asked.

"I'll let you take this one," Cullen said to me.

And so I did. It was easier than I'd thought.

"And this is his sleeping bag?" my son said, after a bit.

I nodded.

"Okay," he said, and laid out the bag next to his sister's. The tent was small, but it would work. There was room for all of us. For all of this.

acknowledgments

IN 1997, WHEN STEPHEN WAS HEADED FOR HIS DOUBLE-LUNG transplant, he and I set out to write a book together about living with CF. But the transplant came sooner than we expected, and life was hectic, and when it wasn't, we wanted a vacation from illness altogether. A few years after he died, I took on the project myself.

The story, with its narrow focus on the three of us (Stephen, me, and CF) holds only a small part of what happened in our lives. Events that were crucial but unrelated to Stephen's illness are mentioned only in passing. I've left out one event that felt impossible to reduce. Our friend Steve (Sam in the book) died in a car accident in April 1998. He lives on in memory, but that's not good enough, and I miss him terribly.

The book could also only hold a small number of the people who were part of the story in its pages. A few had to stand for the rest, and those who do appear come in only here and there. In daily life nothing was further from the truth. It's customary in the acknowledgments to stick to the people who helped with the book, but in this case, I'd like to first acknowledge the people who helped with the life. It was a life that needed a lot of help, and it took place years ago, so it's inevitable that I've missed several people who should be here. I hope they will forgive me. I am indebted to all the people who lived out CF with us, among them:

*   My parents, Ann and Jim Scarboro, my siblings, Catherine, John, and Jean Scarboro, and my aunts, uncles, cousins, and grandparents, for their deep reservoir of love and for seeing me through.

*   Stephen's family—Gus and Fran Evans, Clay and Jody Evans, Tinka and Doug Lambert, and the now-grown Devin, Jamie, and Dane—along with Alix and Carroll Prejean, the McKeons and Schwartzburgs, for their love and support.

*   The friends who made our lives richer and illness less daunting, among them: Joaquin Baca-Asay, Amani King, Josh Kurtz, Caitlin McDonnell, Forest Melchior, Eve Pearlman, and Carla Roitz, there for those first trespasses into swimming pools. Courtney Haught, Liz Johnson, and Kristie Wang, of Hyde Park Boulevard. Cindy Gorman, Steve Kang, Christina Kim, Hilde Myall, Gregg Watkins, Karen Wong, Eric Wright, Kim Wright, and Elizabeth Zirker (Anna in the book), who first made the Bay Area home. Nimmy Abiaka, Wanda Brooks, Sarah Case, Evan Hecox, Shawn Hecox, Lara Justine, Gwen Larsen, Anne McDonnell, Joy Osborne, Britton Shepherd, Tom Van Pelt, and the Zirker family, homes in themselves along the way. The boys at 2307 Piedmont Ave, in particular

Jed Bothell, Moses Cesario, Tristan Gittens, Cyrus Harmon, Todd Havener, Mike Huggard, and Andy Won. Liz Britton, Lisa Dumaw, Gabriel Feldberg, Chris Ford, Laura Hundley, Heather McLaughlin, Nathaniel Pearlman, and Evan Rudall, bright spots in Cambridge. Jennifer Brouhard, Brian Harte, Matt Martin, Marni Nacheff, Alex Perlof, Stuart Saunders, Jono Soglin, Beth Sonnenberg, and Emily Uy, who joined us for post-transplant life.

* Stephen's classmates and professors at the Harvard School for Public Health for their friendship and wonderful support during a difficult time.
* The doctors and nurses at UCSF Hospital and Boston Children's Hospital, in particular Diana Dawson, Ann Fukano, Dr. Jeffrey Golden, Debbie Lallas, Celia Rifkin, Dr. Michael Stulbarg, and Dr. Mary Ellen Wohl, for the terrific care they gave Stephen.
* The teachers, staff, parents, and students at King Middle School in Berkeley, for taking such good care of me during Stephen's final weeks and after his death.

And I am indebted to all those who haven't been named, but helped see us through. Our friends' families, our family friends. In that kind of life, every person who sticks by you matters. In 1996, when Stephen was very, very sick, Hillary Clinton gave her "It Takes a Village" speech. And I remember thinking that unfortunately it wasn't as easy as that—it took a village of kind, smart, generous, and energetic people, with good senses of humor. Stephen and I won the village lottery, and I'm still grateful.

IN WRITING THIS book, I am indebted to Joan Zirker, my excellent first reader, to Aurora Brackett, Michelle Carter, Nona Caspers, Maxine Chernoff, Peter Orner, Suzy Parker, Robin Romm, and Janet Wells for wonderful feedback on early drafts, and to Julia Frey, Phyllis Grant, Lorraine Lupo, and Margaret Ronda for terrific insights that helped me get to the finish line.

I owe deep thanks to Maria Massie for stubbornly believing in this book, especially when I had my doubts, and for helping me find the amazing editor Katie Adams, who improved it immensely. Thanks to all the people at Liveright who helped ferry this book to completion with enthusiasm and care.

I also owe thanks to my family—those mentioned, and those who've come since—Jake Beattie, Gina Gerst, Josie and Joel Gerst, Wylie Gerst, Jennifer Wortman, and the newest members, Naomi and Eli—for their love and support. I am especially grateful to Josie and Joel for the many hours spent taking care of their grandchildren while I wrote. And I owe thanks to the grandchildren themselves, Theo and Tess, for enduring this project and urging me on, noting how many stories they'd managed to write while I was still finishing the one. My deepest thanks goes to Cullen Gerst, for more than I could ever put words to on this page.

about the author

ELIZABETH SCARBORO is the author of two children's novels and a winner of the Olga and Paul Menn Foundation Prize for fiction. She lives in Berkeley, California, with her husband and two children.